DATE DUE

DEMCO 38-296

Elliott Carter

Elliott Carter. Photo: Misha Donat/Boosey & Hawkes.

ELLIOTT CARTER

A Bio-Bibliography

WILLIAM T. DOERING

Bio-Bibliographies in Music, Number 51
Donald L. Hixon, Series Adviser

Greenwood Press
Westport, Connecticut • London

Library of Congress Cataloging-in-Publication Data

Doering, William T.
    Elliott Carter : a bio-bibliography / William T. Doering.
      p. cm.—(Bio-bibliographies in music, ISSN 0742-6968 ; no.
  51)
    Includes discography.
    Includes index.
    ISBN 0-313-26864-9 (alk. paper)
    1. Carter, Elliott, 1908- —Bibliography. 2. Carter, Elliott,
  1908- —Discography. I. Title. II. Series.
  ML134.C19D6 1993
  780'.92—dc20   93-34079
  [B]

British Library Cataloguing in Publication Data is available.

Library of Congress Catalog Card Number: 93-34079
ISBN: 0-313-26864-9
ISSN: 0742-6968

First published in 1993

Greenwood Press, 88 Post Road West, Westport, CT 06881
An imprint of Greenwood Publishing Group, Inc.

Printed in the United States of America

The paper used in this book complies with the
Permanent Paper Standard issued by the National
Information Standards Organization (Z39.48-1984).

10 9 8 7 6 5 4 3 2 1

Contents

Preface

Elliott Carter holds a prominent place in modern music. His compositions have been performed and recorded worldwide. Carter's writings, primarily those appearing in the periodical Modern Music, reveal the thoughts of a major composer and music critic. This book was written, organized and annotated to provide students and scholars better access to the compositions, recordings and writings by and about this distinguished twentieth century American composer.

This book is arranged in five sections: biography, works and performances, discography, bibliography of material by Carter, and bibliography of material about Carter. The first section is a short biography. The purpose of this biography is not to duplicate the other fine biographies available to scholars, but rather to outline the development of Carter's musical career and thus to place the remainder of the work in perspective. The second section is a complete list to date of Carter's works and their significant performances. The section is arranged by genre which is subdivided by the date of completion. Each entry is preceded by a "W" (e.g. W1, W2, etc.) and provides information on the vocal text of the work, dedicatee, medium of performance, and premiere and publication dates. "See" references are provided to facilitate access to the reviews of performances and recordings. The third section is a complete discography of commercially produced recordings and is arranged alphabetically by composition with cross references to the works and performances section. Each entry is preceded by a "D" (e.g. D1, D2, etc.) and provides names of performers, contents of the recording, date of issue, album title, series title, record label number and bibliographic citations for reviews. The fourth section contains a bibliography of writings by Carter and is arranged alphabetically by the title of the article. Some writings have been reprinted. Appropriate citations along with the reprint title are provided. Each entry is preceded by a "B" (e.g. B1, B2, etc.) and includes a short annotation and/or quote from the article. "See" references refer to important citations from other sections of this book. The fifth section is a bibliography of substantial writings about Carter and is arranged by author with anonymous articles interspersed by title. Each entry is preceded by a "C" (e.g. C1, C2, etc.). Each entry includes a short annotation and/or quote from the article. "See" references refer to other sections of the book and are included for reviews of premiere performances.

Several appendices are included. Appendix I provides a list of archival sources valuable to Carter scholarship. Appendix II provides an alphabetical list of Carter's works, and Appendix III is a chronological list of Carter's works. Each entry in Appendix II and III is followed by a "W" number which refers back to the works and performances section. Appendix IV provides addresses current with the publication of this book for publishers of Carter's scores. The book concludes with an index of subjects, and personal, corporate and geographical names.

Throughout this book I have deviated from traditional uses of italics, underlining and bold face type to provide a text which is easier not only to read but also to locate Carter's works within citations. Underlining has been used for titles of books, dissertations and periodicals. I have used italics to highlight Carter's musical works, and have used bold face type to distinguish sections within a particular chapter, such as separating each of Carter's works in the discography.

Acknowledgments

Many thanks go to all the individuals and institutions who have supported me in the writing of this book. The following individuals deserve special recognition for their time, support and encouragement.

Bibliographical Assistance:

I wish to give special recognition to Elliott and Helen Carter who have responded to several letters clarifying dates, performances and other discrepancies. Boosey & Hawkes' Elaine Carroll has been extremely helpful in providing assistance on countless questions. And finally, Harold L. Miller, Reference Archivist, State Historical Society of Wisconsin, who provided helpful advice and reference assistance.

Editorial Assistance:

Proofing bibliographies is not an easy task so a special thanks to my wife Anita Taylor Doering, and Maurice Monhardt, Luther College Music Department, for their efforts. Misha Donat, photographer, has kindly provided the portrait found at the front of this book. Translation of some articles was provided by my wife, Anita, and Elizabeth Jackman Doering. I want to thank the editorial staff at Greenwood Press including: Maureen Melino (Coordinating Editor), Marilyn Brownstein (former Humanities Editor), Don Hixon (Series Adviser) and Mary Blair (former Acquisitions Editor, Music). They have guided me through the publication of this book and have been patient with me during these past years.

Institutional Assistance:

I wish to recognize Luther College for their support in my writing this book. They have been generous in providing me with student assistants, a research grant, and performed the final printing of this book. In particular, Debra Shook showed great patience and expertise with my word processing files. The Luther College Library has given me professional support and encouragement and has assisted me with obtaining materials from other libraries.

I also want to recognize DePauw University for it was while working there that I began researching the book. I also want to thank numerous institutions for the use of their library collections, reference services, and copying facilities: University of Wisconsin-Madison's music and graduate libraries, Luther College (Decorah, IA), University of Wisconsin-La Crosse, Indiana University's music and graduate libraries (Bloomington, IN), Minneapolis Public Library (MN), State Historical Society of Wisconsin (Madison, WI), Northwestern University (Chicago, IL), University of Wisconsin-Eau Claire, University of Wisconsin-River Falls, Des Moines Public Library (IA), La Crosse Public Library (WI), Viterbo College (La Crosse, WI), Madison Public Library (WI), DePauw University (Greencastle, IN), L.E. Phillips Public Library (Eau Claire, WI).

Elliott Carter

Biography

"[Elliott] Carter composes three kinds of music:
discards, studies and masterpieces."[1]

During his lifetime, internationally recognized American composer Elliott Cook Carter, Jr. has composed over three dozen substantial pieces, ranging from stage and choral works to ballets, symphonies, and chamber music. Carter has been the recipient of two Guggenheim Fellowships, two Pulitzer Prizes for Music, and numerous other music awards and honors. Even at age 85, he continues to pioneer trails into new territory in modern American music. Modern music scholars would argue that Carter's greatest influence on twentieth century musical composition is his use and refinement of metric modulation and novel use of sonorities. As David Schiff, a scholar and student of Carter, remarked:

> [To Carter]...any music that is reducible to a few easily imitated tricks fails to achieve the full potential of musical expression. Music has to have the complexity of natural phenomena....And it has to be as intellectually challenging as the best poetry or philosophy.[2]

However, Carter has done more than compose music. Like many of his American contemporaries, he has spent a large amount of his life trying to improve the condition for American composers of modern music, especially in regard to music education. During his long career of over six and a half decades, he has served on numerous faculties, established music curricula, and written and spoken on the need to properly educate Americans, particularly new composers. He has also contributed articles to various music journals and enjoyed a long career as music reviewer and critic.

---

[1]David Schiff, The Music of Elliott Carter (London : Eulenburg Books, 1983), p. 21.

[2]Ibid., p. 19.

Elliott Cook Carter, Jr., one of the premier American composers of concert music in the twentieth century, was born in New York City on December 11, 1908, the son of Elliott Cook Carter, Sr. and Florence Doris Chambers. Although Carter did not come from a particularly musical family, he enjoyed music and learning from a young age. Elliott Jr. decided early in his youth not to pursue the family business for which he had been groomed. This apparently met with disapproval at home.

Carter's paternal grandfather, Eli, began a successful lace importing business after the Civil War in New York City, and his son, Elliott Sr., carried on the tradition and eventually bought out his father's interests. When Elliott Sr. died in 1955, he left the company to its employees. Many Carter scholars use harsh words in describing Carter's parents, suggesting that Carter was virtually cast out by them. He was disinherited when he began serious music study abroad. However, Carter explained that:

> I do remember...taking my father to hear a performance of The Rite of Spring and his saying that 'only a madman' could have written anything like that. Now as I look back on it, though, I see that my parents were really very patient and must have suffered a great deal...they had to sit through my practicing of Scriabin for hours on end, which I imagine they found hard to bear--though they never said so.[3]

While being educated at the Horace Mann School from 1920-1926, young Carter was encouraged by Clifton Furness, music teacher at Horace Mann, to direct serious study to music. Furness recognized his student's interests and talents and introduced him to Charles Ives in 1924. Between Furness and Ives, Carter was exposed to modern music at Carnegie Hall when the Boston Symphony performed there:

> ...I became immediately interested in modern music--up to that time, I had been quite bored with any kind of music, never having heard any modern music.[4]

Although he had taken piano lessons at home, he had not been strongly urged to follow a musical career. Carter credits Ives with pushing him to seriously study composition, and Ives remained a great influence in Carter's musical career. Carter admired Ives' determination to write music for himself and not to impress an audience. Ives wrote a letter of recommendation for Carter to enter Harvard University. In the letter Ives described the young man as an "exceptional boy. He has an instinctive interest in literature and especially music that is somewhat unusual."[5]

---

[3]Allen Edwards, Flawed Words and Stubborn Sounds: A Conversation with Elliott Carter (New York : Norton, 1971), p. 40.

[4]Ibid.

[5]Elliott Carter, "Documents of a Friendship with Ives," Tempo, no. 117 (June 1976), p. 2 ; originals at Yale University Music Library collection.

By this time, Carter had already begun to live a different lifestyle than that of his parents, and he certainly embraced opposing cultural values. Carter was caught up in the avant-garde world of art in Greenwich Village. Katherine Ruth Heyman, a pianist and mystic who held a weekly salon in New York, performed music by Scriabin, Ives, Ravel, Griffes, Schoenberg and others. Teen-aged Carter was most impressed at that time with Scriabin. Carter practiced Scriabin's piano scores diligently and attempted to analyze his works. He enjoyed modern music and was able to purchase new scores during family business trips to Europe. As a result of these jaunts to the Continent, Carter became proficient at several European languages. Before he could write English, Carter learned to speak French at home in training for the family business.

Many scholars agree that Carter began writing music in 1925 or shortly after hearing Stravinsky's The Rite of Spring and being very impressed:

> ...Rite of Spring was a very important and meaningful work, as were several of the works of Varèse...and certainly the later works of Scriabin...as well as Ives' Concord Sonata and some of his songs.[6]

Carter attempted to compose an advanced piano sonata as well as some simpler settings of Joyce's chamber music. After preparatory school, Carter began his studies at Harvard in 1926 and majored in English literature, despite a strong background in the classics. During his undergraduate years, he studied piano with Newton Swift and Hans Ebell, performed with the Harvard Glee Club, and attended as many of the Boston Symphony concerts as he was able. Since Harvard's music department was too conservative for Carter's tastes, the young Elliott took theory courses and oboe lessons at the Longy School.

> ...I began to...discover that the [Harvard] professors...considered Koussevitsky's modernist activities at the Boston Symphony an outright scandal.[7]

It was through Carter's acquaintances that he became familiar with Middle Eastern, Arabic, East Indian, and Chinese music traditions and theory during his undergraduate years, and thus became exposed to non-Western music. Carter even spent a summer transcribing Arab music for the Baron Rudolphe d'Erlanger in Tunisia.

It was during his senior college year when Carter decided to become a composer, although he had entertained the idea before going to Harvard but didn't dare admit this to his parents.[8] After receiving his Bachelor of Arts degree in 1930, Carter continued lessons at Harvard as a graduate student under the direction of Edward Burlingame Hill,

---

[6]Edwards, p. 45.

[7]Ibid.

[8]Ibid.

Gustav Holst (then a visiting professor), and newly appointed professor Walter Piston. Harmony and counterpoint were the focus of Carter's studies.

In 1932, after earning his Master's degree, Carter acted on the suggestion of Piston and began studying privately with Nadia Boulanger in Paris. Thus, Carter's musical training led him to Europe to follow in the footsteps of American composers Aaron Copland, Virgil Thomson, and Piston. During this neoclassical period in the arts, Carter began to develop an interest in the "overt" American styles of Copland and Roger Sessions. However, Carter's main purpose was to learn counterpoint and the basic techniques of Western musical composition. Boulanger used choral music, particularly of Bach, to drive home the lesson. Carter later destroyed all of his compositions written during his Parisian days and many pieces created in of the 1930s.

While in Paris, Carter also earned a *license de contrepoint* from the Ecole Normale de Musique. Carter did not abandon performing music entirely as he sang in a madrigal group directed by Henri Expert and led a chorus of his own. Carter composed incidental music for the Harvard Classical Club's production of Sophocles' *Philocetetes* during his time of study with Boulanger. This piece, for oboe, percussion and men's chorus, was performed at Cambridge, Massachusetts, in the winter of 1933. It was written in Greek, and Carter carefully examined and researched ancient Greek music to incorporate into his first publicly performed composition. He had already explored the Greek language and other classical studies while an undergraduate at Harvard.

Carter returned to the United States in 1935, hoping to find gainful employment during the great Depression.   Carter wrote another piece of incidental music while in Cambridge, Massachusetts, titled Plautus' *Mostellaria* for chamber orchestra and men's voices in Latin. This was performed by the Harvard Classical Club in April 1936. A boisterous excerpt from the score, Tarantella, became a favorite of the Harvard Glee Club for many years. *Tarantella* was later rewritten as a piece for piano four hands and four part men's chorus and performed by the Club April 1937.

In the autumn of 1936 Carter returned to New York City, and he, like many of his peers in the 1930s, launched upon a lengthy career as part-time music reviewer and critic for Modern Music to help earn a regular income. Simultaneously he began to compose a ballet score on the subject of Native American legend Pocahontas which was commissioned by Carter's Harvard associate Lincoln Kirstein.   It was originally composed for piano solo in 1936 and had its debut in Keene, New Hampshire.[9]

The piece was later rewritten, and *Pocahontas*, Carter's first major composition, was successfully premiered in New York on May 24, 1939, by the Ballet Caravan, for which Carter served as musical director from 1937 to 1939. A suite from the score received the Publication of American Music Award from the Juilliard Foundation in 1940 and was later incorporated into Carter's *Symphony #1*. Unfortunately the piece was a bit overshadowed by another ballet on the program that evening--that of Aaron Copland's Billy the Kid.

---

[9]Schiff, Music, p. 97.

Carter and Charles Ives had remained on good terms and Carter had identified with Ives' musical ability throughout his young adulthood. However, as Carter grew professionally and his music began to take on a personality of its own, he began to have mixed feelings about Ives' music. As a music critic for Modern Music, it was Carter's unenviable job to write a review of Ives' Concord Sonata in 1939. At that time, Ives had been heralded by the media as a "great American original" and there was much publicity surrounding the Concord premiere. Carter was forced to give a balanced review of the music and burst the enormous publicity bubble:[10]

> As a whole, the work cannot be said to fill out the broad, elevated design forecast in the composer's preface....In any case, it is not until we have had a much greater opportunity to examine and hear his music, that Ives' position as a composer can be determined. The present canonization is a little premature.[11]

This event created a rift between Carter and the Ives' family. As Schiff noted:

> [This] haunted him both in his subsequent relations with the Ives' family and also in his own evolving senses of creative mission. It would be another decade before Carter could come to terms with Ives' creative legacy and use it in developing his own idiom.[12]

Many years later Carter summarized his feelings towards Charles Ives' music:

> Sometimes, as in the Concord Sonata, his music seems like the work of an extraordinary accomplished and skilled composer....And then there are other pieces that seem to wipe all this aside and do something else.[13]

On July 6, 1939, Carter married Helen Frost Jones, a sculptor and art critic, in Chatham, Massachusetts. A son, David Chambers Carter, was born to the couple on January 4, 1943. The elder Carter accepted a teaching position at St. John's College in Annapolis, Maryland, in 1940.

Carter's next important work, apart from *Pastoral* for English horn and piano, was *The Defense of Corinth* written in 1941. Abraham Skulsky explains that Carter, using a seventeenth century English translation of a text by Rabelais, "uses the chorus in many

---

[10]Ibid., p. 18.

[11]Elliott Carter, "The Case of Mr. Ives," Modern Music, v. 16, no. 3 (March/April 1939), p. 175-176.

[12]Schiff, Music, p. 19.

[13]Edwards, p. 63.

novel ways....The result is extremely lively and spirited, expressing the outspokenly satiric content of the text with great humor."[14]

Carter left his teaching post at St. John's College in 1941 because he felt the demands of teaching were too great to allow enough time for serious composition. At St. John's, Carter supervised all musical endeavors and taught Greek and mathematics. Carter discovered that there simply wasn't enough time to devote to both activities and saw his first priority as composition. During World War II Carter was the music consultant for the Office of War Information and also taught at the Peabody Conservatory from 1946-1948. From there he accepted a post at Columbia University from 1948-1950.

One of two orchestral pieces Carter wrote in the 1940s was *Holiday Overture* written while on vacation on Fire Island in the summer of 1944. Carter composed the piece to celebrate the liberation of Paris from Nazi occupation. *Holiday Overture* won the Independent Music Publishers' Contest in 1945 and was premiered by the Frankfurt Symphony in Frankfurt, Germany, the following year. Part of the contest prize was to be a performance of the winning piece by conductor Sergey Koussevitsky and the Boston Symphony, but the conductor never played the work, and "Carter had to steal the parts from the orchestra's library so they could be duplicated for performance elsewhere."[15] Unfortunately, as with a number of Carter's pieces, conductors felt his works were too technically difficult, structurally complex and modern to be performed. Carter recollected:

> Indeed, I'll never forget taking my *Holiday Overture* to [Aaron] Copland and going over it with him, only to have even him tell me it was just another one of those "typical, complicated Carter scores."[16]

Scholars agree that the two most celebrated compositions written during Carter's 1936-1948 period were his *Piano Sonata* and *The Minotaur* ballet. The *Piano Sonata*, composed in 1945-1946 during Carter's first Guggenheim Fellowship, was noted by critic Arthur Berger as "one of the most distinguished achievements for the keyboard."[17] Incorporated into the *Piano Sonata* was the beginning of what was later to become known as metric modulation.[18]

---

[14]Abraham Skulsky, "Elliott Carter," <u>ACA</u> <u>Bulletin</u>, v. 3, no. 2 (Summer 1953), p. 4.

[15]Schiff, <u>Music</u>, p. 113.

[16]Edwards, p. 58.

[17]Skulsky, p.5 quotes Arthur Berger from an article in the <u>Saturday</u> <u>Review</u> <u>of</u> <u>Literature</u>.

[18]Edwards, p. 91-92, notes that only the term "metric modulation" was new and not the technique. However, Carter is best known for his innovative and optimum use of it.

Skulsky credited Carter with:

> ...coming to grips with the modern piano. For it, he invented a purely
> pianistic style that gives full rein to the virtuoso aspect of the instrument,
> employing its full range of sonorous possibilities.[19]

Richard F. Goldman, in his review which appeared in Musical Quarterly, stated:

> The *Piano Sonata* is a decisive work; it has sweep and scale; there is
> nothing small or fussy about it to detract from its effect. It is dramatic
> and intense, broad and vigorous....moving and original expressiveness
> tending away from neo-classicism.[20]

Carter explained that since his **Piano Sonata** composition, he had been interested in
exploring the sonoric differences between instruments.[21]

The Minotaur, a ballet commissioned again by Lincoln Kirstein, this time for the Ballet
Society, originally began as a collaboration between Carter and choreographer George
Balanchine. The two had worked out the scenes and angular music when Balanchine
took off for Paris to handle a ballet for the Paris Opera. Most of the details of *The
Minotaur* were left to Balanchine's assistant, John Taras.

The premiere took place at the Central High School of Needle Trades in New York City,
March 27, 1947. While the choreography of the ballet was not embraced by the dance
critics, Carter's score received praise from music critics. Skulsky commented:

> ...Carter ventures into the expression of tragic moods in conjunction with
> literary texts. Except for *Pocahontas*, most of his music had hitherto
> been either of a gay or joyous quality or else quietly nostalgic. Now he
> started to explore a domain of feeling new to his music.[22]

Carter's *Sonata for Violoncello and Piano*, composed in 1948, is often noted as a
turning point in Carter's career. It was written for cellist Bernard Greenhouse and was
premiered in February 1950. This was the first piece in which Carter used metric
modulation, and it also revealed his continued experimentation with sonority. Goldman
remarked:

---

[19]Skulsky, p. 5.

[20]Richard F. Goldman, "Current Chronicle: United States: New York," Musical
Quarterly, v. 37, no. 1 (January 1951), p. 85.

[21]Edwards, p. 68.

[22]Skulsky, p. 8.

...the *'Cello Sonata* is far above the common run of contemporary premieres; it is a happy confirmation of the quality of all of Carter's recent work and a happier augury for the future.[23]

This piece marks the end of the neophyte stage of composition for Carter. He had experimented with metric modulation and sonority and had clearly set a course for his future compositions. David Schiff noted that:

Most of the works of 1936 to 1948 display basic conflicts: between experimental innovation and technical discipline, between a politically inspired desire for simplicity and a deep-seated need for complexity of expression.[24]

In the late 1940s, Carter spent:

...a lot of time in the jazz clubs on 52nd Street.... Jazz of that period [the height of the "bebop" era] was very important to me.[25]

David Schiff noted that:

...it is not hard to detect the influence of Bud Powell and Charlie Parker in the Cello Sonata of 1948 and the First String Quartet of 1951. While Carter never mimics jazz, he often captures its rhymthic essence.[26]

Just before writing his first string quartet, Carter composed "compositional studies" titled *Eight Etudes and a Fantasy* (1949) written for woodwind quartet and *Six Pieces for Timpani* (1950). These works prepared him for what he called his "magic mountain" experience. Many percussionists were eager to play the *Pieces*, so Carter published two of the movements in 1960. Over the years, Paul Price and other instructors convinced Carter to publish the remaining four *Pieces*. With the technical expertise of Jan Williams, Carter revised the *Pieces* extensively and wrote another two movements in 1966.[27] The *Eight Pieces* were published in 1968.

---

[23]Goldman, p. 83.

[24]Schiff, <u>Music</u>, p. 76.

[25]David Schiff, "Elliott Carter: America's Much-Honored Composer is Still Challenging Music at Age 75," <u>Ovation</u> (December 1983), p. 15.

[26]Ibid.

[27]Patrick Wilson, "Elliott Carter: Eight Pieces for Four Timpani," <u>Percussive Notes</u>, v. 23, no. 1 (October 1984), p. 65.

The *String Quartet #1*, written in 1950-1951 during his second Guggenheim Fellowship, was a turning point in Carter's attitude toward composition and in the way in which his musical colleagues regarded him. Carter left New York and took up residence near Tucson, Arizona, in the desert to compose a masterpiece that encompassed everything he had learned and experimented with, especially with regard to texture and harmony. Carter doubted any performer would even attempt to play the work or that a musical audience could understand it.[28]

Carter had decided to:

> ...write a work very interesting to myself and to say the hell with the public and with the performers too....So from that point on I decided that I would just write whatever interested me, whatever expressed the conceptions and feelings that I had, without concern for an existing public.[29]

To Carter's surprise, his *String Quartet #1* won the prize at the Liège festival, and he began to gain recognition in Europe. As a result of the success of the piece, he was welcomed as a colleague by international composers. Unfortunately, many Americans hated the piece, and his future in the eyes of American audiences was, at that time, dubious. Schiff noted:

> It took many years to develop a musical language capable of serving Carter's expressive intentions. The mature idiom only emerged fully in the *First String Quartet* of 1951--written fifteen years after Carter's return from Paris.[30]

Carter, in his address to his Harvard classmates on the occasion of their 25th anniversary, reflected on his first internationally recognized piece:

> I decided to let it [the *String Quartet #1*] try its fate in a European contest....I produced forty minutes of string quartet music that was immediately called the hardest piece for the combination ever written....To my utter surprise, the Walden Quartet [of Illinois] learned the work and it won the Liège Prize in September, 1953....My work was submitted under the pseudonym of *Chronometros* since it dealt with unusual divisions of musical time.[31]

---

[28]Edwards, p. 35.

[29]Ibid., p. 35-36.

[30]Schiff, Music, p. 21.

[31]"Elliott Cook Carter," 25th Anniversary Report of the Harvard Class of 1930 (Cambridge, MA : Harvard University Press, 1955), p. 168.

The premiere of the *String Quartet #1* was not held in Liège as was customary for the contest, but at Columbia University in New York by the Walden Quartet of the University of Illinois on February 26, 1953, before the Liège prize had been awarded.

World War II had a tremendous affect on art, culture and music around the world. This change is evident in Carter's compositional style as well. In a 1989 interview, Carter commented:

> Not only the war, but the Depression before it caused a vast change in me and the American music scene. One of the results...was the ever increasing erosion of commonly agreed on aesthetic standards....There was a whole series of philosophical ideas about music reaching a different kind of people and a different kind of audience and being more accessible.[32]

Carter began to develop new rhythmic and harmonic techniques that bridged this "culture gap" between the old avant-garde and high modernism styles. In 1952 Carter was the head of the American ISCM when it hosted an all Webern concert in New York. Although he had always liked the music of Webern, Berg and Schoenberg, Carter grew to appreciate their musical styles even more during this post-World War II era.

From 1953-1954, Carter was a fellow at the American Academy in Rome where he began to write *Variations for Orchestra*. The piece was completed in 1955 and stands out as his only major symphonic work before the *Concerto for Orchestra* (1969). As is typical with technically difficult pieces, particularly symphonic works, *Variations* was not performed by the New York Philharmonic Orchestra until sixteen years after its premiere.

Variations was commissioned by the Louisville Orchestra with financial support of the Rockefeller Foundation. As a result, the piece was tailored to the strengths and limitations of the small string section of the Louisville Orchestra. The work was debuted in April 1956, in Louisville, Kentucky. The composition is most noted for its opposition of instruments and innovative rhythmic structures. *Variations* was revised in 1972.

Orin Moe commented:

> The *Variations* establishes a tactic that will remain. A logical sequence of dramatic events will organize a work at the largest structural level, with an emphasis on process at the medium and small structural level.[33]

Variations marks the end of the intermediate period of Carter's compositional career. The Darmstadt school, the twelve tone system, and total serialization experienced a renaissance following cultural changes in post-World War II Europe. Although Carter

---

[32]Richard Dufallo, "Elliott Carter," Trackings: Composers Speak with Richard Dufallo (New York : Oxford University Press, 1989), p. 279.

[33]Orin Moe, "The Music of Elliott Carter," College Music Symposium, v. 22, no. 1 (Spring 1982), p. 18.

may have been influenced by these methods, he claims to have not analyzed his works in this way or intentionally used these techniques. Following a rhymthic procedures symposium at Princeton University in 1960, Carter wrote an article for Musical Quarterly. When asked by a student regarding serialization, Carter replied:

> ...it is true that like all music, mine goes from one thing to another--the pattern on which serialization is based--but my choices of where to start and where to go are controlled by a general plan of action that directs both the continuity and the expression.[34]

After a writing hiatus of four years, Carter unveiled his *String Quartet #2*. This piece, premiered by the Juilliard Quartet in March 1960, proved to be Carter's official American acknowledgement of his accomplishments. Three major honors were awarded to the work: the Pulitzer Prize for Music (1960), the New York Music Critics' Circle Award (1960-1961), and the UNESCO First Prize (1961). Although commissioned by the Stanley String Quartet of the University of Michigan, the group found it to be too difficult to perform and gave up its first performance rights. Carter returned the commission to the Quartet so the Juilliard Quartet would debut the piece.[35]

Carter saw his second string quartet as a natural progression from the first. Each instrument was afforded its utmost individuality and character. The first violin is "fantastic, ornate and mercurial;" the second violin "laconic, orderly...some-times humorous;" the viola "expressive;" the cello "impetuous."[36]

Howard Taubman, in his New York Times review of the premiere, lauded Carter:

> With his *Second String Quartet* Elliott Carter rivets his right to be regarded as one of the most distinguished of living composers....In the *Second Quartet*, Mr. Carter...has set himself new problems, but one of his fundamental concerns has remained the creative use of polyrhythms. The four instruments have been treated with almost rigorous independence, and yet they interact to enrich one another. The sum is greater than the parts.[37]

Carter taught at Queens College, New York, from 1955-1956, and later at Yale University from 1960-1962. Despite Carter's several forays into various university

---

[34]Elliott Carter, "Shop Talk by an American Composer," Musical Quarterly, v. 46, no. 2 (April 1960), p. 196.

[35]Schiff, Music, p. 240.

[36]Michael Steinberg, "Elliott Carter's Second String Quartet," The Score and I.M.A. Magazine, no. 27 (July 1960), p. 22.

[37]Howard Taubman, "Music: Work by Carter," New York Times, March 26, 1960, p. 14.

teaching positions over the years, he tried to keep the time spent in a classroom to a minimum. In an article from 1969 Carter reflected:

> ...it could be an unhealthy situation for composers to be too much involved with education, especially in a university. For the age level of students, and their preparation is always the same in each new class, from year to year, while the composer changes and develops and naturally grows older.... The American composer, like his colleagues on university faculties, tends to be treated as a commodity...[38]

Following the success of his *String Quartet #2*, Carter completed his next major composition *Double Concerto* for harpsichord and piano with two chamber orchestras in August 1961. The piece was funded by the Fromm Music Foundation and, for the first time, Carter was able to compose for a large group without restriction. He was allowed to hand pick the instrumentalists and was promised adequate rehearsal time.

The piece premiered in September 1961 at the Eighth Congress of the International Society for Musicology. Gustav Meier conducted and Ralph Kirkpatrick and Charles Rosen were soloists on the harpsichord and piano respectively. The *Double Concerto* was recognized with a New York Music Critics' Circle Award for 1961-1962.

Richard F. Goldman noted:

> In the case of Carter's *Concerto*, about eighteen hours of rehearsal were needed to achieve what one of the players described as a performance 'good enough for recording, but slightly risky for live performance.'[39]

At least two premiere reviewers complained of acoustical problems in the auditorium and felt the harpsichord was thin and couldn't lead or carry its chamber orchestra.

Charles Rosen, pianist of the premiere, painfully described the technical problems performers face in playing the *Double Concerto*:

> At one point...traditional notation is stretched beyond its limits and even abandoned, if only briefly....In playing this passage, I have always found it best not to look at the conductor at all and just pray that it will come out right. It generally does, as the extreme speed of the repeated notes at the end demanded by Carter represent the technical limits of the instruments as well as of the performer.[40]

---

[38]Elliott Carter, "The Composer is a University Commodity," College Music Symposium, v. 10 (Fall 1970), p. 68.

[39]Richard F. Goldman, "Current Chronicle: United States: New York," Musical Quarterly, v. 48, no. 1 (January 1962), p. 97.

[40]Charles Rosen, "One Easy Piece," Composer (London), no. 69 (Spring 1980), p. 6.

Rosen also credited conductor Gustav Meier with exclaiming, "I feel more like a traffic cop than a conductor!"[41] Eric Salzman described the Carter work as:

> ...nothing less than an astonishing conception; a breathtaking panorama of flashing textures and rhythms that curve from opening to end with the most extraordinary, imaginative pulse.[42]

One of Carter's early influences, and later friend and colleague, Igor Stravinsky, proclaimed:

> There, the word is out. A masterpiece, by an American composer.[43]

Following a two year professorship at Yale University, Carter again found himself as the composer-in-residence at the American Academy in Rome in 1963 where he began work on a *Piano Concerto* dedicated "To Igor Stravinsky on his 85th birthday with great admiration and friendship." In 1964 Carter was asked by the Ford Foundation and the Berliner Senat to continue a residency in Berlin.

> The Cold War tensions following the construction of the Berlin Wall certainly left their mark on the *Concerto*. Carter remembers the constant sound of machine-gun fire from a U.S. Army target range near his studio--a sound that echoes through the second movement.[44]

Carter finished writing the composition at his studio in Waccabuc, New York, in 1965. The *Piano Concerto* had its debut in January 1967, by the Boston Symphony Orchestra. It was commissioned by Jacob Lateiner through the Ford Foundation, and Lateiner was the pianist at the premiere.

Benjamin Boretz noted in an article:

> ...the Carter *Concerto* does represent a rather extraordinary culmination of ideas inherent in his earlier music, and that it does constitute the most definitively developed instance thus far of a compositional approach that is one of the significant polarities of contemporary American work.[45]

---

[41]Ibid.

[42]Eric Salzman, "Music: Three Distinguished Works," New York Times, September 7, 1961, p. 41.

[43]Igor Stravinsky and Robert Craft, Dialogues and a Diary (New York : Doubleday, 1963), p. 49.

[44]Schiff, Music, p. 227.

[45]Benjamin Boretz, "Music," The Nation, v. 204, no. 14 (April 3, 1967), p. 445.

Arthur Cohn noted:

> ...Elliott Carter...is certainly among the select composers at work today.
> Even when we cannot understand *all* of the sounds he puts together, we
> are under the spell of a dramatic focus that is overwhelming....The *Piano
> Concerto*...is one of the most penetrating contributions he or anyone else
> has made to the music of the 20th century.[46]

And Igor Stravinsky, in a personal letter to Carter in 1968 remarked, "I am more
delighted with it [the *Piano Concerto*] than I can tell you. It is a masterpiece, and I like
it even more than the *Double Concerto*."[47]

Based on a Nobel prize-winning poem <u>Vents</u> (Winds) by French poet St. John Perse,
Carter wrote his *Concerto for Orchestra* in 1968 while composer-in-residence at the
American Academy in Rome.   The score was commissioned by the New York
Philharmonic Symphony Society to celebrate its 125th anniversary.   The work was
dedicated to the New York Philharmonic Orchestra and its musical director, Leonard
Bernstein.

David Schiff noted that the *Concerto* allows for almost every player to become a soloist
at some time.[48]   David Hamilton stated that roles are again assigned to various
performers but that Carter carries this out "in greater depth and detail" than in his other
orchestral works.[49]   Harold Schonberg remarked that following the premiere
performance in February 1970, the piece "received a surprisingly warm welcome."[50]
In an interview with Raymond Ericson, Carter commented that *Concerto for Orchestra*
was the first major work of his to be performed by the Philharmonic.[51]

From 1967-1968, Carter served as professor of musical composition at the Juilliard
School and was appointed Andrew D. White professor-at-large at Cornell University.

----

[46]Arthur Cohn, "Elliott Carter's Piano Concerto," <u>The</u> <u>American</u> <u>Record</u> <u>Guide</u>,
v. 34, no. 10 (June 1968), p. 937.

[47]Letter from Igor Stravinsky to Elliott Carter dated 15 June 1968, reprinted in
Schiff, p. 239.

[48]Schiff, <u>Music</u>, p. 246.

[49]David Hamilton, "Music," <u>The</u> <u>Nation</u>, v. 210, no. 8 (March 2, 1970), p. 254.

[50]Harold Schonberg, "Music: Bernstein Leads Carter Work," <u>New</u> <u>York</u> <u>Times</u>,
February 6, 1970, p. 27.

[51]Raymond Ericson, "Carter on the Record," <u>New</u> <u>York</u> <u>Times</u>, February 1,
1970, section II, p. 23. [Note: David Hamilton, "Carter's Virtuoso Concerto," <u>High</u>
<u>Fidelity</u>, v. 20, no.5 (May 1970), p. 22, gives an inside view of events at the New
York Philharmonic's recording of *Concerto for Orchestra* under the direction of
Leonard Bernstein].

Carter's successful *String Quartet #3* was commissioned by the Juilliard School for the Juilliard Quartet. The *Quartet* was premiered by the Juilliard Quartet at Lincoln Center in January 1973. The musicians were: Robert Mann, Earl Carlyss, Samuel Rhodes and Claus Adam. The piece won the Pulitzer Prize for Music for 1973, thirteen years after Carter's *String Quartet #2* earned a similar award. In a review in the New Yorker, Andrew Porter described the atmosphere of the premiere in the Alice Tully Hall:

> The place was full, the atmosphere electric. All musical New York seemed to be there. It was 'an event'....After the performance, both Carter and his interpreters were cheered.[52]

Carter divided the players into two duos. The first pairs' style was to be intense and impulsive. The second duo was to play in strict time. David Schiff described the *String Quartet #3*:

> The constant superimposition of highly colored textures, tapestry upon tapestry, produces a hallucinatory effect, at once terrifying and captivating. The energy level of the *Third Quartet* and its rhythmic force achieve the peak intensity to be found in all of Carter's chamber music.[53]

David Hamilton described Carter's third quartet as a:

> violent altercation....The conflict ebbs and flows, but at the end of the initial level...violence has returned.[54]

Dedicated to his wife Helen, *Duo for Violin and Piano* was commissioned by the McKim Fund of the Library of Congress. It was finished at the end of April 1974, and was premiered May 1975 in Cooper Union, New York, by the New York Philharmonic Prospective Encounter Concert with Paul Zukofsky on violin and Gilbert Kalish on piano. Schiff noted that Carter "considers it [the *Duo*] his finest composition:"[55]

> In the *Duo*, the contrast between the violin and the piano, both stringed instruments, is fundamentally a gestural one--between stroking and striking.[56]

---

[52]Andrew Porter, "Mutual Ordering," New Yorker, v. 48, no. 50 (February 3, 1973), p. 82.

[53]Schiff, "Elliott Carter: America's Much-Honored Composer is Still Challenging Music at Age 75," p. 52.

[54]David Hamilton, "In Carter's String Quartets, Difficulty Can Hold Delight," New York Times, October 6, 1991, p. 43.

[55]Schiff, Music, p. 270.

[56]Kurt E. and Else Stone (eds.), The Writings of Elliott Carter: An American Composer Looks at Modern Music, (Bloomington, IN : Indiana University Press, 1977), p. 327.

Richard Derby, in a study of the *Duo*, stated:

> Such cross-fertilization and interaction results in a relatively seamless
> growth of music involving a process of constant yet cyclical change....a
> complex, consistent, intensely expressive, perhaps even unsettling--and
> certainly momentous--work of art.[57]

Carter went right back to work, this time in Aspen, Colorado, where he was in residence
with the American Brass Quintet. The piece *Brass Quintet* was commissioned by the
group and was written between May and August 1974. The American Brass Quintet
debuted the composition in a Charles Ives Festival of the BBC to commemorate Ives'
100th birthday. Carter noted in an introductory talk:

> I am particularly happy that the world premiere of my *Brass Quintet*
> should be given as part of the BBC's celebration of Charles Ives'
> hundredth birthday, because it helps to repay the great debt I owe him
> personally and musically.[58]

Andrew Porter commented that the piece "is inspired by the kinds of sound and musical
motion inherent in and traditionally appropriate to ensemble and solo brass."[59] He
described the *Quintet* as a "major addition to the brass chamber literature."[60]

A Mirror on Which to Dwell (six poems of Elizabeth Bishop) was written for soprano
and chamber orchestra and was a return by Carter to the composition of vocal works, a
genre he abandoned after his early days. The work was commissioned by Speculum
Musicae in honor of the U.S. Bicentennial, with grants from the New York State Council
on the Arts, the Mellon Foundation, Milton M. Scofield, Murray Socolof, Fred Sherry
and Bernard E. Brandes. Scored for nine players and a soprano, each poem or song is
different and they are not a continuation of each other. The piece was premiered at
Hunter College in New York City, February 1976, by soprano Susan Davenny Wyner
and Speculum Musicae.

Orin Moe explained:

> The poems are arranged so that they are alternately descriptive and
> emotional, and they are well complemented by Carter's essentially
> dramatic styles....As structurally subtle and complex as any of his music,

---

[57] Richard Derby, "Carter's Duo for Violin and Piano," Perspectives of New
Music, v. 20, no. 1-2 (Fall/Winter 1981-Spring/Summer 1982), p. 167.

[58] Stone, p. 323.

[59] Andrew Porter, ""Duo," New Yorker, v. 51, no. 7 (April 7, 1975), p. 129.

[60] Andrew Porter, "Boris Redivivus," New Yorker, v. 50, no. 5 (December 30,
1974), p. 55.

they [the songs] are nevertheless simply approachable as brilliant readings of arresting poems.[61]

Another score written on the occasion of the American Bicentennial was *A Symphony of Three Orchestras*, completed at the end of December 1976. The New York Philharmonic commissioned the piece through a grant from the National Endowment for the Arts. The work was dedicated to the New York Philharmonic and its musical director, Pierre Boulez, and was premiered February 1977 in Avery Fisher Hall.

The inspiration for the piece was the beginning of Hart Crane's poem The Bridge, which describes the Brooklyn Bridge and New York harbor. Since his Harvard days, Carter had wanted to write a choral work based on the poem. However, he abandoned this idea and used The Bridge instead as a starting point of a symphonic work. The program note included this:

> Although *A Symphony of Three Orchestras* is not in any sense an attempt to express the poem of Hart Crane in music, many of the musical ideas were suggested by it and other works.[62]

Andrew Porter felt that *A Symphony* "is of all Carter's scores the richest in sound."[63] After the premiere, Irving Kolodin described the work as being "of stunning authority and imposing imagination."[64] However, Harold Schonberg's review of the debut was frank:

> ...complex, dissonant and powerful....Mr. Carter has never made concessions to his listeners....The audience took *A Symphony of Three Orchestras* with better grace than is usual. There were hardly any boos, and Mr. Carter got a cordial reception when he bowed from the balcony.[65]

Syringa, a piece that incorporates elements of several genres, was funded through a composer-librettist grant from the National Endowment for the Arts and was dedicated to Sir William and Lady Glock. The premiere took place at Alice Tully Hall, Lincoln

---

[61]Moe, p. 28.

[62]"Symphony of Three Orchestras (1976) : Program Note" quoted by Stone, p. 367.

[63]Andrew Porter, "Great Bridge, Our Myth," New Yorker, v. 53, no. 3 (March 7, 1977), p. 104.

[64]Irving Kolodin, "Carter's Symphony: Beethoven by Maazel," Saturday Review, v. 4, no. 13 (April 2, 1977), p. 37-38.

[65]Harold Schonberg, "Music: Elliott Carter," New York Times, February 18, 1977, section III, p. 11.

Center, in December 1978. Jan DeGaetani was the featured mezzo-soprano, Thomas Paul the bass, and Speculum Musicae the instrumentalists.

John Ashbery, an avant-garde American poet, came to Carter and asked if they could collaborate on a piece. Ashbery sent Carter some of his poetry, and Carter decided to work with Syringa. Carter recollected:

> I began to try to find a way of dealing with the subdued poetic tone in my music, because I think of my work as being more extravagant and exciting; so I decided that I would make Syringa into a duet.[66]

The subject of the poem is the myth of Orpheus. Orin Moe commented:

> Carter contrasts a calm, graceful, smoothly flowing line for mezzo-soprano with a rhythmically agitated, mournful, almost archaic line for bass....the composer assigns the poem to the upper voice and selected texts from the ancient Greek to the lower one.[67]

While at his country home in Waccabuc, New York, and at the American Academy in Rome between June 1979 and April 1980, Carter composed a score for solo piano, the first since his celebrated *Piano Sonata* of 1946. *Night Fantasies* was commissioned by and dedicated to four New York pianists through a grant from the American Music Center. The performers all had had considerable experience and competence in playing Carter's music over a number of years: Paul Jacobs, Gilbert Kalish, Ursula Oppens, and Charles Rosen. At the Bath Festival in England, Ursula Oppens gave the premiere in early June 1980.

Schiff described the structure of the piece:

> ...*Night Fantasies* is built out of many contrasting episodes. Carter, however, collages fragments of his episodes so that they appear, evolve and vanish, sometimes growing imperceptibly out of one another, elsewhere appearing suddenly, sharply interrupting the previous mood.[68]

John McInerney, after hearing Paul Jacobs perform the New York premiere of *Night Fantasies*, commented:

> It is an elaborate, episodic score with deliberate virtuoso intent. Carter has called it a 'sort of contemporary Kriesleriana' and has also likened it

---

[66]Dufallo, p. 280.

[67]Moe, p. 29.

[68]Schiff, Music, p. 315.

to the visions of an insomniac trying vainly to sleep.[69]

In Sleep, In Thunder (six poems of Robert Lowell) was composed for tenor and fourteen instruments and was commissioned by the London Sinfonietta. It premiered in London in October 1982 with Martyn Hill as soloist, but was not performed in the United States until December 1983 at a Speculum Musicae concert in celebration of Carter's 75th birthday. Jon Garrison was the New York soloist. Carter admired Lowell's poetry, and the work is dedicated to the poet's memory. Carter decided to use a group of six unrhymed Lowell sonnets published in 1973 as the text for *In Sleep, In Thunder.*

In a program note, Carter explained:

...what attracted me about these texts were their rapid, controlled changes from passion to tenderness, to humor, and to a sense of loss.[70]

Schiff noted:

Perhaps the key to Carter's portrait of Lowell is volatility. All the poems oscillate in subject and tone; ideas and images recur from one poem to the next but with ironically opposed connotations.... There are no stylistic allusions to past practice, no familiar formal patterns.[71]

Edward Rothstein commented after the U.S. premiere:

Mr. Carter's music managed to celebrate the creation of art out of loss and pain, without becoming indulgent or nostalgic or obvious.[72]

Commissioned by the BBC for the Fires of London (formerly known as the Pierrot Players), *Triple Duo* was a return to purely instrumental ensemble music for Carter. The piece was premiered at the Britain Salutes New York Festival at Symphony Space, New York, and was dedicated to Peter Maxwell Davies, the leader of the Fires. The group called itself a music-theatre ensemble and included a singer, dancer or mime. Andrew Porter described the piece as a:

...'play' for enactment by six instruments, its score a 'scenario' in which three couples--violin and cello, flute and clarinet, piano and percussion--

[69]John McInerney, "Paul Jacobs, Piano: Carter Night Fantasies," High Fidelity/Musical America v. 32, no. 3 (March 1982), p. MA28.

[70]Andrew Porter, "Songs with a Mind," New Yorker v. 59, no. 46 (January 2, 1984), p. 84, quoting Elliott Carter.

[71]David Schiff, "In Sleep, In Thunder: Elliott Carter's Portrait of Robert Lowell," Tempo no. 142 (September 1982), p. 4-5.

[72]Edward Rothstein, "Music: A Tribute to Elliott Carter, 75," New York Times, December 14, 1983, section III, p. 32.

are the characters. They leap onstage abruptly, jauntily as sounds...but the musical gestures are graphic.[73]

Schiff described the composition as:

> ...deceptively lightweight. It begins with a joke; the players are caught in the act of warming up. The winds gurgle and shriek, the strings scratch and pluck, the piano and percussion go bang bang bang....The main formal strategy...is its suppression--and then release--of lyricism.[74]

Guitarist David Starobin commissioned *Changes*, the first solo guitar piece Carter composed. Starobin had asked Carter to consider writing a score for guitar as early as 1979, but Carter had two major compositions to write at that time. He completed a first sketch of *Changes* in April 1983. Starobin premiered the nearly eight minute work at a Speculum Musicae concert at New York's 92nd Street Y on Carter's 75th birthday, December 11, 1983. The piece was originally titled *Micomicon* but Starobin felt the name had connotations of ridicule. After several revisions, the title became *Changes*.

Allan Kozinn noted that during an open rehearsal of the concert Carter explained:

> The title reflects a similarity I hear between the changes in the chordal structures in this piece and the chordal patterns that occur in English bell-ringing--or, 'ringing the changes.' It also has to do with the rapid changes of character I tried to capture in the music.[75]

Andrew Porter described the piece simply as "captivating."[76]   Allan Clive Jones commented:

> Like so many non-guitarist composers, Carter found the unusual tuning and fingering of the instrument...somewhat bothersome. He was at pains to explore the 'natural' character of the instrument and to avoid those things it is patently unsuited for.[77]

---

[73]Andrew Porter, "Thought-Executing Fires," New Yorker, v. 59, no. 12 (May 9, 1983), p. 114.

[74]David Schiff, "Elliott Carter's Harvest Home," Tempo, no. 167 (December 1988), p. 2-3.

[75]Allan Kozinn, "Elliott Carter's Changes," Guitar Review, no. 57 (April 1984), p.2.

[76]Porter, "Musical Events: Songs with a Mind", p. 86.

[77]Allan Clive Jones, "Elliott Carter and the Music of Change," Classical Guitar, v. 3, no. 3 (November 1984), p. 24.

Written in honor of the achievements of Sir William Glock, Carter's *Canon for 4* ("Homage to William") was premiered at the Bath Festival in June 1984, performed by the London Sinfonietta. It was written for the occasion of Glock's retirement as director of the Bath Festival. The work was scored for flute, bass clarinet, violin and violoncello. *Canon* is a short piece, lasting about five minutes. After the American premiere in December 1984 by the Chamber Music Society of Lincoln Center, Andrew Porter commented in his column:

> Initially, the players set out as two couples: flute and clarinet are in step, violin and cello play a two-part invention. Then they become individuals. Quite soon, the texture thins, the pace becomes less emphatic, and group activity turns to conversation....I keep finding new subtleties of construction and feel I have barely touched the surface of its ingenious secrets.[78]

In honor of his long-time friend and colleague, Pierre Boulez, Carter composed another occasional piece *Esprit Rude/Esprit Doux* in celebration of Boulez's 60th birthday. The piece uses a motto based on the letters in the name "Boulez." Scored for flute and clarinet, the performed work lasts about five minutes and was premiered by Boulez's Ensemble InterContemporain, at the end of March 1985, in Baden Baden, Germany.

Riconoscenza, a tribute to Goffredo Petrassi on his 80th birthday, was premiered at the Pontino Festival in Italy, in June 1984 with Georg Mönch as violinist. The title of the piece combines senses of recognition and gratitude. The American premiere featured Eugene Drucker of the Emerson Quartet at a Chamber Music Society of Lincoln Center concert in December 1984--the same concert at which *Canon for 4* received its American debut. Andrew Porter described the work for solo violin as a:

> large adventure in small space...concerned with seeing things in different and varied lights and looking back on what we've just experienced.[79]

An orchestra divided into five groups of four players set the scene for *Penthode*: trumpet, trombone, harp and violin; flute, horn, marimba, and double-bass; oboe, tuba, violin and violoncello; clarinet, bass clarinet, trumpet and vibraphone; and finally bassoon, piano, percussion, and viola. Carter's program note included:

> ...each group has its own repertory of expression characters embodied in its own special field of speeds and musical intervals....*Penthode* is concerned with experiences of connectedness and isolation.[80]

---

[78]Andrew Porter, "Riches in Little Room," New Yorker, v. 60, no. 45 (December 24, 1984), p. 64.

[79]Ibid., p. 62.

[80]Elliott Carter quoted in Andrew Porter, "Discourse Most Eloquent," New Yorker, v. 62, no. 10 (April 28, 1986), p. 96.

The eighteen minute piece was commissioned by and dedicated to Pierre Boulez and L'Ensemble InterContemporain. The group premiered the work in London in July 1985, and in February 1986, they introduced *Penthode* to a U.S. audience in Boston. David Schiff commented that Carter often regretted the fact that orchestras and other large groups could not devote the necessary practice time to his music to perform it successfully. As a result, chamber ensembles have traditionally performed Carter's works at a much higher level. Schiff noted:

> A commission from l'Ensemble InterContemporain ...was an invitation to Carter to write his dream piece--free from normal worries about practical conditions and limits of technique....*Penthode* ... is Carter's luminous response, his vision of a musical utopia.[81]

Completed in 1986, *String Quartet #4* was commissioned by the Composers, Sequoia and Thouvenel Quartets and is dedicated to the Composers Quartet. Fifteen years after the completion of his *String Quartet #3*, Carter again assigned each instrument a distinct personality, but, as Schiff observed, a new "spirit of cooperation" is present.[82] The *Quartet* was premiered by the Composers Quartet in September 1986 in Miami. The piece has four distinct movements: Appassionato, Scherzando, Lento, and Presto. Andrew Porter pointed out that this was something new for Carter: "the dwelling on expressive intervals."[83]

Oboe Concerto was the last major piece Carter wrote in the 1980s. Commissioned by Paul Sacher for Heinz Holliger, the *Concerto* was premiered in Zurich, Switzerland, as part of the Zurich Festival by the Collegium Musicum. Heinz Holliger was the oboist at both the world and American premiere in 1988.

David Schiff explained:

> Again there are two ensembles--the oboe is guarded by a quartet of violas and a percussionist--each with its own material.... [In the *Oboe Concerto*] the soloist is...a blithe spirit, [a] bringer of hope....Through-out the work the oboe is the spirit of lightness...while the orchestra is the bearer of heaviness.[84]

A six minute duo for flute and cello was the subject of Carter's *Enchanted Preludes*. It was written for the occasion of Ann Santen's 50th birthday. At the time, she was music director of WGUC in Cincinnati, Ohio, and she gave considerable air time to

---

[81]Schiff, "Elliott Carter's Harvest Home," p. 5.

[82]Ibid., p. 7.

[83]Andrew Porter, "Quaternion," New Yorker, v. 62, no. 40 (November 24, 1986), p. 116.

[84]David Schiff, "Carter's New Classicism," College Music Symposium, v. 29 (1989), p. 122.

contemporary music.   Carter stated that he attempted to capture Mrs. Santen's "brightness, charm, and irresistible enthusiasm" in the piece.[85]

Three Occasions for Orchestra is actually three separate pieces written in 1986, 1988, and 1989:   "A Celebration of Some 100 x 150 Notes," "Remembrance," and "Anniversary."   "A Celebration" was among a number of three-minute fanfares composed in honor of the Texas sesquicentennial commissioned by the Houston Symphony.

"Remembrance" was dedicated to the memory of Paul Fromm, a patron of new American music who died in 1987, and was commissioned by the Fromm Music Foundation. Oliver Knussen, coordinator of Tanglewood's Festival of Contemporary Music, wanted a companion piece to "A Celebration," and thus, "Remembrance" was created.   The piece was written in 1988 for trombone and orchestra.   The trombone has been described as an:

> 'orator,' declaiming a sonorous tribute against a repeating pattern of static chords.[86]

The third occasion, "Anniversary," was commissioned by the BBC for an Oliver Knussen concert in London in 1989.   The work is dedicated to Carter's wife Helen in celebration of their 50 years of marriage.

Violin Concerto was commissioned by the San Francisco Symphony.   It was written specifically for Ole Böhn, concertmaster of the Oslo Opera Orchestra, and was completed in February 1990.   Böhn and the San Francisco Symphony premiered the piece in May of that year.   Three connected movements form the structure of the concerto: Impulsivo, Angosciato-Tranquillo, and Scherzando.   David Schiff commented:

> Carter imposed two conditions on the music: that the solo part should be at all times audible above the orchestra and yet expressive in character, avoiding any virtuosic display of passage-work.[87]

Elliott Carter continues to compose music after nearly seven decades.   His recent pieces in the 1990s include: *Con Leggerezza Pensosa-Omaggio A Italo Calvino, Scrivo In Vento, Quintet for Piano and Winds, Bariolage, Inner Song*, and *Immer Neu*.

---

[85]Andrew Porter, "Preludes to Felicity," New Yorker, v. 64, no. 17 (June 13, 1988), p. 92.

[86]"Knusson [sic] and the BBCSO," Musical Opinion, v. 113, no. 1345 (January 1990), p. 23.

[87]David Schiff, "Carter's Violin Concerto," Tempo, no. 174 (September 1990), p. 22.

David Schiff, the noted and often quoted Carter scholar, summarized some thoughts on Carter's career with the idea that works written after 1948 (the beginning of Carter's mature period):

> ...challenge the listener with the simultaneous presentation of highly contrasting material. His imagination for superimposed sonorities has been remarkably fertile....
> Possibly the toughest challenge now posed by Carter's music is its very modernity, for at a time when many composers exhibit post-modern or even anti-modernist tendencies, Carter remains faithful to the principles of modernism.[88]

Although best known for his innovative use of the technique of "metric modulation," Carter prefers to call it "tempo modulation." It has been described as one tempo gradually becoming another during a piece, by a change in a combination of markings and note values.

String Quartet #1, written in 1950-1951, marked Carter's "coming of age" as a composer. Richard Morrison in 1990 commented:

> Adjectives that have stuck with his music ever since were born in that moment: complex, dense, intellectual, craggy, difficult. In the 1960s, when such qualities were prized, he was regularly hailed as America's greatest composer. Now, American composers have mostly gone simple, neo-romantic, and minimal....Carter admits he is unsympathetic to present trends.[89]

Bayan Northcott, speaking in the New Grove Dictionary stated:

> ...Carter is all dialectic and movement, displaying a grasp of dynamic form....The result is music of genuine difficulty....There was a period...when Carter's one arguable weakness--the packing of his scenarios with incident to the detriment of dramatic economy--seemed a real stumbling block for orchestras. But younger generations of virtuoso soloists and ensemble players have proved ever more eager to tackle, and quick to master, the unique challenges of each new Carter piece as it appears.[90]

---

[88]Schiff, "Elliott Carter is Still Challenging Music at Age 75," p. 14.

[89]Richard Morrison, "Master of Complexity," The Times (London), March 8, 1990, p. 20.

[90]Bayan Northcott, "Carter, Elliott (Cook, Jr.)," New Grove Dictionary of Music and Musicians (New York : Macmillian, 1980), p. 370.

CHRONOLOGY OF ELLIOTT CARTER

1908	December 11, Elliott Cook Carter, Jr. born in New York City
1920-26	Attended Horace Mann School, New York
1924	Introduced to Charles Ives
1926-32	Attended Harvard; BA in English; MA in Music
	Attended Longy School
1932-35	Attended Ecole Normale de Musique in Paris and studied privately with Nadia Boulanger
1936	Contributor to <u>Modern</u> <u>Music</u> (until 1946)
1937-39	Music director, Ballet Caravan
1939	Married Helen Frost Jones
1940	*Pocahontas* wins Juilliard Publication Award
1940-42	Faculty, St. John's College (Annapolis, MD)
1943	Son David Chambers Carter born
1943-44	Music consultant, Office of War Information
1945	*Canonic Suite* for four alto saxophones awarded a BMI Publication Prize
	Holiday Overture won first prize in the Independent Music Publishers Contest
	Guggenheim Fellowship
1946-48	Faculty, Peabody Conservatory
1948-50	Faculty, Columbia University
1950	Guggenheim Fellowship
	Grant from the National Institute of Arts & Letters
	Tucson, Arizona "magic mountain" experience
1953	*String Quartet #1* wins International Quartet Composition at Liège (Prix de Rome 1953-54)
	Fellowship, American Academy in Rome
1955	Vice president, ISCM
1955-56	Faculty, Queens College (New York)
	Elected member, National Institute of Arts & Letters
	Sonata for flute, oboe, cello and harpsichord receive the Naumburg Prize
1958	Instructor, Salzburg Seminars
1960	*String Quartet #2* wins Pulitzer Prize, New York Music Critics' Circle Award (1960-61), UNESCO Prize (1961) and nominated "best received contemporary classical composition" by the National Academy of Recording Arts & Sciences
1960-62	Faculty, Yale University
1961	*Double Concerto* wins New York Music Critics' Circle Award and the Sibelius Medal
	Honorary doctorate, New England Conservatory of Music
1963	Elected member, American Academy of Arts & Sciences (Boston)
	Composer-in-residence, American Academy in Rome

CHRONOLOGY OF ELLIOTT CARTER, CONTINUED

1964	Composer-in-residence, Ford Foundation, Berlin, West Germany
	Honorary doctorate, Swarthmore College
1965	Received the Brandeis University Creative Arts Award
1966	Faculty, Carleton College (MN)
1967	Received the Harvard Glee Club Medal
	Honorary doctorate, Princeton University
1967-68	Faculty, Juilliard School
	Andrew D. White Professor-at-Large, Cornell University
	Composer-in-residence, American Academy in Rome
1968	Honorary doctorate, Ripon College (WI)
1970	Elected member, American Academy of Arts & Letters
	Honorary doctorates from Oberlin College, Boston, Yale and Harvard Universities
1971	Awarded the Gold Medal of the National Institute of Arts & Letters
	Elected member, National Institute of Arts & Sciences
1973	*String Quartet # 3* receives Pulitzer Prize
1974	Honorary doctorate, Peabody Conservatory
1978	Received the Handel Medallion
1981	Received the Ernest von Siemens Prize
1983	Honorary doctorate, Cambridge University
	Received the Edward MacDowell Medal
1984	Received the George Peabody Medal
1985	Received the National Medal of Arts
1987	Elected commander, Order of Arts & Letters from the French Ministry of Culture
1990	Composer-in-residence, Royal Academy of Music's American Music Festival

Carter has also taught at Dartington, and Tanglewood summer schools, served in the League of Composers, the ISCM, and the ACA, in addition to assisting with music festivals around the world to advance contemporary music.

Works and Performances

The compositions listed here are arranged by genre and subarranged by date of composition. "See" references are included for important citations throughout the rest of this volume. Appendix II is an alphabetical listing of compositions. Appendix III is a chronological listing. Appendix IV contains addresses of publishers of Carter's works as cited below.

STAGE WORKS AND FILM MUSIC

W1.   *Philoctetes* (1931)
Greek text by Sophocles' Philoctetes
Incidental music
For: Baritone, men's chorus, oboe, percussion
Premiere: Sanders Theatre, Harvard University, Cambridge, MA: Harvard
Classical Club; Milman Parry, director; (Harry Levin, Odysseus; Robert
Fitzgerald, Philoctetes), March 15, 1933
Unpublished

W2.   *Mostellaria* (1936)
Latin text by Plautus' Mostellaria
Incidental music
a.   For: Baritone, men's chorus, chamber orchestra
Premiere: Sanders Theatre, Harvard University, Cambridge, MA: Harvard
Classical Club, April 15, 1936
Unpublished
b.   Finale arranged for men's chorus and symphony orchestra and entitled:
Tarantella (See: W29a)
c.   Finale arranged for four-part chorus and piano four-hands (See: W29b)

STAGE WORKS AND FILM MUSIC, CONTINUED

W3.   *Pocahontas* (1936)
       (39 mins.)
       Ballet legend in one act
  a.   For: Piano solo (1936) (See: W53a)
  b.   For: Stage work for orchestra (1939)
       Libretto by: Lincoln Kirstein
       Commissioned by: Lincoln Kirstein for the Ballet Caravan
       Premiere: Martin Beck Theater, New York, NY: Ballet Caravan; Fritz
           Kitzinger, conductor; Lew Christensen, choreographer; Karl Free, scenery
           and costumes; Leda Anchutina, Erick Hawkins, Eugene Loring and Harold
           Christensen, cast, May 24, 1939
       Published by Associated Music Publishers
  c.   Arranged as a suite for orchestra (1939) (See: W10a)

W4.   *The Ball Room Guide* (1937)
       Ballet suite
       Written for Lincoln Kirstein
       Incomplete, withdrawn
       Later the "Polka" section of *The Ball Room Guide* was used in *Prelude,
       Fanfare and Polka* (See: W9)

W5.   *Much Ado About Nothing* (1937)
       Incidental music, Shakespeare
       For: Women's chorus, two violins, two violoncellos
       Withdrawn

W6.   *The Minotaur* (1947)
       (33 mins.)
  a.   Ballet in one act and two scenes
       Libretto by: George Balanchine
       Commissioned by: The Ballet Society
       Premiere: Central High School of Needle Trades, New York, NY: Ballet
           Society; Leon Barzin, conductor; John Taras, choreographer; Joan Junyer,
           scenery and costumes; Elise Reiman, Francisco Moncion, Edward Bigelow
           and Tanaquil LeClerg, cast, March 26, 1947 (See: C13, C241, C258)
       Published by Associated Music Publishers
  b.   Revived as a suite by the Boston Ballet Company and the Boston University
           Symphony Orchestra, choreography by John Butler (See: C62)
  c.   Suite from the Ballet (1947) (See: W13)

ORCHESTRAL

W7.   *Concerto For English Horn And Orchestra* (1937)
       Incomplete, withdrawn

ORCHESTRAL, CONTINUED

W8.   *Symphony* (1937)
Withdrawn

W9.   *Prelude, Fanfare And Polka* (1938)
(6 min.)
For: Small radio orchestra
The "Polka" section was originally part of *The Ball Room Guide* (See: W4)
Awards: BMI Publication Prize, sponsored by the American Composers
Alliance and Broadcast Music, Inc., 1945
Published by Broadcast Music, Inc. and American Composers Alliance, 1944

W10.   *"Pocahontas" Suite* (1939)
(20 mins.)
1. Overture   2. John Smith and [John] Rolfe Lost in the Virginia Forest
3. Princess Pocahontas and her Ladies   4. Torture of John Smith
5. Pavane
a.   For: Orchestra (1939, rev. 1960)
Premiere (1960 rev.): Jacques-Louis Monod recording (See: D92)
Awards: Juilliard Publication Award, 1941 (See: C181)
Published by Kalmus, 1941; Associated Music Publishers, 1961
b.   Originally written for piano solo (1936) (See: W53a)
c.   Revised from stage work for orchestra (1939) (See: W3b)

W11.   *Symphony No.1* (1942 rev. 1954)
(25 mins.)
Dedicated to: Helen Carter
Premiere: Eastman Theater, Kilbourn Hall, Rochester, NY: Eastman-
Rochester Symphony Orchestra; Howard Hanson, conductor, April 27,
1944. Performed as part of the 14th annual Festival of American Music.
Published by Associated Music Publishers, 1961

W12.   *Holiday Overture* (1944 rev. 1961)
(10 mins.)
Premiere: Frankfurt, Germany: Frankfurt Symphony Orchestra; Hans
Blümer, conductor, 1946
American premiere: Baltimore, MD: Baltimore Symphony Orchestra;
Reginald Stewart, conductor, January 7, 1948
Awards: First Prize, Independent Music Publishers Contest, 1945
Published by Arrow Music Press, 1946; Associated Music Publishers, 1946,
1962

W13.   *"The Minotaur" Suite* (1947)
(25 mins.)
Ballet originally written in 1947 (See: W6)
Published by Associated Music Publishers, 1956

ORCHESTRAL, CONTINUED

W14.   *Elegy* (1952)
      (5 mins.)
   a. For: String orchestra
      Premiere: Cooper Union, NY: David Broekman, conductor, March 1, 1953.
         Performed as part of the <u>Music</u> <u>in</u> <u>the</u> <u>Making</u> series.
      Published by Peer International, 1957
   b. Arranged for violoncello and piano (1943) (See: W58a)
   c. Arranged for viola (1961) (See: 58d)
   d. Arranged for string quartet (1946) (See: W58b)

W15.   *Variations For Orchestra* (1954-5, rev. 1972)
      (24 mins.)
      Commissioned by: The Louisville Orchestra with a grant from the Rockefeller
         Foundation
      Premiere: Columbia Auditorium, Louisville, KY: Louisville Orchestra;
         Robert Whitney, conductor, April 21, 1956 (See: C147, C162)
      Premiere (rev.): New York Philharmonic; Lorin Maazel, conductor, April
         1972
      Published by Associated Music Publishers, 1957, corr. ed. 1966

W16.   *Double Concerto* (1961)
      (23 mins.)
   a. For: Harpsichord, piano with two chamber orchestras
      Dedicated to: Paul Fromm
      Commissioned by: The Fromm Music Foundation
      Premiere: Grace Rainey Rogers Auditorium, Metropolitan Museum of Art,
         New York, NY: Ralph Kirkpatrick, harpsichord; Charles Rosen, piano;
         with orchestra; Gustav Meier, conductor, September 6, 1961. Presented
         by the Fromm Music Foundation in conjunction with the Eighth Congress
         of the International Society for Musicology in session at Columbia
         University. (See: C51, C66, C79, C214)
      Awards: New York Music Critics' Circle Citation, 1961/62 (See: C167);
         Sibelius Medal, 1961
      Published by Associated Music Publishers, c1962, 1964
   b. Also revised for piano reduction by Charles Rosen and Ronald Herder, 1964

W17a.   *Piano Concerto* (1964-5)
      (25 mins.)
      Dedicated to: "Igor Stravinsky on his 85th birthday with great admiration and
         friendship"
      Commissioned by: Jacob Lateiner through a grant from the Ford Foundation
      Premiere: Symphony Hall, Boston, MA: Jacob Lateiner, piano; Boston
         Symphony Orchestra; Erich Leinsdorf, conductor, January 6, 1967
         (See: C20, C35, C87, C203, C229, C251)
      Published by Associated Music Publishers, 1967
   b. Reduction for two pianos (1967) (See: W67)

ORCHESTRAL, CONTINUED

W18.   *Concerto For Orchestra*   (1968-9)
(23 mins.)
Inspired by St. John Perse's Nobel Prize winning poem "Vents"
Dedicated to: The New York Philharmonic and its musical director Leonard
Bernstein
Commissioned by: The New York Philharmonic Society for its 125th
Anniversary; however, it was not completed on time
Premiere: Philharmonic Hall, New York, NY: New York Philharmonic
Orchestra; Leonard Bernstein, conductor, February 5, 1970   (See: C38,
C62, C91, C122, C228, C242)
Published by Associated Music Publishers, 1972

W19.   *A Symphony Of Three Orchestras*   (1976)
(17 mins.)
Musical interpretation of Hart Crane's "The Bridge"
Dedicated to: Pierre Boulez and the New York Philharmonic
Commissioned by: The New York Philharmonic under a grant to six
orchestras from the National Endowment for the Arts to write compositions
to honor the American Bicentennial.
Premiere: Avery Fisher Hall, Lincoln Center for the Performing Arts, New
York, NY: New York Philharmonic Orchestra; Pierre Boulez, conductor,
February 17, 1977 (See: C131, C171, C188, C230)
Published by Associated Music Publishers, 1978

W20.   *Penthode*   (1985, rev. Aug 22, 1985)
(18 mins.)
For: Five groups of four instrumentalists
Dedicated to: Pierre Boulez and the l'Ensemble InterContemporain
Commissioned by: l'Ensemble InterContemporain
Premiere: Royal Albert Hall Prom, London, England: l'Ensemble
InterContemporain; Pierre Boulez, conductor, July 26, 1985 (See: C164)
American premiere: Boston, MA: l'Ensemble InterContemporain; Pierre
Boulez, conductor, February 27, 1986 (See: C185)
Published by Hendon Music, 1985

W21.   *A Celebration Of Some 100 x 150 Notes*   (1986)
(3 min.)
Composed as part of *Three Occasions for Orchestra* (See: W26)
Commissioned by: The Houston Symphony Orchestra
Dedicated: In honor of the Texas Sesquicentennial
Premiere: Jesse H. Jones Hall for the Performing Arts, Houston, TX:
Houston Symphony Orchestra; Sergiu Commissiona, conductor, April 10,
1987 (See: C128)

ORCHESTRAL, CONTINUED

Premiere (complete suite): Royal Festival Hall, London, England: BBC Symphony Orchestra; Oliver Knussen, conductor, October 5, 1989 (See: C128)
Published by Hendon Music

W22.   *Oboe Concerto* (1986-7)
(20 mins.)
For: Oboe, concertino group and orchestra
Commissioned by: Paul Sacher for Heinz Holliger
Premiere: Zurich, Switzerland: Heinz Holliger, oboe; Collegium Musicum; Paul Sacher, conductor, June 17, 1988. Performed as part of the Zurich Festival. (See: C113)
American premiere: San Francisco, CA: Heinz Holliger, oboe; San Francisco Symphony Orchestra; Herbert Blomstedt, conductor, November 23, 1988
Published by Hendon Music, 1988

W23.   *Pastoral* (1988)
(12 mins.)
a.   For: English horn, marimba and string orchestra Merion Music
b.   Originally for English horn (or viola or clarinet) and piano (1940) (See: W57a)
c.   Arranged for brass quintet

W24.   *Remembrance* (1988)
(7 mins.)
Composed as part of *Three Occasions for Orchestra* (See: W26)
For: Trombone and large orchestra
Dedicated to: Paul Fromm and the Fromm Music Foundation
Commissioned by: The Fromm Music Foundation in memory of Paul Fromm
Premiere: Theatre-Concert Hall, Tanglewood, Lenox, MA: John DiLutis, trombone; Tanglewood Music Center Orchestra; Oliver Knussen, conductor, August 10, 1988. Performed as part of the Tanglewood Festival. (See: C128, C138, C195)
Premiere (complete suite): Royal Festival Hall, London, England: BBC Symphony Orchestra; Oliver Knussen, conductor, October 5, 1989 (See: C128)
Published by Hendon Music, Associated Music Publishers

W25.   *Anniversary* (1989)
(6 mins.)
Composed as part of *Three Occasions for Orchestra* (See: W27)
Dedicated to: Carter's wife on their 50th wedding anniversary Commissioned by: The BBC
Premiere: St. Louis, MO: St. Louis Symphony Orchestra; Leonard Slatkin, conductor, January 12, 1990

ORCHESTRAL, CONTINUED

Premiere (complete suite): Royal Festival Hall, London, England: BBC Symphony Orchestra; Oliver Knussen, conductor, October 5, 1989 (See: C128, C166)

W26.   *Three Occasions For Orchestra* (1989)
(16 mins.)
1. *A Celebration of Some 100 x 150 Notes* (1986) (See: W21)
2. *Remembrance* (1988) (See: W24)
3. *Anniversary* (1989) (See: W25)
Premiere (complete suite): Royal Festival Hall, London, England: BBC Symphony Orchestra; Oliver Knussen, conductor, October 5, 1989 (See: C128)

W27.   *Violin Concerto* (1990)
(23 min.)
For: Violin and orchestra
Commissioned by: Ole Böhn and the San Francisco Symphony Orchestra
Premiere: Louise M. Davies Symphony Hall, San Francisco War Memorial and Performing Arts Center, San Francisco, CA: Ole Böhn, violin; San Francisco Orchestra; Herbert Blomstedt, conductor, May 2, 1990 (See: C218)
Published by Hendon Music (piano reduction also available), 1990

CHORAL

W28.   *Tom And Lily* (1934)
Comic opera in one act
For: Four solo voices, mixed chorus, chamber orchestra
Withdrawn

W29.   *Tarantella* (1936)
(8 mins.)
Latin text by: Ovid ("Mater, Ades, Florum" from Fasti book V lines 183-199 and 331-337)
Originally the finale from incidental music to *Mostellaria* (See: W2a)
a.   Arranged for four-part men's chorus (TTBB) and symphony orchestra (1936)
Premiere: Symphony Hall, Boston, MA: Harvard Glee Club and Boston "Pops" Orchestra; G. Wallace Woodworth, conductor, May 17, 1937
b.   For: Four-part male chorus (TTBB) and piano four-hands
(8 mins.)
Commissioned by: The Harvard Glee Club
Premiere: Sanders Theatre, Harvard University, Cambridge, MA: Harvard Glee Club; G. Wallace Woodworth, conductor, April 29, 1937
Published in Words and Music: The Composer's View (See: B120a), Associated Music Publishers, 1971

CHORAL, CONTINUED

W30.   ***The Bridge*** (1937)
        Oratorio
        Text by: Hart Crane
        Incomplete

W31.   ***Harvest Home*** (1937)
        (5 min.)
        Text by: Robert Herrick
        For: Mixed chorus (SATB) (a cappella)
        Premiere: NY: Lehman Engel Madrigal Singers, Spring 1938
        Unpublished

W32.   ***Let's Be Gay*** (1937)
        (4 min.)
        Text by: John Gay's "The Beggar's Opera"
        For: Women's chorus (SSAA) and two pianos
        Commissioned by: Nicolas Nabokov
        Premiere: Wells College, Aurora, NY: Wells College Glee Club; Nicholas
            Nabokov, conductor, Spring 1938
        Unpublished

W33.   ***Madrigal Book*** (1937)
        For: 12 madrigals for 3-8 voices
        Most withdrawn
        The section entitled *To Music* was later published separately (See: W34)

W34.   ***To Music*** (1937)
        (7 mins.)
        For: SSAATTBB (a cappella)
        Text by: Robert Herrick's <u>To</u> <u>Music,</u> <u>to</u> <u>Becalm</u> <u>His</u> <u>Fever</u>
        Originally published as part of the *Madrigal Book* (See: W33)
        Premiere: New York: Lehman Engel Madrigal Singers; Lehman Engel,
            conductor, Spring 1938
        Awards: Choral Contest by WPA Federal Music Project in cooperation with
            Carl Fischer, Inc., Columbia Broadcasting Company and the Columbia
            Phonograph Records Company, 1938
        Published by Peer International, 1955

W35.   ***Heart Not So Heavy As Mine*** (1938)
        (6 mins.)
        Text by: Emily Dickinson
        For: SATB (a cappella)
        Commissioned by: The Temple Emanu-El

CHORAL, CONTINUED

Premiere: Temple Emanu-El, New York, NY: Temple Emanu-El Choir; Lazare Saminsky, conductor, March 31, 1939. Performed as part of the Fourth Annual Three-Choir Festival.
Published by Associated Music Publishers, 1939

W36. *The Defense Of Corinth* (1941)
(17 mins.)
Text by: François Rabelais' "Prologue" to Book III of <u>Pantagruel</u> in English translation by Urquhart and Motteux
For: Speaker, men's chorus (TTBB) and piano four-hands
Commissioned by: The Harvard Glee Club
Premiere: Sanders Theatre, Harvard University, Cambridge, MA: Harvard Glee Club; G. Wallace Woodworth, conductor, March 12, 1942
Published by Mercury Music, 1950, 1982; Merion Music

W37. *The Harmony Of Morning* (1944)
(9 mins.)
Text by: Mark Van Doren's <u>Another</u> <u>Music</u>
For: SSAA and chamber orchestra
Commissioned by: The Temple Emanu-El on the occasion of its hundredth anniversary
Premiere: Temple Emanu-El, New York, NY: Temple Emanu-El Choir; Lazare Saminsky, conductor, February 25, 1945. Performed as part of the Centenary Concert. (See: C259)
Published by Associated Music Publishers, 1955, 1986

W38. *Musicians Wrestle Everywhere* (1945)
(4 mins.)
Text by: Emily Dickinson
For: SSATB (a cappella or with string accompaniment)
Premiere (broadcast): WNBC Radio "Story of Music" December 20, 1945
First concert performance: New York Times Hall, New York, NY: Randolph Singers; David Randolph, conductor, February 12, 1946
Published by Music Press, 1948; Mercury Music Corp., 1948; Presser, 1948; Merion Music

W39. *Emblems* (1947)
(16 mins.)
Text by: Allen Tate
For: Men's chorus (TTBB) and piano
Dedicated to: "G. Wallace Woodworth and the Harvard Glee Club."
Commissioned by: The Harvard Glee Club
Premiere (part II only): New York Times Hall, New York, NY: Harvard Glee Club; G. Wallace Woodworth, conductor, April 3, 1951

CHORAL, CONTINUED

Premiere (complete work): Summer Tour of Europe: Colgate College
Singers, Summer European Tour, 1952
Published by Music Press, 1949; Mercury Music Corp., 1949; Merion Music

SOLO VOCAL

W40.   *My Love Is In A Light Attire* (1928)
Text by: James Joyce
Dedicated to: Laura Williams
   a.   For: One voice and piano
Unpublished
   b.   Other Joyce settings (1920s)
lost

W41.   *Tell Me, Where Is Fancy Bred?* (1938)
(3 mins.)
Text by: William Shakespeare's Merchant of Venice
For: Alto voice and guitar
Commissioned by: The Mercury Theatre
Premiere (recording): The Merchant of Venice by Orson Welles and the
Mercury Theatre, Columbia Records, 1938 (See: D141)
Published by Associated Music Publishers, 1972 (guitar part edited by Stanley
Silverman)

W42.   *Three Poems Of Robert Frost* (1943)
(6 mins.)
   1.   *Dust of Snow*
(1.5 mins.)
   a.   For: Medium voice and piano
Published by Associated Music Publishers, 1947, 1975
   b.   Revised for medium voice and guitar (1980)
   2.   *The Rose Family*
(1.5 mins.)
   a.   For: Medium voice and piano
Published by Associated Music Publishers, 1947, 1975
   b.   Revised for medium voice and guitar (1980)
   3.   *The Line Gang*
(3 mins.)
   a.   For: Baritone and piano
Published by Associated Music Publishers, 1975
   b.   Arranged for soprano or tenor voice and chamber orchestra (1975) 1980
Published by Associated Music Publishers
   c.   Arranged for voice and guitar (1980)

SOLO VOCAL, CONTINUED

W43. *Voyage* (1943)
(8 mins.)
Text by: Hart Crane's Infinite Consanguinity
Dedicated: "To Hope and John Kirkpatrick."

   a. For: Medium voice and piano
Premiere: The League of Composers, The Museum of Modern Art, New York, NY: Helen Boatwright, soprano; Helmut Baerwald, piano, March 16, 1947
Published by Valley Music Press, 1945 (Includes: "A commentary on the poem by the composer."); Associated Music Publishers, 1973

   b. Arranged for voice and small orchestra (1975, rev. 1979)

W44. *Warble For Lilac Time* (1943, rev. 1954)
(8 mins.)
Text by: Walt Whitman
For: Soprano (or tenor) and piano, or soprano and small orchestra
Premiere (with chamber orchestra): Saratoga Performing Arts Center, Saratoga Springs, NY: Helen Boatwright, soprano; Yaddo Orchestra; Frederick Fennell, conductor, September 14, 1946
Premiere (with piano): Museum of Modern Art, New York, NY: Helen Boatwright, soprano; Helmut Baerwald, piano, March 16, 1947. Sponsored by The League of Composers.
Published by Peer International, 1956

W45. *The Difference* (1944)
Text by: Mark Van Doren
For: Soprano, baritone and piano
Unpublished

W46. *A Mirror On Which To Dwell* (1975)
(20 mins.)
Text by: Six poems by Elizabeth Bishop
For: Soprano and chamber orchestra
Dedicated to: Susan Davenny Wyner and Speculum Musicae
1. Anaphora 2. Argument 3. Insomnia 4. O Breath 5. Sandpiper
6. View of the Capitol from the Library of Congress
Commissioned: In celebration of the Bicentennial by Speculum Musicae with grants from the New York State Council on the Arts, the Mellon Foundation and four patrons (Milton M. Scofield, Murray Socolof, Fred Sherry and Bernard Brandes).
Premiere: Hunter College Playhouse, New York, NY: Susan Davenny Wyner, soprano; Speculum Musicae; Young Concert Artists; Richard Fitz, conductor, February 24, 1976 (See: C103, C192, C245)
Published by Associated Music Publishers, 1977

SOLO VOCAL, CONTINUED

W47.   *Syringa* (1978)
(20 mins.)
Text by: John Ashbery and ancient Greek poetry
For: Mezzo-soprano, baritone and chamber orchestra
Dedicated to: Sir William Glock and Lady Glock
Commissioned by: Speculum Musicae with a composer-librettist grant from
the National Endowment for the Arts
Premiere: Alice Tully Hall, Lincoln Center for the Performing Arts, New
York, NY: Jan DeGaetani, mezzo-soprano; Thomas Paul, baritone; Scott
Kerney, guitar; Speculum Musicae; Harvey Sollberger, conductor,
December 10, 1978 (See: C47, C173, C187)
Published by Associated Music Publishers, 1980

W48.   *In Sleep, In Thunder* (1981)
(21 mins.)
Text by: Robert Lowell
For: Tenor and 14 players
Dedicated: "In memory of the poet and friend"
Commissioned by: The London Sinfonietta
1. Dolphin   2. Across the Yard   3. La Ignota   4. Dies irae   5. Careless
Night   6. In Genesis
Premiere: St. John's Smith Square, London, England: Martyn Hill, tenor;
London Sinfonietta; Oliver Knussen, conductor, October 27, 1982.
Performed as part of the Music Since 1952 series. (See: C101, C125)
American premiere: Theresa L. Kaufmann Concert Hall, 92nd St. Y, New
York, NY: Jon Garrison, tenor; Speculum Musicae; Robert Black,
conductor, December 11, 1983 (See: C194, C209)
Published by Hendon Music, 1984, c1982

CHAMBER AND INSTRUMENTAL

W49.   *Piano Sonata* (late 1920s)
Withdrawn

W50.   *String Quartet* (1928?)
Withdrawn

W51.   *Sonata* (1934)
For: Flute and piano
Withdrawn

W52.   *String Quartet* (1935)
Withdrawn

CHAMBER AND INSTRUMENTAL, CONTINUED

W53.   *"Pocahontas" Suite* (1936)
    a.   For: Piano solo
        Premiere: Keene State College, Keene, NH: Lew Christensen, choreography;
           Ruthanna Boris, Charles Laskey, Harold Christensen, Erick Hawkins, cast,
           August 17, 1936
        Withdrawn
    b.   Expanded for orchestra (1939) (See: W3b)
    c.   Revised for ballet suite (1939) (See: W10a)

W54.   *String Quartet* (1937)
    Withdrawn

W55.   *Musical Studies* (1938)
    For: Unspecified instruments
    Nos. 1-3 rev. as *Canonic Suite* (See: W56a and b); no. 4, "Andante
    Espressivo" withdrawn

W56.   *Canonic Suite* (1939, rev. 1981)
    (7 mins.)
    1. Fanfare   2. Nocturne   3. Tarantella
    a.   For: Four alto saxophones
        Also called *Suite for Quartet of Alto Saxophones* Originally from *Musical
        Studies* written for Boulanger (See: W55)
        Awards: BMI publication prize, sponsored by the American Composers
           Alliance and Broadcast Music, Inc., 1945
        Published by Broadcast Music, Inc., 1939, 1945; Associated Music Publishers,
        1984
    b.   Arranged for four clarinets (1955-6)
        Published by Associated Music Publishers, 1957, 1969

W57.   *Pastoral* (1940)
    (12 mins.)
    a.   For: English horn (or viola or clarinet) and piano
        Premiere (viola version): New York, NY: Ralph Hersh, viola; Elliott
           Carter, piano, 1942. Performed as part of a League of Composers Concert.
        Premiere (English horn version): New York, NY: ISCM Forum Group,
           Josef Marx, English horn; Elliott Carter, piano, November 12, 1944
        Originally published in New Music v.18, no.3 (April 1945) (See: B97a);
        Merion Music, 1945, 1982
    b.   Arranged for English horn, marimba and string orchestra (1988)
        (See: W23a)
    c.   Arranged for brass quintet

CHAMBER AND INSTRUMENTAL, CONTINUED

W58.   *Elegy* (1943)
       (5 mins.)
       a. For: Violoncello and piano
          Previously entitled: *Adagio for Viola (or Violoncello) and Piano* (1943)
          Published by Peer International, 1962
       b. Arranged for string quartet (1946)
          Premiere: Eliot, Maine: Lanier String Quartet, August 21, 1946
          Published by Peer International, 1958
       c. Arranged for string orchestra (1952) (See: W14a)
       d. Arranged for viola and piano (1961)
          Premiere (viola): Cambridge, MA: George Humphrey, viola; Alice Canady,
             piano, April 16, 1963. Performed as part of the Radcliffe Institute for
             Independent Study, Program of Contemporary Ensemble Music.
          Published by Peer International

W59.   *Piano Sonata* (1945-6, rev. 1982)
       (20 mins.)
       Written on a Guggenheim Fellowship
       Premiere (broadcast): Frick Art Museum, New York, NY: Webster Aitken,
          piano, February 16, 1947. Heard over WNYC Radio.
       First concert performance: New York Times Hall, New York, NY: James
          Sykes, March 5, 1947 (See: C178, C253)
       Published by Music Press, 1948; Mercury Music, 1948; Merion Music

W60.   *Woodwind Quintet* (1948)
       (8 mins.)
       For: Flute, oboe, clarinet, horn and bassoon
       Dedicated to: Nadia Boulanger
       Premiere (broadcast): New York, NY: Martin Orenstein, flute; David
          Abosch, oboe; Louis Paul, clarinet; Pinson Bobo, horn; Mark Popkin,
          bassoon, February 27, 1949. Sponsored by the National Association for
          American Composers and Conductors.
       First concert performance: New York Times Hall, New York, NY: Martin
          Orenstein, flute; David Abosch, oboe; Louis Paul, clarinet; Pinson Bobo,
          horn; Mark Popkin, bassoon, February 27, 1949. Sponsored by the
          National Association for American Composers and Conductors.
          (See: C95, C262)
       Published by American Composers Alliance, 1952; Associated Music
          Publishers, c1952, 1955

W61.   *Sonata For Violoncello And Piano* (1948, rev. 1966)
       (20 mins.)
       Commissioned by: Bernard Greenhouse
       Premiere: New York Times Town Hall, New York, NY: Bernard
          Greenhouse, violoncello; Anthony Makas, piano, February 27, 1950 See:
          C14, C123)

CHAMBER AND INSTRUMENTAL, CONTINUED

Published by the Society for the Publication of American Music, 1953
(See: C168); Associated Music Publishers, corr. ed. 1966

W62.   *Eight Etudes And A Fantasy* (1949-50)
(23 mins.)
For: Woodwind quartet (flute, oboe, clarinet, bassoon)
Written as studies for his orchestration students at
Columbia University
Premiere: Museum of Modern Art, New York, NY: Members
of the New York Woodwind Quintet (Murray Panitz, flute; David Glazer,
clarinet; Jerome Roth, oboe; Bernard Garfield, bassoon), October 28, 1952.
Performed as part of the American Composers Alliance Concert.
(See: C67, C97)
Published by American Composers Alliance, 1952; Associated Music
Publishers, 1959

W63.   [*Six Pieces For Kettle Drums And Orchestra*]   (1950) also called [*Suite for
Timpani*]
a. For: Kettledrums, one player and orchestra
Written as compositional studies
1. saeta   2. moto perpetuo   3. recitative   4. improvisation   5. canaries
6. march
Premiere: Junior Council of the Museum of Modern Art, New York, NY:
Al Howard, May 6, 1952 (See: C41)
Not published but they exist in photocopy
b. *Recitative and Improvisation* (1950)
(3 mins.)
Published by Associated Music Publishers, 1960
c. *Eight Pieces for Four Timpani* (1966)
(23 mins.)
For: One player
Original six pieces revised and two pieces were added:"*adagio*" and "*canto*"
"*Adagio*" and "*canto*" dedicated to Jan Williams
1. saeta   2. moto perpetuo   3. adagio   4. recitative   5. improvisation
6. canto   7. canaries   8. march
Note: "Not more than four are ever to be played as a suite in public."
Published by Associated Music Publishers, 1968

W64.   *String Quartet No.1* (1950-1)
(45 mins.)
Originally entitled: *Chronometros*
Written on a Guggenheim Fellowship and a grant from the National Institute
of Arts and Letters
Dedicated to: The Walden Quartet

CHAMBER AND INSTRUMENTAL, CONTINUED

Premiere: Theresa L. Kaufmann Auditorium, McMillan Theater, Columbia University, New York, NY: Walden String Quartet (Homer Schmitt, Bernard Goodman, violins; John Garvey, viola; Robert Swenson, violoncello), February 26, 1953 (See: C27, C227, C260)

European Premiere: Rome, Italy: Parrenin Quartet, April 1954. Performed at a festival sponsored by the Congress for Cultural Freedom. This performance established Carter's European reputation.

Awards: Liège, Belgium: first prize, Concours International de Composition pour Quatour à Cordes, 1953 (See: C30, C68)

Published by Associated Music Publishers, c1955, 1956

W65.   *Sonata For Flute, Oboe, Violoncello And Harpsichord* (1952)
(18 mins.)
Dedicated to: Sylvia Marlowe
Commissioned by: Sylvia Marlowe for her Harpsichord Quartet
Premiere: Carnegie Recital Hall, New York, NY: Harpsichord Quartet (Sylvia Marlowe, harpsichord; Bernard Greenhouse, violoncello; Claude Monteux, flute; Harry Shulman, oboe), November 10, 1953 (See: C59, C261)
Awards: Walter W. Naumburg Musical Foundation Award, 1956
Published by Associated Music Publishers, c1960, 1962

W66.   *String Quartet No.2* (1959)
(22 mins.)
Commissioned by: The Stanley String Quartet (The Quartet never performed the work due to its difficulty. Carter returned the commission and the Juilliard String Quartet premiered the work. The Stanley String Quartet's name remains on the published score.)
Premiere: Juilliard Concert Hall, Juilliard School, New York, NY: Juilliard String Quartet (Robert Mann, Isidore Cohen, violins; Raphael Hillyer, viola; Claus Adam, violoncello), March 25, 1960 (See: C143, C249, C256, C257)
Awards: Pulitzer Prize for Music, 1960 (See: C85, C237); New York Music Critics' Circle Award, 1960/61 (See: C29, C215); UNESCO Outstanding Musical Work of 1961 (International Rostrum of Composers Award, Paris) (See: C32); Nomination from the National Academy of Recording Arts and Sciences as the year's best contemporary classical composition
Published by Associated Music Publishers, 1961, corr. ed. 1962, 3rd corr. ed. 1981

W67.   *Piano Concerto* (1967)
Reduction for two pianos of the original (See: W17a)
Published by Associated Music Publishers, 1967

CHAMBER AND INSTRUMENTAL, CONTINUED

W68.   *Canon For 3* (1971)
(2 mins.)
For: Three equal instrumental voices   (The score recommends three instruments with different mutes or muted trumpet, clarinet and oboe)
Dedicated: "In memoriam Igor Stravinsky"
Premiere: Alice Tully Hall, Lincoln Center for the Performing Arts, New York, NY: Joel Timm, oboe; Allen Blustein, clarinet; James Stubb, trumpet, January 23, 1972.   Performed as a part of the New and Newer Music series. (See: C108) Associated Music Publishers, 1972
Written at the request of the periodical Tempo in honoring the memory of Igor Stravinsky.   Published in Tempo no.98 (1972) (See: B9)

W69.   *String Quartet No.3* (1971)
(22 mins.)
Dedicated to: The Juilliard String Quartet
Commissioned by: The Juilliard School for the Juilliard String Quartet
Premiere: Alice Tully Hall, Lincoln Center for the Performing Arts, New York, NY: Juilliard String Quartet (Robert Mann, Earl Carlyss, violins; Samuel Rhodes, viola; Claus Adam, violoncello), January 23, 1973 (See: C12, C92, C106, C132, C189, C226)
Awards: Pulitzer Prize, 1973 (See: C238)
Published by Associated Music Publishers, 1973

W70.   *Duo For Violin And Piano* (1973-4)
(18 mins.)
Dedicated to: Carter's wife Helen
Commissioned by: The McKim Fund of the Library of Congress
Premiere: Cooper Union, New York Philharmonic Hall, NY: Paul Zukofsky, violin; Gilbert Kalish, piano, March 5, 1975.   Performed as a part of the Prospective Encounter Concert. (See: C55, C61, C186)
Published by Associated Music Publishers, 1976

W71.   *Brass Quintet* (1974)
(17 mins.)
For: Two trumpets, horn, two trombones
Dedicated to: The American Brass Quintet
Commissioned by: The American Brass Quintet (See: C60)
Premiere (BBC broadcast):   London, England: American Brass Quintet (Robert Biddlecome, Edward Birdwell, Louis Ranger, Raymond Mase, Herbert Rankin), October 20, 1974.   Performed as a part of the Charles Ives Festival.
American premiere: Library of Congress, Washington, D.C.:   American Brass Quintet (Robert Biddlecombe, Edward Birdwell, Louis Ranger, Raymond Mase, Herbert Rankin), November 15, 1974 (See: C93, C184)
Published by Associated Music Publishers, 1976

CHAMBER AND INSTRUMENTAL, CONTINUED

W72.   *A Fantasy About Purcell's "Fantasia Upon One Note"*
(1974)
(3 mins.)
For: Two trumpets, horn, two trombones
Dedicated as a: Christmas present to the American Brass Quintet
Premiere: Carnegie Recital Hall, New York, NY: American Brass Quintet,
   January 13, 1975 (See: C63)
Published by Associated Music Publishers, 1977

W73.   *Birthday Fanfare For Sir William Glock's 70th* (1978)
For: Three trumpets, vibraphone, glockenspiel
Premiere: London, England, May 3, 1978
Unpublished

W74.   *Night Fantasies* (1980)
(20 mins.)
For: Piano
Commissioned by and dedicated to: Paul Jacobs, Ursula Oppens, Gilbert
   Kalish and Charles Rosen with the American Music Center
Premiere: Bath, England: Ursula Oppens, June 2, 1980. Performed as a part
   of the Bath Festival. (See: C83, C112, C233)
American premiere: Theresa L. Kaufmann Concert Hall, 92 St. Y, New
   York, NY: Paul Jacobs, November 11, 1981 (See: C154)
Published by Associated Music Publishers, 1982, Merion Music

W75.   *Triple Duo* (1982-3)
(20 mins.)
For: Violin, violoncello, flute (or piccolo), clarinet (or bass clarinet), piano
   and percussion
"Affectionately dedicated to that ensemble [the Fires of London] and its prime
   mover, Peter Maxwell Davies."
Commissioned by: The BBC for the Fires of London
Premiere: Symphony Space, New York: the Fires of London (Rosemary
   Furness, violin; Jonathan Williams, violoncello; Philipp Davies, flute and
   piccolo; David Campbell, clarinets; Stephen Pruslin, piano; Gregory
   Knowles, percussion), April 23, 1983 (See: C54, C196)
Published by Hendon Music, 3rd corr. ed. 1983

W76.   *Changes* (1983)
(7 mins.)
Originally called *Micomicon*
For: Guitar (edited by David Starobin)
Dedicated to: David Starobin
Commissioned by: David Starobin
Premiere: Theresa L. Kaufmann Concert Hall, 92nd St. Y, New York, NY:
   David Starobin, December 11, 1983 (See: C194)

CHAMBER AND INSTRUMENTAL, CONTINUED

Published by Hendon Music, 1983, 1986

W77.   *Canon For 4, Homage To William [Glock]* (1984)
(5 mins.)
For: Flute, bass clarinet, violin, violoncello
Dedicated: "For the occasion of Sir William Glock's retirement from the Bath Festival"
Premiere: Bath, England: London Sinfonietta, June 8, 1984. Performed as part of the Bath Festival.
American premiere: Chamber Music Society of Lincoln Center (Paula Robison, flute; Virgil Blackwell, clarinet; Philip Setzer, violin; David Finckel violoncello), December 9, 1984 (See: C193)
Published by Hendon Music, c1984, 1986

W78.   *Esprit Rude/Esprit Doux (Rough Breathing/Smooth Breathing)* (1984)
(5 mins.)
For: Flute, clarinet
Dedicated: "Pour Pierre Boulez en célébration de son soixantième anniversaire"
Premiere: Baden Baden, Germany: Members of l'Ensemble InterContemporain, March 31, 1985
Published by Hendon Music, 1985

W79.   *Riconoscenza Per Goffredo Petrassi* (1984)
(5 mins.)
For: Violin
Dedicated to: Goffredo Petrassi on his 80th birthday
Premiere: Latina, Italy: Georg Mönch, June 15, 1984. Performed as part of the Pontino Festival.
American premiere: Sponsored by the Chamber Music Society of Lincoln Center (Eugene Drucker, first violinist of the Emerson Quartet), December 9, 1984 (See: C193)
Published by Hendon Music, 1984

W80.   *String Quartet No.4* (1985-6)
(24 mins.)
Dedicated to: The Composers Quartet
Commissioned by: The Composers, Sequoia and Thouvenel Quartets
Premiere: Miami, FL: (Matthew Raimondi, Anahid Ajemian, Jean Dane, Mark Shuman), September 17, 1986. Performed as part of the Composers String Quartet Festival. (See: C191)
Published by Hendon Music, 1986

W81.   *Birthday Flourish* (1988)
(2 minutes)

CHAMBER AND INSTRUMENTAL, CONTINUED

    a. For: Five trumpets in C
        Premiere: Louise M. Davies Symphony Hall, San Francisco War Memorial
        and Performing Arts Center, San Francisco, CA: Members of the San
        Francisco Symphony; Herbert Blomstedt, conductor, September 14, 1988
    b. Arranged for brass quintet

W82.   *Enchanted Preludes* (1988)
        (6 mins.)
        For: Flute and violoncello
        Commissioned by: Harry Santen as a 50th birthday present for his wife Ann
        Santen
        Premiere: Merkin Concert Hall, Bard College, NY: Da Capo Chamber
        Players (Patricia Spencer, flute; Andrzej Emelianoff, violoncello), May 16,
        1988 (See: C105, C190)
        Published by Hendon Music

W83.   *Con Leggerezza Pensosa-Omaggio A Italo Calvino* (1990)
        (5 mins.)
        For: E♭ Clarinet (or B♭ Clarinet), violin and violoncello
        Premiere: Latina, Italy: Ciro Scarponi, clarinet; Jorge Risi, violin; Luigi
        Lanzillotta, violoncello, September 29, 1990. Sponsored by the Italian
        Institute for Musicological Research.
        U.K. Premiere: London, England: Queen Elizabeth Hall, London
        Sinfonietta; Oliver Knussen, conductor, February 10, 1991
        Published by Hendon Music (E♭), 1991; Boosey and Hawkes (B♭), 1991

W84.   *Scrivo In Vento* (1991)
        (5 minutes)
        For: Solo flute
        Premiere: Avignon, France: Robert Aitken, flute, JunE 20, 1991.
        Performed as part of the Avignon Festival.
        Published by Hendon Music, 1991

W85.   *Quintet* (1992)
        (18 minutes)
        For: Piano and winds (oboe, clarinet, bassoon, horn)
        Premiere: Cologne, Germany: KolnMusik, September 13, 1992

W86.   *Bariolage* (1992)
        (5 mins.)
        Composed as part of *Trilogy* (See: W89)
        For: Solo harp
        Premiere: Salle Patino, Geneva, Switzerland: Ursula Holliger, harp, March
        23, 1992
        Premiere (complete suite): Pontino, Italy: Heinz Holliger, oboe; Ursula
        Holliger, harp. Performed as part of the Pontino Festival, June 1992.

CHAMBER AND INSTRUMENTAL, CONTINUED

W87.   *Inner Song* (1992)
       (5 mins.)
       Composed as part of *Trilogy* (See: W89)
       For: Solo oboe
       Premiere: Witten, Germany: Heinz Holliger, oboe, April 25, 1992.
           Performed as part of the Witten Festival.
       Premiere (complete suite): Pontino, Italy: Heinz Holliger, oboe; Ursula
           Holliger, harp. Performed as part of the Pontino Festival, June 1992.

W88.   *Immer Neu* (1992)
       (5 mins.)
       Composed as part of *Trilogy* (See: W89)
       For: Oboe and harp
       Premiere: Pontino, Italy: Heinz Holliger, oboe; Ursula Holliger, harp.
           Performed as part of the Pontino Festival, June 1992.
       Premiere (complete suite): Pontino, Italy: Heinz Holliger, oboe; Ursula
           Holliger, harp. Performed as part of the Pontino Festival, June 1992.

W89.   *Trilogy* (1992)
       For: Oboe and harp
       I. *Bariolage* (See: W86) II. *Inner Song* (See: W87)
           III. *Immer Neu* (See: W88)
       Premiere: Pontino, Italy: Heinz Holliger, oboe; Ursula Holliger, harp.
           Performed as part of the Pontino Festival, June 1992.

Discography

Included below are all commercial recordings of Carter's works arranged alphabetically. Record label, performers, recording date, accompanying works and some reviews of the recordings are provided. Cross references are made to pertinent citations found elsewhere in this book.

Brass Quintet (W71)

D1.   Odyssey Y 34137 (lp, stereo) 1976
         American Brass Quintet (Robert Biddlecome, Edward Birdwell, Louis Ranger, Raymond Mase, Herbert Rankin)
         Recorded March 31-April 1, 1975
         Notes by Elliott Carter
         Modern American Music series
         With: Elliott Carter's *Eight Pieces for Four Timpani* (D28); *A Fantasy About Purcell's Fantasies Upon One Note* (D45)
         See: New Records (January 1977), p.9; Saturday Review of Literature (November 13, 1976), p.52

Canon for 4: Homage to William (W77)

D2.   New Albion Records NA019 CD (cd) 1989
         California E.A.R. Unit (Erika Duke, Lorna Eder, Arthur Jarvinen, Amy Knoles, Robin Lorentz, Gaylord Mowrey, James Rohrig, Rand Steiger, Dorothy Stone) with Toby Holmes, Theresa Tunnicliff
         Notes by Ruth Dreier
         With: Arthur Jarvinen's Egyptian Two Step; Rand Steiger's Quintessence; Michael Torke's The Yellow Pages; Karlheinz Stockhausen's Dr. K-Sextet; Elliott Carter's *Enchanted Preludes* (D38); *Esprit Rude/Esprit Doux* (D41); Louis Andriessen's Hoketus

D3.   GM Recordings GM 2020 CD (cd) 1990
       Da Capo Chamber Players
       Recorded February 5, 1988, at Merkin Concert Hall, New York
       Album title: Perle/Carter
       With: Elliott Carter's *Enchanted Preludes* (D40); George Perle's Sonata for
           Cello and Piano; Lyric Piece, Cello and Piano; Elliott Carter's *Pastoral,
           Clarinet and Piano* (D75); George Perle's Sonata a Quatro, Flute/Alto
           Flute, Clarinet, Violin and Cello; Elliott Carter's *Esprit Rude/Esprit Doux*
           (D43)

Canon for 3: In Memoriam Igor Stravinsky (W68)

D4.   Desto DC 7133 (lp, stereo) 1972
       Phoenix PHCD 115 (cd) 1990
       Gerard Schwarz, Louis Ranger, Stanley Rosenzweig
       Note: Two versions, once on three trumpets (straight mute, solotone mute,
           and cup mute), once on fluegelhorn, cornet and trumpet
       Notes by Gerard Schwarz
       Album title: New Music for Trumpet: Played by Gerard Schwarz
       Album title on CD: Gerard Schwarz Performs New Music for Trumpet
       With: Richard Moryl's Salvos; Charles Whittenberg's Polyphony; Stefan
           Wolpe's Solo Piece; Henry Brant's Concerto for Trumpet and Nine
           Instruments
       See: Fanfare (March/April 1991), p.493

D5.   Crystal S 361 (lp, stereo) 1976
       Thomas Stevens, Mario Guarneri, Roy Poper
       Notes by Thomas Stevens
       Album title: Music for Trumpet
       Recital series
       With: Igor Stravinsky's Fanfare for a New Theater; Paul Hindemith's Sonata
           (1939); Chou Wen-Chung's Soliloquy of a Bhiksuni; Robert Hall Lewis'
           Monophony VII; Harold Budd's New Work #5
       See: New Records (February 1977), p.15

Changes (W76)

D6.   Bridge Records BDG 2004 (lp) 1984
       David Starobin, guitar
       Recorded March-April 1984, at Holy Trinity Episcopal Church, New York
           City
       Notes by William K. Bland
       Album title: New Music with Guitar
       With: Tōru Takemitsu's Toward the Sea; John Anthony Lennon's Another's
           Fandango; David Del Tredici's Acrostic Song; Barbara Kolb's Songs
           Before an Adieu

D7.   Bridge Records BCD 9009 (cd) 1988
       Changes, Reissue of D6
       David Starobin, guitar
       Notes by William K. Bland
       Album title: New Music with Guitar
       With: Stephen Sondheim's Sunday Song Set; Milton Babbitt's Composition
           1984; Tōru Takemitsu's Toward the Sea; John Anthony Lennon's Another's
           Fandango; Barbara Kolb's Songs Before an Adieu; William Bland's
           Victoria Fantasy; Hans Werner Henze's Carillon, Récitatif, Masque

Concerto for Orchestra (W18)

D8.   Columbia M 30112 (lp, stereo) 1970
       New York Philharmonic, Leonard Bernstein, conductor
       Recorded on February 11, 1970, in New York
       Notes by Elliott Carter
       With: William Schuman's In Praise of Shahn
       See: Rollingstone no.80 (April 15, 1971), p.46; High Fidelity v.21, no.3
           (March 1971), p.82; New Records (February 1971), p.2; New York Times
           (February 7, 1971), IV, p.26; Saturday Review of Literature (January 30
           1971), p.54

D9.   ICME 1 (lp) 1974
       Various orchestras
       Notes by Igor Buketoff and John Vinton
       Album title: The International Contemporary Music Exchange, Inc. Presents
           the Outstanding Orchestral Compositions of the United States
       With: Earle Brown's Available Forms II; Aaron Copland's Appalachian
           Spring; George Crumb's Echoes of Time and the River; Lukas Foss's Time
           Cycle; Roy Harris's Symphony No.3; Charles Ives's Symphony No.4; Carl
           Ruggles's Sun-Treader; William Schuman's Symphony No.6; Roger
           Sessions's Symphony No.3; Samuel Barber's Knoxville: Summer of 1915;
           Henry Cowell's Synchrony; Jacob Druckman's Windows; Lou Harrison's
           Symphony on G; Alan Hovhaness's Mysterious Mountain; Wallingford
           Riegger's Symphony No.3, op.42; George Rochberg's Symphony No.2;
           Gunther Schuller's Seven Studies on Themes of Paul Klee; Virgil
           Thomson's The Plow that Broke the Plains; Edgard Varèse's Arcana;
           Charles Wuorinen's Piano Concerto (1966)

D10.   Composers Recording CRI SD 469 (lp, stereo) 1982
       Concerto, reissue of D8
       Notes by David Schiff
       Album title: Music of Elliott Carter
       American Contemporary series
       With: Elliott Carter's *Syringa* (D135)

See: American Record Guide (May 1983), p.15; Consumer Research Bulletin
(March 1983), p.43; Fanfare v.6, no.3 (January/February 1983), p.134;
New York Times (November 21, 1982), VIII, p.19; New Records
(December 1982), p.12; High Fidelity v.33, no.9 (September 1983), p.69-
70, 113 (See: C88)

The Defense of Corinth (W36)

D11.   Harvard Glee Club F-HGC 64 (lp, mono) 1964
Harvard Glee Club; Radcliffe Choral Society; Elliot Forbes, conductor;
Thomas G. Gutheil, narrator)
Album title: Annual Spring Concert, April 24, 1964
With: Heinrich Schutz's Deutsches Magnificat; Johannes Brahms's Funf
Gesange, op.104; Hans Leo Hassler's Chromatic Motet: Ad Dominum,
cum Tribularer Clamavi; Samuel Barber's Reincarnations

D12.   Vox Box SVBX 5353 (lp, stereo) 1977
Jan Opalach, speaker; Edward Green, piano; Mark Sutton Smith, piano; Gregg
Smith Singers; Texas Boys Choir; Columbia University Men's Glee Club;
Peabody Conservatory Concert Singers; Gregg Smith, conductor
Notes by Gregg Smith
Album title: America Sings (1920-1950)
With: Samuel Barber's A Stopwatch and an Ordnance Map; Leonard
Bernstein's Choruses from 'The Lark'; Elliott Carter's *Musicians Wrestle
Everywhere* (D64); Aaron Copland's Two Pieces for Treble Choir; Henry
Cowell's Luther's Coral to His Son; Irving Fine's The Choral New Yorker;
Lukas Foss's Behold I Build an House; George Gershwin's Two Madrigals;
Charles Ives's Two Election Songs; Walter Piston's Psalm and Prayer of
David; Wallingford Riegger's Who Can Revoke; William Schuman's
Prelude; Charles Seeger's Chant; Roger Sessions's Turn, O Liberstad;
Louise Talma's Let's Touch the Sky; Virgil Thomson's Four Southern
Hymns; Virgil Thomson's Alleluia
See: New Records (December 1977), p.8; New York Times (July 1, 1979),
IV, p.22

D13.   GSS Recordings GSS 103 (lp, stereo) 1984
Men's Choruses and Women's Choir of the Gregg Smith Singers; The Long
Island Symphonic Choral Association; Columbia University Men's Glee
Club; Gregg Smith, conductor
The Choral Masters series v.1
With: Elliott Carter's *Tarantella* (D140); *Emblems* (D37); *Harmony of
Morning* (D47); *Heart not so Heavy as Mine* (D50); *Musicians Wrestle
Everywhere* (D66); *To Music* (D149)

Double Concerto (W16)

D14.   Epic LC 3830 (lp, mono) 1962
         Epic BC 1157 (lp, stereo) 1962
         Ralph Kirkpatrick, harpsichord; Charles Rosen, piano; English Chamber
             Orchestra; Gustav Meier, conductor
         Recorded September 7-8, 1961
         Notes by Elliott Carter
         Twentieth-Century Composers series
         With: Leon Kirchner's Concerto for Violin, Cello, Ten Winds and Percussion
         See: Music Magazine v.164, no.6 (July 1962), p.43-44; High Fidelity (June
             1962), p.56; Hi/Fi Stereo Review (June 1962), p.66; Musical America
             (August 1962), p.29; New York Times (July 22, 1962), X, p.8; Saturday
             Review of Literature (April 28, 1962), p.48

D15.   H.M.V. ALP 2052 and ASD 601 (1965)
         Double Concerto, Reissue of D14
         Notes by Elliott Carter
         With: Elliott Carter's *Piano Sonata* (D81)

D16.   Columbia MS 7191 (lp, stereo) 1968
         CBS 72717 (1969)
         CBS S 34 61093 (1970)
         Paul Jacobs, harpsichord; Charles Rosen, piano; English Chamber Orchestra;
             Frederik Prausnitz, conductor
         Recorded January 4, 1968
         Notes by Elliott Carter
         Music of Our Times series
         With: Elliott Carter's *Variations for Orchestra* (D153)
         See: High Fidelity/Musical America v.19, no.2 (February 1969), p.85; Stereo
             Review (March 1969), p.90; Saturday Review of Literature (December 28,
             1968), p.52; Records and Recordings v.11, no.5 (February 1968), p.21-23;
             American Record Guide v.37, no.11 (July 1971), p.756-759 (See: C36)

D17.   Nonesuch H-71314 (lp, stereo) 1975
         Nonesuch 71314-4 SR (cassette) 1975
         Paul Jacobs, harpsichord; Gilbert Kalish, piano; Contemporary Chamber
             Ensemble; Arthur Weisberg, conductor
         Notes by Elliott Carter
         With: Elliott Carter's *Duo for Violin and Piano* (D18)
         See: Tempo no.116 (March 1976), p.29; Consumer Research Bulletin
             (February 1976), p.43; High Fidelity (March 1976), p.82; New Records
             (December 1975), p.7; Musical Quarterly v.63, no.2 (April 1977), p.287-
             289 (See: C4)

D17a.   Elektra Nonesuch 79183-2 (cd) 1992
         Paul Jacobs, harpsichord; Gilbert Kalish, piano; Contemporary Chamber
            Ensemble; Arthur Weisberg, conductor
         With: Elliott Carter's *Sonata for Flute, Oboe and Harpsichord* (D104a);
            Sonata for Violoncello and Piano (D109b)

Duo for Violin and Piano (W70)

D18.   Nonesuch H 71314 (lp, stereo) 1975
         Nonesuch 71314-4 SR (cassette) 1975
         Paul Zukofsky, violin; Gilbert Kalish, piano
         Recorded March 1975
         Notes by Elliott Carter
         With: Elliott Carter's *Double Concerto* (D17)
         See: Tempo no.116 (March 1976), p.29; Consumer Research Bulletin
            (February 1976), p.43; High Fidelity (March 1976), p.82; New Records
            (December 1975), p.7; Musical Quarterly v.63, no.2 (April 1977), p.287-
            289 (See: C4)

D19.   Sony S2K 47229 (47256, 47257) (cd) 1991
         Robert Mann, violin; Christopher Oldfather, piano
         With: Elliott Carter's *String Quartet No.1* (D113); *String Quartet No.2*
            (D119); *String Quartet No.3* (D125), *String Quartet No.4* (D129)
         See: American Record Guide (March/April 1992), p.43; Fanfare
            (March/April 1992), p.170; Gramophone (April 1992), p.94

Eight Etudes and a Fantasy (W62)

D20.   Composers Recording CRI 118 (lp, mono) 1958
         Composers Recording SD 118 (lp, stereo) 1958
         Composers Recording CAS 118 (cassette) 1958
         New York Woodwind Quintet members (Murray Panitz, flute; Jerome Roth,
            oboe; David Glazer, clarinet; Bernard Garfield, bassoon)
         Notes by Peggy Glanville-Hicks
         With: Quincy Porter's String Quartet No.8
         See: High Fidelity v.8, no.5 (May 1958), p.54; HiFi and Music Review (May
            1958), p.66; Library Journal (March 1 1958), p.747; Hi-Fi Music at Home
            (April 1959), p.29; New York Times (May 18, 1958), X, p.15

D21.   Concert-Disc M 1229 (lp, mono) 1963
         Concert-Disc CS 229 (lp, stereo) 1963
         New York Woodwind Quintet members (Samuel Baron, flute; Ronald
            Roseman, oboe; David Glazer, clarinet; Arthur Weisberg, bassoon)
         Notes by Samuel Baron
         Concert-Disc Connoisseur series
         With: Gunther Schuller's Woodwind Quintet; Irving Fine's Partita for Wind
            Quintet

See: High Fidelity (November 1963), p.83; Hi/Fi Stereo Review (December 1963), p.78; New Records (October 1963), p.7; New York Times (January 26, 1964), X, p.18

D22.   Candide CE 31016 (lp, stereo) 1969
Vox STGBY 644 (1971)
CBS S 34 61145 (1970)
Decca (1974)
Dorian Wind Quintet members (Karl Kraber, flute; Charles Kuskin, oboe; William Lewis, clarinet; Jane Taylor, bassoon)
Notes by William B. Ober
With: Elliott Carter's Woodwind Quintet (D158); Hans Werner Henze's Quinetett
See: New Records (September 1969), p.7

D23.   [Eight Etudes only]
Classics Record Library SQM 80-5731 (lp, stereo) 1975
Chamber Music Society of Lincoln Center members (Paula Robison, flute; Leonard Arner, oboe; Gervase de Peyer, clarinet; Loren Glickman, bassoon)
Notes by Harris Goldsmith
Album title: The Chamber Music Society of Lincoln Center
With: Ludwig van Beethoven's String Trio in G, op.9, no.1; Robert Schumann's Fantasy Pieces for Clarinet and Piano, op.73; W.A. Mozart's Piano Quartet in E Flat, K.493; J.S. Bach's Concerto in C Minor for Oboe, Violin, Strings and Continuo; Gabriel Fauré's Two Pieces for Flute and Piano: Sicilienne, op.78; Fantasy, op.79; Moritz Moszkowski's Suite in G Minor for Two Violins and Piano, op.71; Robert Schumann's Andante and Variations for Two Pianos, Two Cellos and Horn; Joseph Haydn's String Trio in G, op.53, no.1; Gabriel Fauré's Dolly Suite for Piano Duet, op.56; Johannes Brahms's Two Songs for Contralto, Piano and Viola, op.91; Camille Saint-Saëns' Caprice on Danish and Russian Airs for Flute, Oboe, Clarinet and Piano, op.79

D24.   Columbia Special Products C 10159 (lp, mono) 197-?
First two movements only
Eight Etudes, Reissue of D20
Album title: Music Appreciation. Record 8
With: Charles Ives' Second Piano Sonata: 1st movement; Aaron Copland's Appalachian Spring: parts I-IV; William Billings' New-England Psalm-Singer: When Jesus Wept; William Schuman's England Triptych: When Jesus Wept

D25.   Musical Heritage Society MHS 4876 (lp, stereo) 1983
Eight Etudes and a Fantasy, Reissue of D22
Recorded in 1966 at Capitol Records Studio "B"
Notes by David Schiff

Album title: Chamber Music
With: Elliott Carter's *String Quartet No.3* (D121)
See: Strad v.100, no.1193 (September 1989), p.773-774

D26.   Musical Heritage Society MHS 824704X (MHS 4704-4705) (lp, stereo) 1983
Musical Heritage Society MHC 226704W (cassette) 1983
Eight Etudes and a Fantasy, Reissue of D23
Notes by Michael Keeley
Album title: Three Centuries of Chamber Music
With: J.S. Bach's Concerto in C Minor for Oboe, Violin, Strings and
Continuo, S.1060; Joseph Haydn's String Trio in G Major, op.53, no.1;
Moritz Moszkowski's Suite in G Minor for Two Violins and Piano, op.71;
Gabriel Fauré's Two Pieces for Flute and Piano; Dolly: Suite for Piano
Duet, op.56; Camille Saint-Saëns' Caprice on Danish and Russian Airs,
op.79

D27.   River City Studios 44711 (lp) 1985
La Sonore Wind Quintet
Recorded at First Presbyterian Church, Mt. Pleasant, MI
Album title: 20th Century Chamber Music
With: Jean Francaix's Quintette

D27a.   Stradivarius STR 33304 (cd) 1991
Quintetto Arnold
Recorded October 22-23 and November 19-20, 1990, at Chiesa della
Misericordia, Turin, Italy
Notes by Paolo Petazzi
Album title: Musica per Quartetto e Quintetto a Fiati
With: Elliott Carter's *Woodwind Quintet* (D164); Franco Donatoni's Blow;
Gyeorgy Kurtág's Quintetto per Fiati, op.2; Gyeorgy Ligeti's Zehn Stücke
für Bläserquintett
See: Fanfare (July/August 1992), p.358

Eight Pieces for Four Timpani (W63)

D28.   Odyssey Y 34137 (lp, stereo) 1976
Morris Lang, timpani
Recorded May 28 and June 23-24, 1975
Notes by Elliott Carter
Modern American Music series
With: Elliott Carter's *Brass Quintet* (D1); *A Fantasy About Purcell's
Fantasia Upon One Note* (D45)
See: New Records (January 1977), p.9; Saturday Review of Literature
(November 13, 1976), p.52

D29.   ["Recitative," "Moto perperuo," "Saeta," and "Improvisation" only] Erato
STU 71106 (lp, stereo) 1978
Sylvio Gualda, timpani

Recorded April 1977, L'Eglise du Liban, Paris
Notes by Gerard Mannoni
Album title: Percussion v.2
With: Iannis Xenakis' Psappha; Nguyen Thien Dao's May

D30.   BIS LP-256 (lp, stereo) 1984
Gert Mortenson, timpani
Recorded January 14, 1982, in a live concert at Studio 2 Danmarks Radio
Album title: Neue Musik für Schlagzeug
With: Per Nörgard's I Ching; Iannis Xenakis' Psappha

Elegy (string quartet version) (W58)

D31.   Golden Crest NEC 115 (lp, quadrophonic) 1977
Composers Quartet (Matthew Raimondi, violin; Anahid Ajemian, violin; Jean
    Dane, viola; Michael Rudiakov, violoncello)
Notes by composers
Album title: The Composer's String Quartet Plays Literature of American
    Contemporary Composers
New England Conservatory series
With: Gunther Schuller's String Quartet No.1; Igor Stravinsky's Double
    Canon for String Quartet; Henry Cowell's Quartet Euphometric; Richard
    Swift's String Quartet IV

D32.   S23555 Entr'acte (digital)
Kronos Quartet
With: Elliott Carter's *String Quartet No.2* (D117); Lukas Foss' Quartet No.1;
    Bernard Herrmann's Echoes

D33.   Etcetera KTC 1065-1066 (cd) 1988
Arditti String Quartet
Recorded June 1988, in St. Silas Church, Kentish Town, London
Notes by David Harvey
Album title: The Music for String Quartet
With: Elliott Carter's *String Quartet No.1* (D112); *String Quartet No.4*
    (D128); *String Quartet No.2* (D118); *String Quartet No.3* (D123)
See: Tempo no.173 (June 1990), p.57-59; Musical America v.109, no.6
    (November 1989), p.8-10; Neue Zeitschrift für Musik v.151, no.1 (January
    1990), p.46-47

Elegy (viola version) (W58d)

D34.   ECM 1316 (on all formats) 1986
ECM 827 744-1; ECM 1-25043; ECM 25043-1 (lp) 1986
ECM 827 744-2 (cd) 1986
ECM 4-25043 (on container: ECM 25043-4) (cassette) 1986
Kim Kashkashian, viola; Robert Levin, piano

Recorded in New York
Album title: Elegies
ECM New series
With: Benjamin Britten's Lachrymae; Ralph Vaughan Williams' Romanze;
Alexander Glasunov's Elegie op.44; Franz Liszt's Romance Oubliée; Zoltán
Kodály's Adagio c-dur; Henri Vieuxtemps' Elegie op.30

D34a.   Crystal Records CD 636 (cd) 1991
Paul Cortese, viola; Jon Klibonoff, piano
Recorded June 10-12, 1991, at Concordia College, Bronxville, New York
With: William Bergsma's Fantastic Variations on a Theme from Tristan; Alan
Hovaness' Chahagir for Viola Solo; George Rochberg's Sonata for Viola
and Piano; Vincent Persichetti's Parable for Solo Viola. Infanta Marina

Elegy (string orchestra version) (W14)

D35.   Nonesuch D 79002 (lp,stereo) 1980
Nonesuch 79002-2 (cd) 1980
Elektra/Asylum/Nonesuch D1-79002 (cassette) 1980
Los Angeles Chamber Orchestra; Gerard Schwarz, conductor
Recorded April 2, 1980, at Ambassador Auditorium, Pasadena, California
Notes by Elliott Carter and Eric Salzman
Album title: American Music for Strings
With: Samuel Barber's Serenade for Strings; Irving Fine's Serious Song;
David Diamond's Rounds for String Orchestra
See: Consumer Research Bulletin (March 1981), p.43; Fanfare (March/April
1981), p.232; New York Times (March 29, 1981), IV, p.31; Stereo Review
(February 1981), p.111

D36.   New Editions
Colgate College Singers

Emblems (W39)

D37.   GSS Recordings GSS 103 (lp, stereo) 1984
Men's Choruses and Women's Choir of the Gregg Smith Singers; The Long
Island Symphonic Choral Association; Columbia University Men's Glee
Club; Gregg Smith, conductor
The Choral Masters series v.1
With: Elliott Carter's *Tarantella* (D140); *The Harmony of Morning* (D47);
Heart Not so Heavy as Mine (D50); *Musicians Wrestle Everywhere* (D66);
To Music (D149); *The Defense of Corinth* (D13)

Enchanted Preludes (W82)

D38.   New Albion Records NA019 CD (cd) 1989
California E.A.R. Unit (Erika Duke, Lorna Eder, Arthur Jarvinen, Amy
Knoles, Robin Lorentz, Gaylord Mowrey, James Rohrig, Rand Steiger,

Dorothy Stone) with Theresa Tunnicliff, clarinet
Recorded September 15-16, 1988, at SUNY Purchase
Notes by Ruth Dreier
With: Arthur Jarvinen's Egyptian Two Step; Rand Steiger's Quintessence;
Michael Torke's The Yellow Pages; Karlheinz Stockhausen's Dr. K-Sextet;
Elliott Carter's *Esprit Rude/Esprit Doux* (D41); *Canon for Four* (D2); Louis
Andriessen's Hoketus

D39.   ECM New Series ECM 1391 (cd) 1990
ECM New Series ECM 839 617-2 (cd) 1990
ECM New Series ECM 839 617-4 (cassette) 1990
Thomas Demenga, violoncello; Philippe Racine, flute
Recorded April 1989 in Zurich
Notes by Heinz Holliger
With: J.S. Bach's Suite No.3 in D for Solo Violoncello BWV 1009; Elliott
Carter's *Esprit Rude/Esprit Doux* (D42); *Riconoscenza* (D97); *Triple Duo*
(D151)
See: Tempo no.173 (June 1990), p.57-59; Fanfare (January/February 1992),
p.152

D40.   GM Recordings GM 2020CD (cd) 1990
Da Capo Chamber Players
Recorded September 15-16, 1988, at SUNY Purchase
Album title: Perle/Carter
With: Elliott Carter's *Canon for Four* (D3); George Perle's Sonata for Cello
and Piano; Lyric Piece, Cello and Piano; Elliott Carter's *Pastorale,
Clarinet and Piano* (D75); George Perle's Sonata a Quatro, Flute/Alto
Flute, Clarinet, Violin and Cello; Elliott Carter's *Esprit Rude/Esprit Doux*
(D43)

Esprit Rude/Esprit Doux (W78)

D41.   New Albion Records NA019 CD (cd) 1989
California E.A.R. Unit (Erika Duke, Lorna Eder, Arthur Jarvinen, Amy
Knoles, Robin Lorentz, Gaylord Mowrey, James Rohrig, Rand Steiger,
Dorothy Stone) with Toby Holmes, Theresa Tunnicliff
Notes by Ruth Dreier
With: Arthur Jarvinen's Egyptian Two Step; Rand Steiger's Quintessence;
Michael Torke's The Yellow Pages; Karlheinz Stockhausen's Dr. K-Sextet;
Elliott Carter's *Enchanted Preludes* (D38); *Canon for Four* (D2); Louis
Andriessen's Hoketus

D42.   ECM New Series ECM 1391 (cd) 1990
ECM New Series ECM 839 617-2 (cd) 1990
ECM New Series ECM 839 617-4 (cassette) 1990
Philippe Racine, flute; Ernesto Molinari, clarinet
Recorded April 1989, in Zurich
Notes by Heinz Holliger

With: J.S. Bach's Suite No.3 in D for Solo Violoncello BWV 1009; Elliott
Carter's *Enchanted Preludes* (D39); *Riconoscenza* (D97); *Triple Duo*
(D151)
See: Tempo no.173 (June 1990), p.57-59; Fanfare (January/February 1991),
p.152

D43.   GM Recordings GM 2020CD (cd) 1990
Da Capo Chamber Players
Recorded February 5, 1988, at Merkin Concert Hall, New York
Album title: Perle/Carter
With: Elliott Carter's *Enchanted Preludes* (D40); *Canon for Four* (D3);
George Perle's Sonata for Cello and Piano; Lyric Piece, Cello and Piano;
Elliott Carter's *Pastorale, Clarinet and Piano* (D75); George Perle's
Sonata a Quatro, Flute/Alto Flute, Clarinet, Violin and Cello

D44.   Erato ECD 75553 (cd) 1990
Erato 2292-45364-2 (cd) 1990
Sophie Cherrier, flute; André Trouttet, clarinet
Recorded under the composer's supervision, December 1987, IRCAM, Espace
de projection, Paris
Notes by Elliott Carter
With: Elliott Carter's *Oboe Concerto* (D71); *A Mirror on Which to Dwell*
(D62); *Penthode* (D76)
See: Tempo no.173 (June 1990), p.57-59; Fanfare (July/August 1991), p.134;
Musical America (July 1991), p.71

A Fantasy About Purcell's "Fantasia Upon One Note" (W72)

D45.   Odyssey Y 34137 (lp, stereo) 1976
American Brass Quintet (Louis Ranger, Raymond Mase, Edward Birdwell,
Herbert Rankin, Robert Biddlecome)
Recorded March 31 - April 1, 1975
Notes by Elliott Carter
Modern American Music series
With: Elliott Carter's *Eight Pieces for Four Timpani* (D28); *Brass Quintet*
(D1)
See: New Records (January 1977), p.9; Saturday Review of Literature
(November 13, 1976), p.52

D45a.   Capriccio 10361 (cd)
Frankfurt Radio Orchestra; Brass Ensemble; Lutz Köhler, conductor
With: J.S. Bach's (arr. Mowat) Brandenburg Concerto No.3; Henry Purcell's
Fantasies; Aaron Copland's Fanfare for the Common Man; Samuel Barber's
Mutation from Bach; Handel's (arr. Howarth) Music for the Royal
Fireworks
See: Fanfare (March/April 1992), p.132

D45b.   Hyperion CDA66517 (cd) 1991
London Gabrieli Brass Ensemble; Christopher Larkin, conductor
Recorded in All Hallows, Gospel Oak, London, July 14-15, 1991
With: Charles Ives' From the Steeples and the Mountains; Samuel Barber's
Mutations from Bach; Roy Harris' Chorale for Organ and Brass; Virgil
Thomson's Family Portrait; Henry Cowell's Grinnell Fanfare; Tall Tale;
Hymn and Fuguing Tune no.12; Rondo; Philip Glass' Brass Sextet; Carl
Ruggles' Angels; Charles Ives' Processional: Let There be Light

The Harmony of Morning (W37)

D46.   Vox Box SVBX 5354 (lp, stereo) 1979
Gregg Smith Singers; Orpheus Ensemble; Peabody Conservatory Chorus and
Texas Boys' Choir; Gregg Smith, conductor
Notes by Gregg Smith
Album title: America Sings: American Choral Music. After 1950
With: William Bergsma's Riddle Me This; Giuseppe Chihara's Lie Lightly,
Gentle Earth; Jacob Druckman's Madrigale; Lou Harrison's Mass (to St.
Anthony); Michael Hennagin's The House on the Hill; Andrew Imbrie's On
the Beach at Night; Carolyn Madison's Two Pieces; William Mayer's The
Eve of St. Agnes; Edmund Najera's In Dulci Jubilo; Ned Rorem's Missa
Brevis; Ronald Roxbury's Four Motets; William Schuman's Mail Order
Madrigals; Gregg Smith's Legend; Donald Waxman's Thomas Hardy Songs

D47.   GSS Recordings GSS 103 (lp, stereo) 1984
Men's Choruses and Women's Choir of the Gregg Smith Singers; The Long
Island Symphonic Choral Association; Columbia University Men's Glee
Club; Gregg Smith, conductor
The Choral Masters series v.1
With: Elliott Carter's *Tarantella* (D140); *Emblems* (D37); *Heart Not so Heavy
as Mine* (D50); *Musicians Wrestle Everywhere* (D66); *To Music* (D149);
The Defense of Corinth (D13)

Heart Not So Heavy As Mine (W35)

D48.   American Musical Heritage MIA 116 (1961)
The Society for the Preservation of the American Musical Heritage Hamline
A Cappella Choir; Robert Holliday, conductor
Album title: Choral Music in 20th-Century America
Music in America series
Choral Music of the Twentieth Century series

D49.   Nonesuch H 1115 (lp, mono) 1966
Nonesuch H 71115 (lp, stereo) 1966
Canby Singers; Edward Tatnall Canby, conductor
Notes by Edward Tatnall Canby
Album title: The Dove Descending

With: Johannes Brahms' Ach, Arme Welt, op.110, no.2; Ich Aber bin Elend, op.110, no. 1; Das Mädchen, op. 93a, no.2; O Süsser Mai, op.93a, no.3; Elliott Carter's *Musicians Wrestle Everywhere* (D63); Don Carlo Gesualdo's O Vos Omnes; Hans Hassler's Cantata Domino; O Aufenhalt Meins Leben; Paul Hindemith's 6 Chansons; Frauenklage; Claudio Monteverdi's Ohimése Tanto Amatel; Zeffiro Torna; Claude Sermisy's Au Joly Boys; Igor Stravinsky's The Dove Descending Breaks the Air; Peter Warlock's Corpus Christi

See: High Fidelity (September 1966), p.112; HiFi/Stereo Review (October 1966), p.138; New Records (July 1966), p.7

D50.   GSS Recordings GSS 103 (lp, stereo) 1984
Men's Choruses and Women's Choir of the Gregg Smith Singers; The Long Island Symphonic Choral Association; Columbia University Men's Glee Club; Gregg Smith, conductor
The Choral Masters series v.1
With: Elliott Carter's *Tarantella* (D140); *Emblems* (D37); *The Harmony of Morning* (D47); *Musicians Wrestle Everywhere* (D66); *To Music* (D149); *The Defense of Corinth* (D13)

Holiday Overture (W12)

D51.   Composers Recordings SD 475 (lp, stereo) 1982
American Composers Orchestra; Paul Dunkel, conductor
Recorded February 1982, in Walt Whitman Auditorium, Brooklyn College
Notes by David Schiff
Album title: Elliott Carter: The Early Years
American Historic series
With: Elliott Carter's *Symphony No.1* (D131); *Pocahontas Suite* (D94)
See: American Record Guide (May 1983), p.16; Consumer Research Bulletin (March 1983), p.43; Fanfare (January/February 1983), p.132-134; New Records (December 1982), p.4; New York Times (December 21, 1982), VIII, p.19; High Fidelity v.33, no.9 (September 1983), p.69-70, 113 (See: C88)

D52.   Composers Recordings ACS 6003 (cassette) 1985
Holiday Overture, Reissue of D51
American Composers Orchestra; Paul Dunkel, conductor
Album title: Music of Elliott Carter
Anthology series
With: Elliott Carter's *Syringa* (D136); *Symphony No.1* (D132)

D53.   CRI CD 610 (cd) 1991
Holiday Overture, reissue of D51
Notes by David Schiff
Album title: The Music of Elliott Carter
CRI American Masters series

With: Elliott Carter's *Pocahontas Suite* (D95); *Syringa* (D138)
See: American Record Guide (March/April 1992), p.42

In Sleep, In Thunder (W48)

D54.   Wergo WER 60124 (lp, stereo) 1985
Elektra/Asylum/Nonesuch 79110 (cd) 1985
Elektra/Asylum/Nonesuch 79110-1 (lp, stereo) 1985
Elektra/Asylum/Nonesuch 79110-4 SR (cassette) 1985
Martyn Hill, tenor; London Sinfonietta; Oliver Knussen, conductor
Recorded February 29, 1984, in Rosslyn Hill Chapel, Hampstead, London
Notes by David Schiff
With: Elliott Carter's *Triple Duo* (D150)
See: Tempo no.158 (September 1986), p.34-35

D55.   Bridge Records BCD 9014 (cd) 1989
Jon Garrison, tenor; Speculum Musicae; Robert Black, conductor
Recorded October 20-21, 1987, in New York
Album title: The Vocal Works (1975-1981)
With: Elliott Carter's *Three Poems of Robert Frost* (D146); *A Mirror on
Which to Dwell* (D61); *Syringa* (D137)
See: Musical America v.110, no.6 (September 1990), p.70-71; Tempo no.173
(June 1990), p.57-59; Nats Journal v.47, no.2 (1990), p.48; American
Music v.8, no.4 (1990), p.492-494; American Record Guide
(January/February 1990), p.40; Musical America (March 1990), p.70

The Minotaur (W6)

D56.   Elektra Nonesuch 9 79248-2; 79178; 79047 (cd) 1990
New York Chamber Symphony; Gerard Schwarz, conductor
Recorded December 6, 1988, at the Manhattan Center, New York City
Notes by Lloyd Schwartz
With: Elliott Carter's *Three Poems of Robert Frost*: "Dust of Snow," "The
Rose Family" (D147); *Piano Sonata* (D89)
See: Fanfare (July/August 1991), p.134; Musical America (July 1991), p.71

The Minotaur Suite (W13)

D57.   Mercury MG 50103 (lp, mono) 1956
Mercury MRL 2515 (1956)
Eastman-Rochester Symphony Orchestra; Howard Hanson, conductor
Recorded on January 22, 1956
Notes by David Hall
Olypian series
With: Colin McPhee's Tabuh-Tabuhan

See: New Yorker v.32, no.14 (May 26, 1956), p.130 or p.120-1; American Record Guide (July 1956), p.177; Consumer Research Bulletin (July 1956), p.35; High Fidelity (July 1956), p.44; Hi-Fi Music at Home (July/August 1956), p.28; New Records (July 1956), p.4

D58.   Mercury Golden Imports SRI 75111 (lp, electronically altered to simulate stereo) 1978
Minotaur Suite Reissue of D57
With: Henry Cowell's Symphony No.4; Wallingford Riegger's New Dance
See: Fanfare (March/April 1979), p.46; New Records (February 1979), p.3

A Mirror on Which to Dwell (W46)

D59.   Radio France IRCAM (cassette) 1978
[excerpts] "Argument" and "Sandpiper" only
Deborah Cook; Ensemble InterContemporain; Pierre Boulez, conductor
Album title: Pierre Boulez Presents
Le Temps Musical series 3
With: Olivier Messiaen's Études de rythme: Mode de valeurs et d'intensités

D60.   Columbia M 35171 (lp, stereo) 1980
Columbia MT 35171 (cassette) 1980
CBS Masterworks 76812
Susan Davenny Wyner, soprano; Speculum Musicae; Richard Fitz, conductor
Recorded at CBS Recording Studios, New York
Notes by Elliott Carter
With: Elliott Carter's *A Symphony of Three Orchestras* (D134)
See: Tempo no.143 (December 1982), p.30-31 (See: C98); Fanfare (January/February 1981), p.98; New Records (January 1981), p.1; Stereo Review (April 1981), p.103; High Fidelity/Musical America v.31, no.8 (August 1981), p.52,55 (See: C89)

D61.   Bridge Records BCD 9014 (cd) 1989
Christine Schadeberg, soprano; Speculum Musicae; Donald Palma, conductor
Recorded December 2-3, 1988, in New York
Album title: The Vocal Works (1975-1981)
With: Elliott Carter's *Three Poems of Robert Frost* (D146); *Syringa* (D137); *In Sleep, In Thunder* (D55)
See: Musical America v.110, no.6 (September 1990), p.70-71; Tempo no.173 (June 1990), p.57-59; NATS Journal v.47, no.2 (1990), p.48; American Music v.8, no.4 (1990), p.492-494; American Record Guide (January/February 1990), p.40; Musical America (March 1990), p.70

D62.   Erato ECD 75553 (cd) 1990
Erato 2292-45364-2 (cd) 1990
Phyllis Bryn-Julson, soprano; Ensemble InterContemporain; Pierre Boulez, conductor
Notes by Elliott Carter

Recorded under the composer's supervision, December 1987, IRCAM, Espace de projection, Paris

With: Elliott Carter's *Oboe Concerto* (D71); *Esprit Rude/Esprit Doux* (D44); *Penthode* (D76)

See: Tempo no.173 (June 1990), p.57-59; Fanfare (July/August 1991), p.134; Musical America (July 1991), p.71

Musicians Wrestle Everywhere (W38)

D63.   Nonesuch H 1115 (lp, mono) 1966
Nonesuch H 71115 (lp, stereo) 1966
Canby Singers; Edward Tatnall Canby, conductor
Notes by Edward Tatnall Canby
Album title: The Dove Descending
With: Johannes Brahms' Ach, Arme Welt, op.110, no.2; Ich Aber bin Elend, op.110, no. 1; Das Mädchen, op. 93a, no.2; O Süsser Mai, op.93a, no.3; Elliott Carter's *Heart not so Heavy as Mine* (D49); Claudio Gesualdo's O Vos Omnes; Hans Hassler's Cantata Domino; O Aufenhalt Meins Leben; Paul Hindemith's 6 Chansons; Frauenklage; Claudio Monteverdi's Ohimése Tanto Amatel; Zeffiro Torna; Claude Sermisy's Au Joly Boys; Igor Stravinsky's The Dove Descending Breaks the Air; Peter Warlock's Corpus Christi
See: High Fidelity (September 1966), p.112; HiFi/Stereo Review (October 1966), p.138; New Records (July 1966), p.7

D64.   Vox Box SVBX 5353 (lp, stereo) 1977
Gregg Smith Singers; Gregg Smith, conductor
Notes by Gregg Smith
Album title: America Sings (1920-1950)
With: Samuel Barber's A Stopwatch and an Ordnance Map; Leonard Bernstein's Choruses from 'The Lark'; Elliott Carter's *Defence of Corinth* (D12); Aaron Copland's Two Pieces for Treble Choir; Henry Cowell's Luther's Coral to His Son; Irving Fine's The Choral New Yorker; Lukas Foss' Behold I Build a House; George Gershwin's Two Madrigals; Charles Ives' Two Election Songs; Walter Piston's Psalm and Prayer of David; Wallingford Riegger's Who Can Revoke; William Schuman's Prelude; Charles Seeger's Chant; Roger Sessions' Turn, O Liberstad; Louise Talma's Let's Touch the Sky; Virgil Thomson's Four Southern Hymns; Virgil Thomson's Alleluia
See: New Records (December 1977), p.8; New York Times (July 1, 1979), IV, p.22

D65.   Deutsche Grammophon 2530 912 (lp, stereo) 1978
Tanglewood Festival Chorus; John Oliver, conductor
Notes by Michael Steinberg
Album title: American Choral Music of the 20th Century

With: Charles Ives' Psalms 24, 67 and 90; Jacob Druckman's Antiphonies; Aaron Copland's In the Beginning.
See: Fanfare (November/December 1979), p.153; Stereo Review (December 1979), p.154

D66.   GSS Recordings GSS 103 (lp, stereo) 1984
Men's Choruses and Women's Choir of the Gregg Smith Singers; The Long Island Symphonic Choral Association; Columbia University Men's Glee Club; Gregg Smith, conductor
The Choral Masters series v.1
With: Elliott Carter's *Tarantella* (D140); *Emblems* (D37); *The Harmony of Morning* (D47); *Heart Not so Heavy as Mine* (D50); *To Music* (D149); *The Defense of Corinth* (D13)

Night Fantasies (W74)

D67.   Nonesuch 79047 (lp, stereo) 1983
Elektra/Asylum/Nonesuch SR 79047; Nonesuch 9 79047-4 G (cassette) 1983
Paul Jacobs, piano
Recorded in August 1982, at the RCA Studio "A" in New York
Notes by Elliott Carter and Paul Jacobs
With: Elliott Carter's *Piano Sonata* (D86)
See: Stereo Review v.48 (November 1983), p.78; Clavier v.27, no.2 (February 1988), p.46-7; Hamilton. Elliott

D68.   Etcetera ETC 1008 (lp, stereo) 1983
Etcetera KTC 1008 (cd) 1988
Etcetera ET 331; TC 1008 (cassette) 1983
Charles Rosen, piano
Notes by Charles Rosen
Album title: Piano Works
With: Elliott Carter's *Piano Sonata* (D88)
See: Stereo Review v.48 (November 1983), p.78; High Fidelity v.33, no.9 (September 1983), p.69-70, 113 (See: C88)

D69.   Bridge Records BCD 9001 (cd) 1986
Bridge Records BCS 7001 (cassette) 1986
Aleck Karis, piano
Recorded February 6-8, 1984, at Holy Trinity Episcopal Church, New York City
Notes by Aleck Karis
American Pianists series 1
With: Frederic Chopin's Fantasie, op.49; Robert Schumann's Carnival, op.9; Elliott Carter's *Piano Sonata* (D87)

D70.   Music & Arts CD-604 (cd) 1989
Ursula Oppens, piano
Recorded at State University of New York, Purchase

Notes by Susan Feder

Album title: American Piano Music of Our Times

With: Conlon Nancarrow's Tango; William Bolcom's The Dead Moth Tango; Michael Sahl's Tango from the Exiles Café; Julius Hemphill's Parchment; John Adams' Phrygian Gates; Lukas Foss' The Curriculum Vitae Tango; David Jaggard's Tango

See: Keyboard v.16, no.2 (February 1990), p.24

D70a.   Neuma 450-76 (cd) 1991

Stephen Drury, piano

Recorded at Jordan Hall, New England Conservatory, Boston, MA, July 1990

Notes by Stephen Drury

Album title: Contemporary Piano Music

With: John Cage's Etudes Australes (Book 1)

See: American Record Guide (July/August 1992), p.114; Fanfare (July/August 1992), p.136

Oboe Concerto (W22)

D71.   Erato ECD 75553 (cd) 1990

Erato 2292-45364-2 (cd) 1990

Heinz Holliger, oboe; l'Ensemble InterContemporain; Pierre Boulez, conductor

Recorded under the composer's supervision, December 1987, IRCAM, Espace de projection, Paris

Notes by Elliott Carter

With: Elliott Carter's Esprit Rude/Esprit Doux (D44); A Mirror on Which to Dwell (D62); Penthode (D76)

See: Tempo no.173 (June 1990), p.57-59; Fanfare (July/August 1991), p.134; Musical America (July 1991), p.71

Pastoral for Clarinet and Piano (W57)

D72.   Orion ORS 77275 (lp, stereo) 1977

John Russo, clarinet; Lydia Walton Ignacio, piano

Notes by C. Jacueline Hogue

With: John Russo's Larghetto; Sonata No.4; François Devienne's Sonata No.1; John Davidson's Introduction and Dance

See: New Records (January 1978), p.7

D73.   Grenadilla GS 1018 (lp, stereo) 1978

Elsa Ludewig-Verdehr, clarinet; David Liptak, piano

Notes by Rosario Mazzeo

With: Mario Castelnuovo-Tedesco's Sonata for Clarinet and Piano, op.128; Vincent Frohne's Study for Clarinet Solo, op.17

See: Fanfare (March/April 1980), p.72; New Records (October 1979), p.4

D74.   Golden Crest Records RE 7075 (lp, stereo) 1982
        Keith Wilson, clarinet; Donald Currier, piano
        Album title: Music for Clarinet
        Recital series
        With: Paul Hindemith's Sonata for Clarinet and Piano; Quincy Porter's
            Quintet for Clarinet and Strings
        See: Fanfare (March/April 1983), p.332; New Records (February 1983), p.5

D75.   GM Recordings GM 2020CD (cd) 1990
        Da Capo Chamber Players
        Recorded September 15-16, 1988, at SUNY Purchase
        Album title: Perle/Carter
        With: Elliott Carter's *Enchanted Preludes* (D40); *Canon for Four* (D3);
            George Perle's Sonata for Cello and Piano; Lyric Piece, Cello and Piano;
            George Perle's Sonata a Quatro, Flute/Alto Flute, Clarinet, Violin and
            Cello; Elliott Carter's *Esprit Rude/Esprit Doux* (D43)

D75a.   CRS Master Recordings CD 9255 (cd) 1992
        John Russo, clarinet; Lydia Walton Ignacio, piano
        Album title: Contemporary/Classic Masters
        With: John Russo's Sonata no.4 for Clarinet and Piano; Larghetto for
            Clarinet, Viola and Piano; François Devienne's Sonata no.1 for Clarinet
            and Piano; Robert Dusek's Gray Dawn; John Davidson's Introduction and
            Dance; David Hush's Partita no.1 for Violoncello Solo; Carl Harrison's
            Songs from a Child's Garden

Penthode (W20)

D76.   Erato ECD 75553 (cd) 1990
        Erato 2292-45364-2 (cd) 1990
        l'Ensemble Intercontemporain; Pierre Boulez, conductor
        Recorded under the composer's supervision, December 1987, IRCAM, Espace
            de projection, Paris
        Notes by Elliott Carter
        With: Elliott Carter's *Oboe Concerto* (D71); *Esprit Rude/Esprit Doux* (D44);
            A Mirror on Which to Dwell (D62)
        See: Tempo no.173 (June 1990), p.57-59; Fanfare (July/August 1991), p.134;
            Musical America (July 1991), p.71

Piano Concerto (W17)

D77.   RCA Victor LM 3001 (lp, mono) 1968
        RCA Victor LSC 3001 (lp, stereo) 1968
        RCA RB/SB 6756 (1968)
        Jacob Lateiner, piano; Boston Symphony Orchestra; Erich Leinsdorf,
            conductor
        Recorded from tapes of the first two performances January 7-8, 1967, at
            Boston Symphony Hall (See: W17a)

Notes by Michael Steinberg
With: Michael Colgrass' As Quiet As
See: High Fidelity v.18, no.5 (May 1968), p.67-8; American Record Guide
      v.34, no.10 (June 1968), p.936-937,945 (See: C35); HiFi/Stereo Review
      (June 1968), p.80; New Records (June 1968), p.6; New York Times
      (March 1, 1967), IV, p.30; Musical Quarterly v.55, no.4 (October 1969),
      p.559-572 (See: C251); New York Times (January 7, 1967), p.21:1
      (See: C229)

D78.   New World Records NW 347 (lp, stereo) 1986
        New World Records NW 347-2 (cd) 1986
        New World Records NW 347-4 (cassette) 1986
        Ursula Oppens, piano; Cincinnati Symphony Orchestra; Michael Gielen,
            conductor
        Recorded in Music Hall, Cincinnati, Ohio, October 5th and 6th, 1984
        Notes by David Schiff
        With: Elliott Carter's *Variations for Orchestra* (D154)

Piano Sonata (W59)

D79.   American Recording Society ARS-25 (lp, mono) 1952
        Beveridge Webster, piano
        Note: "Produced expressly for the American Recording Society by the Ditson
            Musical Foundation."
        200 Years of American Music series
        With: Elliott Carter's *Sonata for Violoncello and Piano* (D105)
        See: New York Times (March 30, 1952), X, p.6; Saturday Review of
        Literature (March 29, 1952), p.48

D80.   Epic LC 3850 (lp, mono) 1962
        Epic BC 1250 (lp, stereo) 1962
        Charles Rosen, piano
        Recorded on April 25, 1961
        Notes by Charles Rosen
        With: Elliott Carter's *Pocahontas Suite* (D93)
        See: High Fidelity (February 1963), p.78; HiFi/Stereo Review (March 1963),
        p.68; New Records (January 1963), p.4; New York Times (May 12, 1963),
        X, p.10; Saturday Review of Literature (December 29, 1962), p.58; New
        Yorker v.39 (June 8, 1963), p.163-165

D81.   HMV ALP 2052 and ASD 601 (1965)
        Charles Rosen, piano
        Recorded on April 25, 1961
        Notes by Charles Rosen
        With: Elliott Carter's *Double Concerto* (D15)

D82.   Desto D 419 (lp, mono) 1965
Desto DST 6419 (lp, stereo) 1965
Piano Sonata, reissue of D79
With: Elliott Carter's *Sonata for Violoncello and Piano* (D106)
See: Pan Pipes (January 1966), p.41

D83.   Dover HCR 5265 (lp, mono) 1966
Dover HCR-ST 7014; HCR-ST 7265 (lp, stereo) 1966
Beveridge Webster, piano
Notes by Roger Kamien
Album title: Modern American Piano Music
With: Aaron Copland's Piano Variations; Roger Sessions' Second Sonata for
Piano
See: Consumer Research Bulletin (January 1967), p.14; High Fidelity
(November 1966), p.110; HiFi/Stereo Review (December 1966), p.114;
New Records (November 1966), p.12; New York Times (October 30,
1966), IV, p.20; Stereo Review (December 19, 1966), p.74

D84.   Valois MB 755 (lp, stereo) 1966
Noel Lee, piano
Notes by Noel Lee
With: Aaron Copland's Piano Variations; Roger Sessions' Second Sonata

D85.   Orion ORS 79342 (lp, stereo) 1979
Evelinde Trenkner, piano
Recorded at the Pleshakov-Kaneko Music Institute, Palo Alto, California
Notes by Evelinde Trenkner
With: Franz Liszt's Praludium und Fuge uber den Names Bach; Alfredo
Casella's Due Ricercari sul Nome BACH; Arthur Honegger's Preludio,
Arioso et Fughette sur le Nom de BACH
See: Fanfare (May/June 1980), p.67; New Records (February 1980), p.12

D86.   Elektra/Asylum/Nonesuch 79047 (lp, stereo) 1983
Elektra/Asylum/Nonesuch SR 79047; Nonesuch 9 79047-4 G (cassette) 1983
Paul Jacobs, piano
Recorded at the RCA Studio "A" in New York in August 1982
Notes by Elliott Carter and Paul Jacobs
With: Elliott Carter's *Night Fantasies* (D67)
See: Stereo Review v.48 (November 1983), p.78; Clavier v.27, no.2
(February 1988), p.46-47; Hamilton. Elliott

D87.   Bridge Records BCD 9001 (cd) 1986
Bridge Records BCS 7001 (cassette) 1986
Aleck Karis, piano
Recorded at Holy Trinity Episcopal Church, New York City, February 6-8,
1984
Notes by Aleck Karis

American Pianists series
With: Frederic Chopin's Fantasie, op.49; Robert Schumann's Carnival,
op.91; Elliott Carter's *Night Fantasies* (D69)

D88.   Etcetera ETC 1008 (lp) 1983
Etcetera KTC 1008 (cd) 1988
Etcetera ET 331; TC 1008 (cassette) 1983
Charles Rosen, piano
Notes by Charles Rosen
Album title: Piano Works
With: Elliott Carter's *Night Fantasies* (D68)
See: Stereo Review v.48 (November 1983), p.78; High Fidelity v.33, no.9
(September 1983), p.69-70, 113 (See: C88)

D89.   Elektra Nonesuch 9 79248-2; 79178; 79047 (cd) 1990
Piano Sonata, reissue of D86
New York Chamber Symphony; Gerard Schwarz, conductor
Notes by Lloyd Schwartz
With: Elliott Carter's *The Minotaur* (D56); *Three Poems of Robert Frost*:
"Dust of Snow," "The Rose Family" (D147)
See: Fanfare (July/August 1991), p.134; Musical America (July 1991), p.71

D90.   Virgin Classics VC 791163-2 (cd) 1991
Peter Lawson, piano
Recorded November-December, 1989, Abbey Road Studio No.1, London
Album title: American Piano Sonatas Vol. One
With: Aaron Copland's Piano Sonata; Charles Ives' Three Page Sonata;
Samuel Barber's Piano Sonata, op.26

D91.   Factory FACD 256 (cd)
With: Ligeti's Etudes, bk.1; Martland's Kgakala; Olivier Messiaen's Le
Courlis Cendre
See: Fanfare (May/June 1991), p.352

D91a.   Continuum CCD 1028-1029 (cd) 1991
John McCabe, piano
Recorded in Rosslyn Hill Chapel, London, September 3-11, 1990
Notes by Calum MacDonald and John McCabe
Album title: Transatlantic Piano
With: John Adams' Phrygian Gates; André Previn's The Invisible Drummer;
George Rochberg's Carnival Music; Richard Rodney Bennett's Noctuary;
Aaron Copland's Sonata

D91b.   CDM LDC 278 1067 (cd) 1991
Noel Lee, piano
Recorded September 9-11, 1991, Eglise Luthérienne Saint-Pierre, Paris
Notes by Noel Lee
Album title: Musique Américaine pour Piano

With: Louis Moreau Gottschalk's Souvenir de Porto-Rico, op.31; The Dying
Poet (Le Poète Mourant); Grand Scherzo, op.57; Edward MacDowell's Sea
Pieces (Marines), op.55; Aaron Copland's Variations; John Cage's In a
Landscape

D92.   Program Promotions PP-2 (cd) 1992
Michael Kieran Harvey, piano
Recorded in Mittagong, N.S.W. Australia
Album title: Inspired 20th Century Piano Music
With: Igor Stravinsky's Trois Movements de Pétrouchka; Graham Hair's
Under Aldebaran; Carl Vine's Piano Sonata

Pocahontas Suite (W10)

D93.   Epic LC 3850 (lp, mono) 1962
Epic BC 1250 (lp, stereo) 1962
Zürich Radio Orchestra; Jacques Monod, conductor
Notes by Charles Rosen
With: Elliott Carter's *Piano Sonata* (D80)
See: New Yorker v.39 (June 8, 1963), p.163-165; New Records (January
1963), p.4; New York Times (May 12, 1963), X, p.10; High Fidelity
(February 1963), p.78; HiFi/Stereo Review (March 1963), p.68; Saturday
Review of Literature (December 29, 1962), p.58

D94.   Composers Recordings SD 475 (lp, stereo) 1982
American Composers Orchestra; Paul Dunkel, conductor
Recorded February 1982, in Walt Whitman Auditorium, Brooklyn College
Notes by David Schiff
Album title: Elliott Carter: The Early Years
American Historic series
With: Elliott Carter's *Holiday Overture* (D51); *Symphony No.1* (D131)
See: American Record Guide (May 1983), p.16; Consumer Research Bulletin
(March 1983), p.43; Fanfare (January/February 1983), p.132-134; New
Records (December 1982), p.4; New York Times (December 21, 1982),
VIII, p.19; High Fidelity v.33, no.9 (September 1983), p.69-70, 113
(See: C88)

D95.   CRI CD 610 (cd) 1991
Pocahontas, reissue of D92
Notes by David Schiff
Album title: The Music of Elliott Carter
CRI American Masters series
With: Elliott Carter's *Holiday Overture* (D53); *Syringa* (D138)
See: American Record Guide (March/April 1992), p.42

Riconoscenza Per Goffredo Petrassi (W79)

D96.   New World Records NW 333 (lp, stereo) 1986
        Maryvonne Le Dizes-Richard, violin
        Recorded January 1985, IRCAM, Centre-Georges-Pompidou, Paris
        Notes by Tim Page
        Album title: Hidden Sparks
        With: Tod Machover's Hidden Sparks; Ralph Shapey's Fantasy for Violin and
            Piano; John Melby's Concerto for Violin and Computer-Synthesized Tape

D97.   ECM New Series ECM 1391 (cd) 1990
        ECM New Series ECM 839 617-2 (cd) 1990
        ECM New Series ECM 839 617-4 (cassette) 1990
        Hansheinz Schneeberger, violin
        Recorded April 1989, in Zurich
        Notes by Heinz Holliger
        With: J.S. Bach's Suite No.3 in D for Solo Violoncello BWV 1009; Elliott
            Carter's *Esprit Rude/Esprit Doux* (D42); *Enchanted Preludes* (D39); *Triple
            Duo* (D151)
        See: Tempo no.173 (June 1990), p.57-59; Fanfare (January/February 1992),
            p.152

Sonata for Flute, Oboe, Violoncello and Harpsichord (W65)

D98.   Columbia ML 5576 (lp, mono) 1960
        Columbia MS 6176 (lp, stereo) 1960
        Anabel Brieff, flute; Josef Marx, oboe; Lorin Bernsohn, violoncello; Robert
            Conant, harpsichord
        Recorded on May 16, 1957
        Record commissioned by the Walter W. Naumburg Foundation
        Notes by Michael Steinberg
        With: Harold Shapero's String Quartet No.1
        See: New York Times July 23, 1961; High Fidelity (January 1961), p.74;
            New Records (December 1960), p.11; New Republic (February 13, 1961),
            p.21; Saturday Review of Literature (December 17, 1960), p.43
            (See: C43)

D99.   Decca DL 10 108 (lp, mono) 1965
        Decca DL 710 108 (lp, stereo) 1965
        Samuel Baron, flute; Ronald Roseman, oboe; Alexander Kouguell, violoncello;
            Sylvia Marlowe, harpsichord
        Notes by Sylvia Marlowe
        Decca Gold Record Label series
        With: Ned Rorem's Lovers, a Narrative for Harpsichord, Oboe, 'Cello, and
            Percussion; Manuel de Falla's Concerto for Harpsichord, Flute, Clarinet,
            and 'Cello; Henri Sauguet's Suite Royale
        See: HiFi/Stereo Review (July 1965), p.68; New Records (September 1965),
            p.15; New York Times (May 23, 1965), X, p.15

D100.   Nonesuch H 71234 (lp, stereo) 1969, 1973, 1977
         Harvey Sollberger, flute; Charles Kuskin, oboe; Fred Sherry, violoncello; Paul
             Jacobs, harpsichord
         Notes by Elliott Carter
         With: Elliott Carter's *Sonata for Violoncello and Piano* (D107)
         See: Stereo Review v.24, no.3 (March 1970), p.86-87; High Fidelity v.20,
             no.2 (February 1970), p.84; Reprinted in: American Musical Digest v.1
             no.5 (1970), p.45; American Record Guide v.36, no.7 (March 1970),
             p.498; Tempo no.105 (June 1973), p.40-41; New York Times (December
             21, 1969), IV, p.26

D101.   Deutsche Grammophon 2530 104 (lp, stereo) 1971
         Boston Symphony Chamber Players (Doriot Anthony Dwyer, flute; Ralph
             Gomberg, oboe; Jules Eskin, violoncello; Robert Levin, harpsichord)
         Notes by Sheila Keats
         Album title: American Chamber Music: 20th Century
         With: Charles Ives' Largo for Violin, Clarinet and Piano; Quincy Porter's
             Quintet for Oboe and String Quartet
         See: High Fidelity (August 1971), p.96; Library Journal (June 1, 1971),
             p.1954; The Monthly Letter (May 1971), p.11; Stereo Review (September
             1971), p.103

D102.   Serenus SRS 12056 (lp, stereo) 1974
         Sonata, reissue of D99
         Album title: Sylvia Marlowe Plays Harpsichord Music of the 20th Century
         Notes by Sylvia Marlowe
         With: Ned Rorem's Lovers, a Narrative for Harpsichord, Oboe, 'Cello, and
             Percussion; Manuel de Falla's Concerto for Harpsichord, Flute, Clarinet,
             and 'Cello; Henri Sauguet's Suite Royale

D103.   Columbia CML 5576; CMS 6176 (1974) (1968?, AML 7176) Special Service
             Records (AMS 6176? n.d.)
         Sonata, reissue of D98
         With: Harold Shapero's String Quartet No.1

D104.   Golden Crest NEC 109 (lp, stereo) 1975
         New England Conservatory of Music Chamber Players (Jolie Troob, flute;
             Cheryl Priebe, oboe; Gloria Johns, violoncello; Christopher Kies,
             harpsichord); John Heiss, conductor
         Notes by John Heiss
         Album title: Contemporary American Music
         Contemporary Chamber Music series v.9
         With: Milton Babbitt's Composition for 4 Instruments; Igor Stravinsky's
             Fanfare for Two Trumpets; Henry Brandt's Angels and Devils.

D104a.   Elektra Nonesuch 79183-2 (cd) 1992
         Harvey Sollberger, flute; Charles Kuskin, Oboe; Fred Sherry, violoncello;
         Paul Jabobs, harpsichord
         With: Elliott Carter's *Double Concerto* (D17a); *Sonata for Violoncello and
         Piano* (D109b)

Sonata for Violoncello and Piano (W61)

D105.   American Recording Society ARS-25 (lp, mono) 1952
         Bernard Greenhouse, violoncello; Anthony Makas, piano
         Note: "Produced expressly for the American Recording Society by the Ditson
         Musical Foundation."
         200 Years of American Music series
         With: Elliott Carter's *Piano Sonata* (D79)
         See: New York Times (March 30, 1952), X, p.6; Saturday Review of
         Literature v.35, no.13 (March 29, 1952), p.48

D106.   Desto D 419 (lp, mono) 1965
         Desto DST 6419 (lp, stereo) 1965
         Sonata, reissue of D105
         With: Elliott Carter's *Piano Sonata* (D82)
         See: Pan Pipes (January 1966), p.41

D107.   Nonesuch H 71234 (lp, stereo) 1969, 1973, 1977
         Joel Krosnick, violoncello; Paul Jacobs, piano
         Notes by Elliott Carter
         With: Elliott Carter's *Sonata for Flute, Oboe, Violoncello and Harpsichord*
         (D100)
         See: Stereo Review v.24, no.3 (March 1970), p.86-87; High Fidelity v.20,
         no.2 (February 1970), p.84; Reprinted in: American Musical Digest v.1,
         no.5 (1970), p.45; American Record Guide v.36, no.7 (March 1970),
         p.498; Tempo no.105 (June 1973), p.40-41; New York Times (December
         21, 1969), IV, p.26

D108.   Golden Crest RE 7081 (lp, stereo) 1979
         Michael Rudiakov, violoncello; Ursula Oppens, piano
         Album title: The Art of Michael Rudiakov
         Recital series
         With: J.S. Bach's Suite, Violoncello Unaccompanied no.1, G major, S.1007
         See: American Record Guide (September 1979), p.16; Stereo Review
         (October 1979), p.130

D109.   Finlandia FACD 362 (cd) 1988
         Anssi Karttunen, violoncello; Tuija Hakkila, piano
         Recorded in Jarvenpaa Hall, September-December 1987
         Notes by Anssi Karttunen
         Album title: Contemporary Music for Cello and Piano

With: Jouni Kaipainen's Trois Morceaux de l'aube, op.15; Edison Dehisov's Cello Sonata; Paavo Heininen's Serenade op.31, no.1; Erik Bergman's Quo Vadis, op.102

D109a.   Musikproduktion Dabringhaus und Grimm MD+G L 3397 (cd) 1992
Tilmann Wick, violoncello; Heasook Rhee, piano
Recorded at the Fürstliche Reitbahn, Arolsen, March 1992
Album title: Cellosonaten von 1948 (Cello Sonatas of 1948)
With: Nikolaj Miaskovsky's Sonate für Violoncello und Klavier, Nr.2, op.81; Francis Poulenc's Sonate für Violoncello und Klavier
See: American Record Guide (July/August 1992), p.256; Fanfare (July/August 1992), p.340

D109b.   Elektra Nonesuch 79183-2 (cd) 1992
Joel Krosnick, violoncello; Paul Jacobs, piano
With: Elliott Carter's *Double Concerto* (D17a); *Sonata for Flute, Oboe, Violoncello and Harpsichord* (D104a)

String Quartet No.1 (W64)

D110.   Columbia ML 5104 (lp, mono) 1956
Columbia CML 5104 (lp, mono) 1968
Columbia AML 5104 (1974)
Walden Quartet of the University of Illinois (Homer Schmitt, violin; Bernard Goodman, violin; John Garvey, viola; Robert Swenson, violoncello)
Recorded on February 2, 1955
Notes by Elliott Carter and William Glock
American Music Series no. 1
See: New York Times (December 9, 1956), II, p.106:19, Musical Quarterly v.43, no.1 (January 1957), p.130-132; American Record Guide (September 1956), p.2; Consumer Research Bulletin (October 1956), p.35; High Fidelity (September 1956), p.56; Hi-Fi Music at Home (September/October 1956), p.35; The Nation (October 6, 1956), p.296; New Records (September 1956), p.5

D111.   Nonesuch H 71249 (lp, stereo) 1970, 1972
Nonesuch 32803 (1975)
Nonesuch D1007 (cassette) 1970
Advent D 1007 (cassette) 1974
Elektra/Nonesuch 71249-2 (cd) 198-?
Composers Quartet (Matthew Raimondi, violin; Anahid Ajemian, violin; Jean Dupouy, viola; Michael Rudiakov, violoncello
Recorded April 21-23, 1970
Notes by Elliott Carter
With: Elliott Carter's *String Quartet No.2* (D115)

See: Tempo no. 105 (June 1973), p.40-41; Stereo Review v.26, no.2 (February 1971), p.89; London Times (January 22, 1972); High Fidelity v.21, no.2 (February 1971), p.76-78; New Records (January 1971), p.6; New York Times (February 7, 1971), IV, p.27; American Record Guide v.37, no.11 (July 1971), p.756-759 (See: C36)

D112.   Etcetera KTC 1065-1066 (cd) 1988
Arditti String Quartet
Recorded June 1988, in St. Silas Church, Kentish Town, London
Notes by David Harvey
Album title: The Works for String Quartet
With: Elliott Carter's *String Quartet No.4* (D128); *String Quartet No.2* (D118); *String Quartet No.3* (D123); *Elegy for String Quartet* (D34)
See: Neue Zeitschrift für Musik v.151, no.1 (January 1990), p.46-47; Tempo no.173 (June 1990), p.57-59; Musical America v.109, no.6 (November 1989), p.8-10

D113.   Sony S2K 47229 (47256, 47257) (cd) 1991
Juilliard String Quartet (Robert Mann, violin; Joel Smirnoff, violin; Samuel Rhodes, viola; Joel Krosnick, violoncello)
With: Elliott Carter's *String Quartet No.2* (D119); *String Quartet No.3* (D125); *String Quartet No.4* (D129); *Duo for Violin and Piano* (D19)
See: American Record Guide (March/April 1992), p.43; Fanfare (March/April 1992), p.170; Gramophone (April 1992), p.94

String Quartet No.2 (W66)

D114.   RCA Victor LM 2481 (lp, mono) 1961
RCA Victor LSC 2481 (lp, stereo) 1961
Juilliard String Quartet (Robert Mann, violin; Isidore Cohen, violin; Raphael Hillyer, viola; Claus Adam, violoncello)
Notes by Michael Steinberg
With: William Schuman's String Quartet No.3
See: High Fidelity (July 1961), p.54; HiFi/Stereo Review (July 1961), p.67; New Records (May 1961), p.6; New York Times (May 7, 1961), II, p.19 (See: C215); Saturday Review of Literature (May 27, 1961), p.40

D115.   Nonesuch H 71249 (lp, stereo) 1970, 1972
Nonesuch NON 32803 (1975)
Nonesuch D1007 (cassette) 1970
Advent D 1007 (cassette) 1974
Elektra/Nonesuch 71249-2 (cd) 198-?
Composers Quartet (Matthew Raimondi, violin; Anahid Ajemian, violin; Jean Dupouy, viola; Michael Rudiakov, violoncello)
Recorded April 21-23, 1970
Notes by Elliott Carter
With: Elliott Carter's *String Quartet No.1* (D111)

See: Tempo no. 105 (June 1973), p.40-41; Stereo Review v.26, no.2
(February 1971), p.89; London Times (January 22, 1972); High Fidelity
v.21, no.2 (February 1971), p.76-78; New Records (January 1971), p.6;
New York Times (February 7, 1971), IV, p.27; American Record Guide
v.37, no.11 (July 1971), p.756-759 (See: C36)

D116.   Columbia M 32738 (lp, stereo) 1974
Columbia MQ 32738 (lp, quadraphonic) 1974
Juilliard String Quartet (Robert Mann, violin; Earl Carlyss, violin; Raphael
    Hillyer, viola; Claus Adam, violoncello)
Recorded February 19-20, 1969
Notes by Elliott Carter and Robert Hurwitz
Modern American Music series
With: Elliott Carter's String Quartet No.3 (D120)
See: High Fidelity v.24, no.7 (July 1974), p.73-75 (See: C94); New Records
    (July 1974), p.6; New York Times (April 21, 1974), IV, p.26; Stereo
    Review (September 1974), p.116; Musical Newsletter v.4, no.3 (Summer
    1974), p.3-11 (See: C163)

D117.   Entr'acte S23555 (digital)
Kronos Quartet
With: Elliott Carter's Elegy for String Quartet (D32); Lukas Foss' Quartet
    No.1; Bernard Herrmann's Echoes

D118.   Etcetera KTC 1065-1066 (cd) 1988
Arditti String Quartet
Recorded June 1988, in St. Silas Church, Kentish Town, London
Notes by David Harvey
Album title: The Works for String Quartet
With: Elliott Carter's String Quartet No.1 (D112); String Quartet No.4
    (D128); String Quartet No.3 (D123); Elegy for String Quartet (D34)
See: Neue Zeitschrift für Musik v.151, no.1 (January 1990), p.46-47; Tempo
    no.173 (June 1990), p.57-59; Musical America v.109, no.6 (November
    1989), p.8-10

D119.   Sony S2K 47229 (47256, 47257) (cd) 1991
Juilliard String Quartet (Robert Mann, violin; Joel Smirnoff, violin; Samuel
    Rhodes, viola; Joel Krosnick, violoncello)
With: Elliott Carter's String Quartet No.1 (D113); String Quartet No.3
    (D125); String Quartet No.4 (D129); Duo for Violin and Piano (D19)
See: American Record Guide (March/April 1992), p.43; Fanfare
    (March/April 1992), p.170; Gramophone (April 1992), p.94

String Quartet No.3 (W69)

D120.   Columbia M 32738 (lp, stereo) 1974
Columbia MQ 32738 (lp, quadraphonic) 1974

Juilliard String Quartet (Robert Mann, violin; Earl Carlyss, violin; Samuel
   Rhodes, viola; Claus Adam, violoncello)
Recorded November 19-21, 1973
Notes by Elliott Carter and Robert Hurwitz
Modern American Music series
With: Elliott Carter's *String Quartet No.2* (D116)
See: High Fidelity v.24, no.7 (July 1974), p.73-75 (See: C94); New Records
   (July 1974), p.6; New York Times (April 21, 1974), IV, p.26; Stereo
   Review (September 1974), p.116; Musical Newsletter v.4, no.3 (Summer
   1974), p.3-11 (See: C163)

D121.   Musical Heritage Society MHS 4876 (lp, stereo) 1983
Composers String Quartet (Matthew Raimondi, violin; Anahid Ajemian,
   violin; Jean Dane, viola; Mark Shuman, violoncello)
Recorded at Vangaurd Sound Studio, New York, N.Y.
Notes by David Schiff
Album title: Chamber Music
With: Elliott Carter's *Eight Etudes and a Fantasy* (D25)
See: Strad v.100, no.1193 (September 1989), p.773-774

D122.   RCA Red Seal RS 9006 (lp, stereo) 1983
Arditti String Quartet
Recorded February 1982, Henry Wood Hall, London
With: Brian Ferneyhough's Quartet No.2; Jonathan Harvey's Quartet No.2

D123.   Etcetera KTC 1065-1066 (cd) 1988
Arditti String Quartet
Recorded June 1988, in St. Silas Church, Kentish Town, London
Notes by David Harvey
Album title: The Works for String Quartet
With: Elliott Carter's *String Quartet No.1* (D112); *String Quartet No.4*
   (D128); *String Quartet No.2* (D118); *Elegy for String Quartet* (D34)
See: Neue Zeitschrift für Musik v.151, no.1 (January 1990), p.46-47; Tempo
   no.173 (June 1990), p.57-59; Musical America v.109, no.6 (November
   1989), p.8-10

D124.   RCA London RL 70883 (cd) 1990

D125.   Sony S2K 47229 (47256, 47257) (cd) 1991
Juilliard String Quartet (Robert Mann, violin; Joel Smirnoff, violin; Samuel
   Rhodes, viola; Joel Krosnick, violoncello)
With: Elliott Carter's *String Quartet No.1* (D113); *String Quartet No.2*
   (D119); *String Quartet No.4* (D129); *Duo for Violin and Piano* (D19)
See: American Record Guide (March/April 1992), p.43; Fanfare
   (March/April 1992), p.170; Gramophone (April 1992), p.94

String Quartet No.4 (W80)

D126.   Music and Arts CD 606 (cd) 1991
Composer's Quartet
With: Milton Babbitt's Quartet for Strings, no.5; Laurence Powell's Quartet
for Strings 1982
See: American Record Guide (May/June 1991), p.44;Fanfare (May/June
1991), p.150

D127.   Nonesuch
Kronos Quartet

D128.   Etcetera KTC 1065-1066 (cd) 1988
Arditti String Quartet
Recorded June 1988, in St. Silas Church, Kentish Town, London
Notes by David Harvey
Album title: The Works for String Quartet
With: Elliott Carter's *String Quartet No.1* (D112); *String Quartet No.2*
(D118); *String Quartet No.3* (D123); *Elegy for String Quartet* (D34)
See: Musical America v.109, no.6 (November 1989), p.8-10, 80, 89; Neue
Zeitschrift für Muzik v.151 (January 1990), p.46-47; Tempo no.173 (June
1990), p.57-59

D129.   Sony S2K 47229 (47256, 47257) (cd) 1991
Juilliard String Quartet (Robert Mann, violin; Joel Smirnoff, violin; Samuel
Rhodes, viola; Joel Krosnick, violoncello)
With: Elliott Carter's *String Quartet No.1* (D113); *String Quartet No.2*
(D119); *String Quartet No.3* (D125); *Duo for Violin and Piano* (D19)
See: American Record Guide (March/April 1992), p.43; Fanfare
(March/April 1992), p.170; Gramophone (April 1992), p.94

Symphony No.1 (W11)

D130.   Louisville LOU 611 (lp, mono) 1961
Louisville Orchestra; Robert Whitney, conductor
Louisville First Edition series
With: Alexei Haieff's Divertimento
See: High Fidelity (September 1961),p.85; New York Times (July 23, 1961),
X, p.8; Saturday Review of Literature (May 27, 1961), p.42

D131.   Composers Recordings SD 475 (lp, stereo) 1982
American Composers Orchestra; Paul Dunkel, conductor
Recorded February 1982, in Walt Whitman Auditorium, Brooklyn College
Notes by David Schiff
Album title: Elliott Carter: The Early Years
American Historic series
With: Elliott Carter's *Holiday Overture* (D51); *Pocohontas Suite* (D94)

See: American Record Guide (May 1983), p.16; Consumer Research Bulletin
(March 1983), p.43; Fanfare (January/February 1983), p.132-134; New
Records (December 1982), p.4; New York Times (December 21, 1982),
VIII, p.19; High Fidelity v.33, no.9 (September 1983), p.69-70, 113
(See: C88)

D132. Composers Recordings ACS 6003 (cassette) 1985
Symphony, reissue of D131
Notes by David Schiff
Album title: Music of Elliott Carter
Anthology series
With: Elliott Carter's *Syringa* (D136); *Holiday Overture* (D52)

D133. CRI CD 552 (cd) 1988
Symphony, reissue of D131
Notes by Susan Feder
With: Francis Thorne's Symphony No.5; Nicolas Roussakis's Fire and Earth
and Water and Air

A Symphony of Three Orchestras (W19)

D134. Columbia M 35171 (lp, stereo) 1980
Columbia MT 35171 (cassette) 1980
CBS Masterworks 76812
New York Philharmonic; Pierre Boulez, conductor
Recorded February 1977
Notes by Elliott Carter
With: Elliott Carter's *A Mirror on Which To Dwell* (D60)
See: Tempo no.143 (December 1982), p.30-31 (See: C98); Fanfare
(January/February 1981), p.98; New Records (January 1981), p.1; Stereo
Review (April 1981), p.103; High Fidelity/Musical America v.31, no.8
(August 1981), p.52,55 (See: C89)

Syringa (W47)

D135. Composers Recordings SD 469 (lp, stereo) 1982
Jan DeGaetani, mezzo-soprano; Thomas Paul, baritone; Speculum Musicae
and The Group for Contemporary Music; Harvey Sollberger, conductor
Recorded in New York in May 1981
Notes by David Schiff
Album title: Music of Elliott Carter
American Contemporary series
With: Elliott Carter's *Concerto for Orchestra* (D10)
See: Consumer Research Bulletin (March 1983), p.43; Fanfare v.6, no.3
(January/February 1983), p.134; New Records (December 1982), p.12;
New York Times (November 21, 1982), VIII, p.19; American Record
Guide (May 1983), p.15; High Fidelity v.33, no.9 (September 1983), p.69-
70, 113 (See: C88)

D136.   Composers Recordings ACS 6003 (cassette) 1985
Syringa, reissue of D135
Album title: Music of Elliott Carter
Anthology series
With: Elliott Carter's *Holiday Overture* (D52); *Symphony No.1* (D132)

D137.   Bridge Records BCD 9014 (cd) 1989
Katherine Ciesinski, mezzo-soprano; Jan Opalach, bass-baritone; Speculum
   Musicae; William Purvis, conductor
Recorded December 5-6, 1988, in New York
Album title: The Vocal Works (1975-1981)
With: Elliott Carter's *Three Poems of Robert Frost* (D146); *A Mirror in
   Which to Dwell* (D61); *In Sleep, In Thunder* (D55)
See: Musical America v.110, no.6 (September 1990), p.70-71; Tempo no.173
   (June 1990), p.57-59; NATS Journal v.47, no.2 (1990), p.48; American
   Music v.8, no.4 (1990), p.492-494; American Record Guide
   (January/February 1990), p.40; Musical America (March 1990), p.70

D138.   CRI CD 610 (cd) 1991
Syringa, reissue of D135
Notes by David Schiff
Album title: The Music of Elliott Carter
CRI American Masters series
With: Elliott Carter's *Holiday Overture* (D53); *Pocahontas Suite* (D95)
See: American Record Guide (March/April 1992), p.42

Tarantella (W29)

D139.   Carillon 118 (lp, mono) 1961
Harvard University Glee Club; Elliot Forbes, conductor
Album title: Harvard in Song

D140.   GSS Recordings GSS 103 (lp, stereo) 1984
Men's Choruses and Women's Choir of the Gregg Smith Singers; The Long
   Island Symphonic Choral Association; Columbia University Men's Glee
   Club; Gregg Smith, conductor
The Choral Masters series v.1
With: Elliott Carter's *Emblems* (D37); *The Harmony of Morning* (D47); *Heart
   not so Heavy as Mine* (D50); *Musicians Wrestle Everywhere* (D66); *To
   Music* (D149); *The Defense of Corinth* (D13)

Tell Me, Where is Fancy Bred? (W41)

D141.   Columbia MC 6-1 (lp, 78, mono) 1938
Wexler Colla-Negri (From the Orson Welles Mercury Theatre production of
   "Merchant of Venice")

D142.   Turnabout TV 34727 (lp, stereo) 1978
Rosalind Rees, soprano; David Starobin, guitar
Notes by William Bland
Album title: 20th Century Music for Voice and Guitar
With: William Schuman's Orpheus with his Lute; Andrew Imbrie's Tell Me,
Where is Fancy Bred?; Harold Blumenfeld's Rilke; Lou Harrison's
Serenade; Igor Stravinsky's Four Songs; William Bland's Song for David;
Barbara Kolb's The Sentences; John Cage's The Wonderful Widow of
Eighteen Springs; Gregg Smith's Steps
See: New Records (March 1979), p.13; New York Times (April 5, 1979),
III, p.11; Musical Quarterly v.66, no.1 (January 1980), p.153-154

Three Poems of Robert Frost (W42)

D143.   "The Rose Family" and "Dust of Snow" only
Hargail HN 708 (lp, 78, mono) 1947
William Hess, tenor; Robert Fizdale, piano
Album title: American Songs
With: Theodore Chandler's The Dove; Three Epitaphs

D144.   Unicorn RHS 353 (lp, stereo) 1978
Unicorn UN1-72017 (lp, stereo) 1978
Meriel Dickinson, mezzo-soprano; Peter Dickinson, piano
Recorded March 28, 1977, All Saints Church, Petersham, Surrey, England
Album title: An American Anthology
With: George Gershwin's I Got Rhythm; Aaron Copland's In Evening Air;
Night Thoughts; Poet's Song; Elliott Carter's *Voyage* (D155); Virgil
Thomson's Two by Marianne Moore; John Cage's Five Songs; Virgil
Thomson's Portrait of F.B. (Francis Blood); George Gershwin's A Foggy
Day in London Town; They All Laughed
See: Gramophone (August 1978), p.367; New Records (August 1979), p.12;
New York Times (July 22, 1979), IV, p.21; Stereo Review (September
1979), p.104

D145.   "Dust of Snow," "The Rose Family" only
Elektra/Nonesuch 79178-2; (9 79178-2 on container) (cd) 1988
Elektra/Nonesuch 4-79178 (cassette) 1988
Jan DeGaetani, mezzo-soprano; Gilbert Kalish, piano
Recorded December 21-23, 1987, at the American Academy and Institute of
Arts and Letters, New York
Album title: Songs of America: On Home, Love, Nature, and Death
With: Stephen Foster's Beautiful Child of Song; Charles Wakefield Cadman's
The Moon Drops Low: from Four American Indian Songs; Ruth
Crawford's (Seeger) Home Thoughts; White Moon; Joy; Milton Babbitt's
The Widow's Lament in Springtime; Warren Benson's American Primitive:
from Three Solitary Songs; George Crumb's The Sleeper; Irving Fine's My
Father: from Mutability; Carrie Jacobs-Bond's Nothin' But Love; I Love
You Truly; Her Greatest Charm; Sergius Kagen's The Junk Man; Mario

Davidovsky's Lost; John Cage's Little Four Paws: from Five Songs for Contraalto; William Schuman's Dozing on the Lawn: from Time to the Old; Charles Ives' Song: She is not Fair; The All-Enduring; Rebecca Clarke's Lethe; Ned Rorem's Interlude: from Poems of Love and the Rain; Samuel Alder's Time, You Old Gypsy Man; Stanley Walden's Grandma (Millie): from Suite, Three Ladies; Aaron Jay Kernis' Stein x Seven, no.6; William Bolcom's Waitin: from Cabaret Songs; Aaron Copland's There Came a Wind Like a Bugle: from Twelve Poems of Emily Dickinson; Charles Ives' Sunrise

D146.   Bridge Records BCD 9014 (cd) 1989
Patrick Mason, baritone; Speculum Musicae; David Starobin, conductor
Recorded October 21, 1981, in New York
Album title: The Vocal Works (1975-1981)
With: Elliott Carter's *A Mirror in Which to Dwell* (D61); *Syringa* (D137); *In Sleep, In Thunder* (D55)
See: Musical America v.110, no.6 (September 1990), p.70-71; Tempo no.173 (June 1990), p.57-59; American Record Guide (January/February 1990), p.40; Musical America (March 1990), p.70; NATS Journal v.47, no.2 (1990), p.48; American Music v.8, no.4 (1990), p.492-494

D147.   "Dust of Snow" and "The Rose Family" only
Elektra Nonesuch 79248-2; 79178; 79047 (cd) 1990
Three Poems, reissue of D145
Notes by Lloyd Schwartz
With: Elliott Carter's *The Minotaur* (D56); *Piano Sonata* (D89)
See: Fanfare (July/August 1991), p.134; Musical America (July 1991), p.71

To Music (W34)

D148.   New World Records NW 219 (lp, stereo) 1977
University of Michigan Chamber Choir; Thomas Hillbish, conductor
Recorded in Hill Auditorium, University of Michigan, Ann Arbor
Notes by Robert Morgan
Recorded Anthology of American Music series
With: Randall Thompson's Americana; Seymour Shifrin's The Odes of Shang
See: American Record Guide (August 1978), p.43; Fanfare (May/June 1978), p.27; Stereo Review (July 1978), p.102

D149.   GSS Recordings GSS 103 (lp, stereo) 1984
Rosalind Rees, soprano; Men's Choruses and Women's Choir of the Gregg Smith Singers; The Long Island Symphonic Choral Association; Columbia University Men's Glee Club; Gregg Smith, conductor
The Choral Masters series v.1
With: Elliott Carter's *Tarantella* (D140); *Emblems* (D37); *The Harmony of Morning* (D47); *Heart not so Heavy as Mine* (D50); *Musicians Wrestle Everywhere* (D66); *The Defense of Corinth* (D13)

Triple Duo (W75)

D150.   Wergo WER 60124 (lp, stereo) 1985
Elektra/Asylum/Nonesuch 79110-1 (lp, stereo) 1985
Elektra/Asylum/Nonesuch 79110 (cd) 1985
Elektra/Asylum/Nonesuch 79110-4 SR; 9 79110-4 (cassette) 1985
Fires of London
Recorded November 5, 1984, in St, Luke's Church, Hampstead, London
Notes by David Schiff
With: Elliott Carter's *In Sleep, In Thunder* (D54)
See: Tempo no.158 (September 1986), p.34-35

D151.   ECM New Series ECM 1391 (cd) 1990
ECM New Series ECM 839 617-2 (cd) 1990
ECM New Series ECM 839 617-4 (cassette) 1990
Hansheinz Schneeberger, violin; Thomas Demenga, violoncello; Philippe
Racine, flute; Ernesto Molinari, clarinet; Paul Cleemann, piano; Gerhard
Huber, percussion; Jurg Wyttenbach, conductor
Recorded October 1988, in Basel, Switzerland
Notes by Heinz Holliger
With: J.S. Bach's Suite No.3 in D for Solo Violoncello BWV 1009; Elliott
Carter's *Esprit Rude/Esprit Doux* (D42); *Enchanted Preludes* (D39);
Riconoscenza (D97)
See: Tempo no.173 (June 1990), p.57-59; Fanfare (January/February 1992),
p.152

Variations for Orchestra (W15)

D152.   Lousiville LOU 58-3 (lp, mono) 1958
Louisville Orchestra; Robert Whitney, conductor
Notes by Elliott Carter
Commissioning series
With: Everett Helm's Second Piano Concerto
See: High Fidelity August 1958), p.46; Hi-Fi Music at Home (September
1958), p.27; New York Times (September 7, 1958), X, p.21

D153.   Columbia MS 7191 (lp, stereo) 1968
CBS 72717 (1969)
CBS S 34 61093 (1970)
Paul Jacobs, harpsichord; Charles Rosen, piano; English Chamber Orchestra;
New Philharmonia Orchestra; Frederik Prausnitz, conductor
Recorded March 1967
Notes by Elliott Carter
Music of Our Time series
With: Elliott Carter's *Double Concerto* (D16)

See: High Fidelity/Musical America v.19, no.2 (February 1969), p.85; Stereo
Review (March 1969), p.90; Saturday Review of Literature (December 28,
1968), p.52; Records and Recordings v.11, no.5 (February 1968), p.21-23;
American Record Guide v.37, no.11 (July 1971), p.756-759 (See: C36)

D154.   New World Records NW347 (lp, stereo) 1986
New World Records NW 347-2 (cd) 1986
New World Records NW 347-4 (cassette)
Cincinnati Symphony Orchestra; Michael Gielen, conductor
Recorded in Music Hall, Cincinnati, Ohio, October 22,1985
Notes by David Schiff
With: Elliott Carter's *Piano Concerto* (D78)

Voyage (W43)

D155.   Unicorn RHS 353 (lp, stereo) 1978
Unicorn UN1-72017 (lp, stereo) 1978
Meriel Dickinson, mezzo-soprano; Peter Dickinson, piano
Recorded March 28, 1977, All Saints Church, Petersham, Surrey, England
Album title: An American Anthology
With: George Gershwin's I Got Rhythm; Elliott Carter's *Three Poems of*
Robert Frost (D144); Aaron Copland's In Evening Air; Night Thoughts;
Poet's Song; Virgil Thomson's Two by Marianne Moore; John Cage's Five
Songs; Virgil Thomson's Portrait of F.B. (Francis Blood); George
Gershwin's A Foggy Day in London Town; They All Laughed
See: Gramophone (August 1978), p.367; New Records (August 1979), p.12;
New York Times (July 22, 1979), IV, p.21; Stereo Review (September
1979), p.104

Woodwind Quintet (W60)

D156.   Classic Editions CE 2003 (lp, mono) 1953
New Art Wind Quintet (Andrew Lolya, flute; Melvin Kaplan, oboe; Irving
Neidich, clarinet; Tina Di Dario, bassoon; Elizabeth Bobo, french horn)
Notes by Elliott Carter
Album title: An American Woodwind Symposium
With: Roger Goeb's Quintet for Woodwinds; Ingolf Dahl's Allegro and
Arioso; Vincent Persichetti's Pastoral for Quintet of Wind Instruments;
Walter Piston's Three Pieces; Henry Cowell's Suite for Woodwind Quintet;
Wallingford Riegger's Woodwind Quintet, op.51
See: Bulletin of American Composers Alliance v.4, no.2 (1954), p.21;
American Record Guide (May 1954), p.302; High Fidelity (July 1954),
p.57; New York Times (March 14, 1954), X, p.8; Saturday Review of
Literature (February 27, 1954), p.71

D157.   RCA Victor LM 6167; SPS 33-417 (lp, mono) 1966
RCA Victor LSC 6167 (lp, stereo) 1966
RCA RB/SB 6692 (1967)
Boston Symphony Chamber Players (Doriot Anthony Dwyer, flute; Ralph
Gomberg, oboe; Gino Cioffi, clarinet; Sherman Walt, bassoon; James
Stagliano, French horn
Notes by Peter Ustinov
Album title: The Boston Symphony Chamber Players
With: W.A. Mozart's Quartet, Flute and Strings, D Major, K.285; Quartet,
Oboe and Strings, F Major, K.370. Johannes Brahms' Quartet, Piano and
Strings, no.3, C Minor, op.60; Ludwig van Beethoven's Serenade, Flute,
Violin, Viola, D Major, op.25; Irving Fine's Fantasia for String Trio;
Aaron Copland's Vitebsk, Study on Jewish Themes; Walter Piston's
Divertimento for Nine Instruments
See: Gramophone (February 1967), p.431; High Fidelity (December 1966),
p.81; The Monthly Letter (March 1967), p.9; New Records (October
1966), p.6

D158.   Candide CE 31016 (lp, stereo) 1969
CBS S 34 61145 (1970)
Vox STGBY 644 (1971)
Decca (1974)
Dorian Wind Quintet (Karl Kraber, flute; Charles Kuskin, oboe; William
Lewis, clarinet; Jane Taylor, bassoon; Barry Benjamin, french horn)
Notes by William B. Ober
With: Elliott Carter's Eight Etudes and a Fantasy (D22); Hans Werner
Henze's Quintett
See: New Records (September 1969), p.7

D159.   Vox SVBX 5307 (lp, stereo) 1977
Dorian Wind Quintet (Karl Kraber, flute; Jerry Kirkbride, clarinet; Charles
Kushkin, oboe; Jane Taylor, bassoon; Barry Benjamin, french horn)
Recorded in 1976
Album title: The Avant Garde Woodwind Quintet in the U.S.A.
With: Samuel Barber's Summer Music for Woodwind Quintet; Arthur
Berger's Quartet in C Major for Woodwinds; Luciano Berio's Children's
Play for Woodwind Quintet; Irving Fine's Partita for Wind Quintet; Lukas
Foss's The Cave of the Winds; Mario Davidovsky's Synchronism No.8;
Jacob Druckman's Delizie Contente Che l'alme Beate; Gunther Schuller's
Quintet Woodwinds & Horn; Karel Husa's Preludes, Flute, Clarinet &
Bassoon

D160.   Melbourne Records SMLP 4040 (1980)
Yorkwinds (Stewart Douglas, flute; Lawrence Cherney, oboe; Harcus
Hennigar, horn; Gerald Robinson, bassoon)
Recorded at the Club Harmonie, Toronto, March 16, 17 and 18, 1980
Album title: The York Winds Play Music

New Music series no. 16
With: Brian Cherney's Notturno; Bernard Heiden's Sinfonia for Woodwind
Quintet; John Rea's Reception and Offering Music

D161.   Musical Heritage Society 4782 (lp, stereo) 1983
Soni Ventorum Wind Quintet
Album title: 20th Century Works for Wind Ensemble
With: Samuel Barber's Summer Music, op.31; Irving Fine's Partita, 1948;
Joseph Goodman's Scherzo for Wind Quintet, 1979

D162.   KM Records KM 15131 (198-?)
Travis Chamber Players (United States Air Force Band of Golden Gate
Recorded in the Community Center, Davis, California
With: Ludwig van Beethoven's (arr. Kinningham) Zapfenstreich; March in
C for Military Band; Richard Strauss' Serenade, op.7; Ferenc Farkas'
Antiche Danze Ungheres I; Harry Breuer's (arr. Woelfel) Bit' O Rhythm;
Wilke Renwick's Dance; Jean Joseph Mouret's Rondeau; Jean Baptiste
Lully's Overture to "Cadmus et Hermione;" John Philip Sousa's
Washington Post March

D163.   Premiere PRCD 1006 (cd) 1990
Boehm Quintette (Sheryl, Henze, flute; Phyllis Lanini, oboe; Steve Hartman,
clarinet; Joseph Anderer, horn; Robert Wagner, bassoon)
Album title: American Winds, volume one
With: Walter Piston's Woodwind Quintet; Irving Fine's Partita; Ellie
Siegmeister's Ten Minutes for Four Players; Vincent Persichetti's Pastoral;
Walter Piston's Three Pieces for Flute, Clarinet & Bassoon
See: Fanfare (January/February 1991), p.402

D164.   Stradivarius STR 33304 (cd) 1991
Quintetto Arnold
Recorded October 22-23 and November 19-20, 1990, at Chiesa della
Misericordia, Turin, Italy
Notes by Paolo Petazzi
Album title: Musica per Quartetto e Quintetto a Fiati
With: Franco Donatoni's Blow; Gyeorgy Kurtág's Quintetto per Fiati, op.2;
Elliott Carter's Eight Etudes and a Fantasy (D27a); Gyeorgy Ligeti's Zehn
Stücke für Bläserquintett
See: Fanfare (July/August 1992), p.358

Bibliography of Material by Carter

This chapter covers a broad range of entries all written by Carter. Many entries originated from his years as a music critic for Modern Music. Also included are citations to numerous interviews. There have been two book length compilations of Carter's writings. Else and Kurt Stone have reprinted many of Carter's writings in their book entitled The Writings of Elliott Carter (See: B133). Enzo Restagno has also translated 33 writings into Italian in his book entitled Carter (See: B10).

B1.   "Acceptance by Mr. Carter of the Gold Medal for Music." Proceedings of the American Academy of Arts and Letters and the National Institute of Arts and Letters 2nd series, no.22 (1972), p.34.

        Carter's acceptance letter upon receiving the Institute's Gold Medal for Music in 1971.

B2.   "Un Altro Passo Avanti (1958)." See: "Un Paso Adelante" B97.

B3.   "An American Destiny." Listen v.9, no.1 (November 1946), p.4-6. Reprinted In: Boston Symphony Program Notes 82nd season, 6th program (November 2, 1962), p.355-356, 358, 360-366. Reprinted In: Stone, p.143-150. Reprinted as: "Un Destino Americano (Charles Edward Ives)," In: Restagno, p.145-150.

        A study of the life and musical philosophy of Charles Ives.

B4.   "American Figure, With Landscape." Modern Music v.20, no.4 (May/June 1943), p.219-225. Reprinted in condensed version with preface In: Lederman, Minna. The Life and Death of a Small Magazine (Modern Music, 1924-1946). Brooklyn College, NY: Institute for Studies in American Music (ISAM Monographs, no.18), p.43-46. Reprinted In: Stone, p.87-93.

A tribute to Henry Franklin Belknap Gilbert, 1868-1928. A review of his tragic, yet determined and compelling life, his musical career, and nationalistic style. In the condensed version the preface discusses Frederick Jacobi and the magazine's broad concern as to whether Carter should have the great responsibility of writing the Forecast and Review column.

B5.   "American Music on the New York Scene." Modern Music v.17, no.2 (January/February 1940), p.93-101. Reprinted In: Stone, p.68-74. Reprinted as: "La Musica Americana Sulla Scena New Yorchese, 1940," In: Restagno, p.104-108.

Review of performances of American music in New York including Roy Harris' Third Symphony which "stands out as the most striking and thoroughly unusual score." The All-Sessions Concert at the Composers' Forum Laboratory is said to be a "clear demonstration that Sessions, during his whole life as a composer, has shunned the easy effect and the immediate appeal, has fought to keep his music honest, serious, conscientious to the limit of his power." Music by Piston, Schuman, Carpenter, Hanson, Hill, Thomson and Diamond and a program of 20th century harpsichord music announced by Ralph Kirkpatrick, and recent performances by the New York Philharmonic are also reviewed briefly.

B6.   "Are My Ears on Wrong?--A Profile of Charles Ives." BBC-TV/Open University; David M. Thompson, producer. Solana Beach, CA: Media Guild, 1982.

A 16mm film which contains "[d]ramatizations and actual archival film footage and photographs [which] combine to relate the life of American composer Charles Ives and to document the musical background which influenced his work. Composers Aaron Copland and Elliott Carter reminisce about Ives and discuss his music."

B7.   "At the Hall of Music." Modern Music v.16, no.4 (May/June 1939), p.242-3. Reprinted In: Stone, p.58-59.

Review of music at the Hall of Music during the 1939 New York World's Fair. "These concerts . . . prove that outside the traditional repertory of our symphony orchestras there are lots of scores worth hearing, both old and new. Never again will we believe our conductors when they return from summer vacations abroad with news that no works of any interest are being written. Every foreign concert at the Fair has proved just the opposite."

B8.   "Le Basi Ritmiche della Musica." See: "The Rhythmic Basis of American Music" B105.

B9.   "Canon for 3 [Muted Trumpets]: In Memoriam Igor Stravinsky." Tempo
       no.98 (1972), between pages 22-23.

       Full musical score written under the title "In Memoriam Igor Stravinsky,
       Canon and Epitaphs Set 2." (See: W68)

B10.   Carter. Edited by Enzo Restagno. Torino: EDT/Musica, 1989. Interview
       reprinted as: Elliott Carter: In Conversation with Enzo Restagno for
       Settembre Musica 1989. Translated by Katherine Silberblatt Wolfthal.
       Brooklyn, NY: Institute for Studies in American Music, Conservatory of
       Music, Brooklyn College of the City University of New York, 1991.

       A translation into Italian of 33 of Carter's writings. These writings range
       from program notes from concerts and liner notes from recordings to journal
       articles. A 79 page interview by Enzo Reslagno is also included as well as a
       works list and discography.

B11.   "The Case of Mr. Ives." Modern Music v.16, no.3 (March/April 1939),
       p.172-176. Reprinted In: Perspectives of New Music v.2, no.2 (1964),
       p.27-29. Reprinted In: Stone, p.48-51. Reprinted as: "Il Caso Ives," In:
       Restagno, p.93-99.

       Review of Charles Ives' Concord Sonata. Carter was "sadly disappointed."

B12.   "Il Caso Ives." See: "The Case of Mr. Ives" B11.

B13.   "The Changing Scene, New York 1940." Modern Music v.17, no.4
       (May/June 1940), p.237-241. Reprinted In: Stone, p.81-85.

       Review of New York performances during the first half of the spring season.
       The premiere of Piston's Violin Concerto is described as a "highly successful
       work, distinguished in feeling, personality and imagination, excellent in
       musical handling." John Kirkpatrick's perennial All-American Concert at
       Town Hall is reviewed, except for Sessions' Piano Sonata, as having "been
       chosen with an eye to special character rather than musical perfection." The
       League of Composers' program of North and South American music is
       described as having work too varied in character and thus, making it
       impossible to compare works. The League's first Young Composers Concert
       is also reviewed as presenting "several able and interesting works." Britten's
       Violin Concerto is described as having a "very skillful and original
       orchestration that had many really inventive and striking moments." Carter
       stated the premiere of Bernard Herrmann's Moby Dick is "uncommonly good
       . . . stern, vigorous and highly effective in the illustrative style."

B14.   "Charles Ives Remembered." In: Charles Ives Remembered: An Oral
       History. Edited by Vivian Perlis. New Haven: Yale University Press,
       1974. p.131-145. Reprinted In: Stone, p.258-269.

Reminiscences of Charles Ives written after an interview with Vivian Perlis and based on Carter's long friendship with Ives which is documented through numerous letters.

B15.   "La Chiusura della New York Primavera, 1938." See: "Season's End: New York, Spring, 1938" B110.

B16.   "La Chiusura della Stagione 1937 a New York." See: "Season's End in New York" B109.

B17.   "The Composer is a University Commodity." College Music Symposium v.10 (Fall 1970), p.68-70. Reprinted In: Stone, p.279-282.

One of 22 responses by composers to statements made by Igor Stravinsky to Robert Craft. Carter writes about the current role of composer as educator in the college setting. Carter discusses the problem of universities doing little for the advancement of the composer, the problem of an overabundance of composers willing to teach, and the hiring of foreign composers as educators instead of American composers.

B18.   "Composers by the Alphabet." Modern Music v.19, no.1 (November/December 1941), p.70-71.

Review of the book Great Modern Composers by Oscar Thompson which Carter describes as "not of much value."

B19.   "The Composer's Viewpoint." National Music Council Bulletin v.7, no.1 (September 1946), p.10-11. Reprinted In: Stone, p.140-143.

Carter stresses the importance of composing, publishing and performing "durable music . . . for it is the achievement of high musical quality that rouses the enthusiasm of each of us."

B20.   "Conversation with Elliott Carter." Edited by Benjamin Boretz. Perspectives of New Music v.8, no.2 (Spring/Summer 1970), p.1-22.

One of ten interviews with American composers conducted under the auspices of the School of Continuing Education of New York University. The interviews emphasize issues of interest to "nonspecialists." In particular, "the significance of the 'medium' of a musical composition with respect to the perception of the whole." The interview with Carter spends considerable time discussing Carter's Double Concerto.

B21.   "Coolidge Crusade; WPA; New York Season." Modern Music v.16, no.1 (November/December 1938), p.33-38. Reprinted In: Stone, p.39-43.

Carter comments on Elizabeth Sprague Coolidge's continued "intelligent and laudable crusade for modern music." Carter continues by reviewing recent New York performances, among them being Hindemith's St. Francis which Carter labels as "an important musical event." Carter then briefly reviews several other performances and concerts, among them: Copland's Music for the Theatre, Stravinsky's Les Noces and Symphonie de Psaumes, Diamond's Overture and Trio, the Westminster Choir School Festival and Schuman's Pioneers and Second Symphony.

B22.   "Creators on Creating: Elliott Carter." Edited by Leighton Kerner. Saturday Review v.7, no.16 (December 1980), p.38-42.

A nontechnical interview between Kerner and Carter in which Carter discusses "his methods of composition and work habits, his acoustic influences, his work-in-progress and the importance and vitality of contemporary music."

B23.   "Cronache d'Attualità: Italia." See: "Current Chronicle: Italy" B26.

B24.   "Cronache d'Attualità: New York 1959." See: "Current Chronicle: United States: New York" B28.

B25.   "Current Chronicle: Germany." Musical Quarterly v.46, no.3 (July 1960), p.367-371. Reprinted In: Stone, p.212-216.

Reviews of two German opera premieres about Russia: Nicolas Nabokov's Der Tod des Grigori Rasputin performed by Nicolas Nabokov at Cologne, and Dmitri Shostakovitch's Lady Macbeth of Mzensk performed at the Dusseldorf Opera. Shostakovitch's piece, in its only version to date (1960), was first performed in the United States in 1936. It was abruptly withdrawn before World War II. Even though the score was being rewritten and its performance forbidden by the composer, a previously unknown score was discovered.

B26.   "Current Chronicle: Italy." Musical Quarterly v.45, no.4 (October 1959), p.530. Reprinted In: Stone, p.173-184. Reprinted as: "Cronache d'Attualità: Italia," In: Restagno, p.163-173.

Review of the International Society for Contemporary Music festival in Rome. The role of the festival is also discussed. "Occasionally some of the works on the programs have been disappointing, yet at each festival enough were important or remarkable and enough more contained moments of special musical interest."

B27.   "Current Chronicle: New York." Musical Quarterly v.52, no.1 (January 1966), p.93-101. Reprinted In: Stone, p.248-255.

Review of a Juilliard concert featuring the premiere of Edvard Steuermann's Cantata for mixed chorus and orchestra. Steuermann's musical life is examined as well as the cantata of which Carter says "casts a mark of highly sensitive, beautifully connected phrases over the whole text."

B28.   "Current Chronicle: United States: New York." Musical Quarterly v.45, no.3 (July 1959), p.375-381. Reprinted In: Stone, p.166-173. Reprinted as: "Cronache d'Attualità: New York 1959," In: Restagno, p.157-162.

Review of Roger Sessions' Violin Concerto recently performed by the New York Philharmonic and Tossy Spivakovsky, Violin.

B29.   "Czech Composer: Bohuslav Martinu, the Man and His Works." Saturday Review (January 20, 1945), p.16-17.

A review of a book-length biography written by Milos Safranek and published by Alfred Knopf in 1944. Due to the author's lack of a musical background, Carter notes that "[i]t is still up to the musical world to evaluate Martinu's music at its true worth."

B30.   "Un Destino Americano (Charles Edward Ives)." See: "An American Destiny" B3.

B31.   "Documenti di un'Amicizia con Ives." See: "Documents of a Friendship with Ives" B32.

B32.   "Documents of a Friendship with Ives." Tempo no.117 (June 1976), p.2-10. Reprinted In: Parnassus v.3, no.2 (Spring/Summer 1975), p.300-315. Reprinted In: Stone, p.331-343. Reprinted as: "Documenti di un'Amicizia con Ives," In: Restagno, p.224-234.

Selected letters are presented from the Ives Collection at Yale University which reveal the "history of a warm and inspiring friendship" between Carter and Charles Ives during Carter's years as a student and his early years as a composer.

B32a.   "Electronic Music Lauded by Carter." New York Times (June 18, 1960), p.12:4.

Carter, in a recent address at the annual convention of the American Symphony Orchestra League, calls for a better understanding of electronic music.

B33.   "Elliott Carter." Edited by Allan Kozinn. Fugue v.3 (April 1979), p.32-36.

An interview conducted by Allan Kozinn in celebration of Carter's 70th birthday. Kozinn asks Carter about his compositions, specifically Syringa, and the methods employed when developing musical plots in composing. Carter also discusses the state of the symphony and experimental music in the United States.

B34.   "Elliott Carter." Edited by Marvin A. Wolfthal. La Musica v.3, no.14 (October 1979), p.232-233.

An interview by Marvin Wolfthal printed in Italian.

B35.   "Elliott Carter." Edited by Ruth Dreier. Musical America v.108, no.10 (October 1988), p.6, 8-10.

A result of a 1988 interview Ruth Dreier had with Carter. Emphasis is placed on performance difficulties of Carter's music and with his new *String Quartet No. 4.*

B36.   "Elliott Carter." In: The Orchestral Composer's Point of View: Essays on Twentieth-Century Music by Those Who Wrote It. Edited by Robert Stephan Hines. Norman, Oklahoma: University of Oklahoma, 1970, p.39-61. Reprinted In: Stone, p.282-300. Reprinted as: "Il Punto di Vista del Compositore di Musica per Orchestra," In: Restagno, p.196-211.

Carter looks at the problems in writing music for the orchestra including a lack of financial support, poorly rehearsed performances, the inaccessibility of the music to the listener, and the oftentimes difficult new music. Carter then discusses the problems of the orchestra itself. The size of the orchestra reflects the taste of romantic music and not that of contemporary music. Lastly, Carter examines his own musical techniques in his orchestral compositions.

B37.   "Elliott Carter." Soundpieces: Interviews with American Composers. Edited by Cole Gagne and Tracy Caras. Metuchen, NJ: Scarecrow, 1982. p.87-100.

Cole Gagne interviewed Carter in 1975 and asked about his education, musical influences, contemporaries, and his compositions.

B38.   "Elliott Carter." In: Trackings: Composers Speak with Richard Dufallo. New York: Oxford University Press, 1989. p.269-285.

An interview with Carter on May 29, 1986. The interview focuses on Carter's early development and education as a composer, and, in particular, the role Charles Ives played in his development.

B39.   "Elliott Carter and Leon Kirchner; Two American Composers Tell How Their Music Reflects the World." Center for Cassette Studies, 1971.

An audio cassette interview in which Carter and Kirchner compare their music to earlier classical music and demonstrate that their music is based in real world experiences.

B40.   Elliott Carter: In Conversation with Enzo Restagno for Settembre Musica 1989. See: Carter B10.

B41.   "Elliott Carter: Musician of the Month." Edited by Patrick Smith. High Fidelity/Musical America v.23, no.8 (August 1973), p.MA4-5.

Patrick Smith reviews his conversations with Elliott Carter, who had at that time just received the 1972 Pulitzer Prize for Music. Carter stresses the need for formal education and the opportunity for young American composers to experiment with their music.

B42.   "Elliott Carter Objects [Letter in Answer to an Article by Harold Schonberg]." New York Times (October 20, 1968), II, p.20:5.

Carter and other panelists respond to an article appearing in the New York Times on September 22 and 29, 1968, regarding the future of the symphony as a medium. The panel discussion was actually held two years before the article was published. Carter clarifies several comments he made in the original discussion of which he had no previous knowledge of its publication or broadcast. (See: C254)

B42a.   "Elliott Cook Carter." In: 25th Anniversary Report of the Harvard Class of 1930. Cambridge, MA: Harvard University Press, 1955, p.165-169.

An autobiographical sketch which Carter wrote for the occasion.

B42b.   "Elliott Cook Carter." In: 50th Anniversary Report of the Harvard Class of 1930. Cambridge, MA: Harvard University Press, 1980, p.836-838.

An autobiographical sketch which Carter wrote for the occasion.

B43.   "Elliott Carter Talking to Raffaele Pozzi." Translated by Louise Forster. Tempo no.167 (December 1988), p.14-17. Originally printed in the Roman magazine Piano-Time. (I could not verify this.)

This interview originally took place when Carter attended the 1984 Pontino Festival for the world premiere of his Riconoscenza. The interview concentrates on Carter's musical development and the United States as the rising musical center.

B44.   "Expressionism and American Music." Perspectives of New Music v.4, no.1 (Fall/Winter 1965), p.1-13. Reprinted In: Perspectives on American Composers. Edited by Benjamin Boretz and Edward T. Cone. New York: W.W. Norton, 1971, p.217-229. Reprinted In: Stone, p.230-243.

A detailed account of "the disturbing fact that the world of serious music here [in America] is still thought of as an outpost of that European world which Americans have so often found more attractive than the reality of what they have at home. [That] we have no genuine interest in looking at our own situation realistically . . . and developing ourselves for what we really are, but are always trying to gain admission into the European musical world."

B45.   "Fallacy of the Mechanistic Approach. [Review of Joseph Schillinger's 'The Schillinger System of Musical Composition.']" Modern Music v.23, no.3 (Summer 1946), p.228-230. Reprinted In: Stone, p.118-121.

Review of the book: System of Musical Composition by Joseph Schillinger. Carter states that the basic philosophic fallacy with the book is "the assumption that the 'correspondences' between patterns of art and patterns of the natural world can be mechanically translated from one to the other by the use of geometry or numbers. When this conception is carried to even greater lengths in the belief that music will stimulate reactions if it follows the graphic projection of geometric patterns of 'mechanical and bio-mechanical trajectories,' one can only feel that the whole idea is arbitrary in the extreme."

B46.   "Films and Theatre." Modern Music v.20, no.3 (March/April 1943), p.205-207. Reprinted In: Stone, p.86.

Review of the films: The Siege of Leningrad and Yankee Doodle Dandy which Carter calls "fresh, vigorous and hearty" and short reviews of two theatre productions: Sidney Kingsley's The Patriots and Thorton Wilder's The Skin of Our Teeth.

B47.   "Fine Inverno, New York, 1937." See: "Late Winter: New York, 1937" B71.

B47a.   Flawed Words and Stubborn Sounds: A Conversation with Elliott Carter. Edited by Allen F. Edwards. New York: Norton, 1971.

An interview with Elliott Carter based upon the series of lectures Carter gave as the Ward Lucas Visiting Professor of Music at Carleton College in 1966. The interview begins with a discussion of European and American attitudes toward "serious" music. Also discussed are: the acceptance of American composers in the United States and abroad, Carter's personal musical development, the technical characteristics of Carter's music, and current trends in musical compositions.

B48.   "For Pierre on His Sixtieth." In: Pierre Boulez: Eine Festschriften zum 60. Geburtstag am 26. Marz 1985. Edited by Josef Hausler. Vienna: Universal Edition, 1985. p.12-13. Printed along with German translation as: "Für Pierre zum Sechzigsten." p.14-15. Reprinted as: "Per Pierre, in Occasione dei Suoi Sessant' Anni," In: Restagno, p.261-262.

A tribute to Pierre Boulez on his birthday.

B49.   "Foreword." In: <u>Richard Franko Goldman: Selected Essays and Reviews, 1948-1968</u>. Edited by Dorothy Klotzman. New York: Institute for Studies in American Music, Department of Music, School of Performing Arts, Brooklyn College, 1980. p.vii-ix. Reprinted as: "In Memory of Richard Franko Goldman," In: <u>American Music Center Newsletter</u> v.22, no.4 (Fall 1980), p.13.

Foreword for a compilation of writings by composer, conductor, and critic Richard Goldman.

B50.   "The Function of the Composer [In Teaching the General College Student]." <u>Bulletin of the Society for Music in the Liberal Arts College</u> v.3, no.1, suppl. 3 (1952). Reprinted In: Stone, p.150-158.

Carter details several problems in teaching music to the general student in an academic environment. He describes his involvement in an integrated course structure at St. John's College which brought interdisciplinary concepts to the student.

B51.   "Für Pierre zum Sechzigsten." See: "For Pierre on His Sixtieth" B48.

B52.   "Further Notes on the Winter Season." <u>Modern Music</u> v.16, no.3 (March/April 1939), p.176-179. Reprinted In: Stone, p.51-54.

Carter reviews recent (1939) New York performances including: Jean Françaix's Piano Concerto which "is so much like its predecessor that it is very hard to think of something new to say." Bela Bartok's Rhapsody for Clarinet and Violin "proved that a good new work if played by performers with the reputations of Joseph Szigeti and Benny Goodman can have great success," Igor Stravinsky's Concerto for Two Pianos "sounds even better than it looks on paper, and proves to be one of Stravinsky's finest works." Aaron Copland's Sextet, an arrangement of his Short Symphony, "goes the limit in rhythmic invention . . . and gives further evidence of the strong inventive and imaginative qualities of this individual composer and of his great skill." Vladimir Dukelsky's Dédicaces is labeled as "inferior" by Carter. Carter ends by noting that Hendrik Willem van Loon "has recently published five very interesting, vituperative 'Deliberate Reflections' on the situation of the American musician" appearing in the <u>Greenwich Times</u> January 10-14, 1939.

B53.   "A Further Step." See: "Un Paso Adelante" B97.

B54.   "Gabriel Fauré." <u>Listen</u> v.6, no.1 (May 1945), p.8-9, 12. Reprinted In: Stone, p.107-110. Reprinted In: Restagno, p.123-126.

Written upon the one hundredth anniversary of Fauré's birth, the article highlights Fauré's musical career.

B55. "The Genial Sage." In: Paul Rosenfeld: Voyager in the Arts. Edited by Jerome Mellquist and Lucie Wiece. New York: Creative Age Press, 1948. p.163-165.

A reminiscence of critic Paul Rosenfeld.

B56. "Homage to Ravel." Modern Music v.15, no.2 (January/February 1938), p.96. Reprinted In: Stone, p.21.

A homage to the music of Maurice Ravel.

B57. "IGNM-Jury vor Neuen Problemen." See: "Sixty Staves to Read" B112.

B58. "Igor Stravinsky, 1882-1971." Proceedings of the American Academy of Arts and Letters and the National Institute of Arts and Letters 2nd series, no.22 (1972), p.84-86. Reprinted In: Stone, p.306-308.

A tribute to Stravinsky upon his death in which Carter expresses his grief. "In mourning his death, musicians of succeeding generations suffer this loss as a loss of part of their world. The horizon has suddenly become narrower. For while each generation has tended to live out its particular version of the twentieth century, Stravinsky encompassed them all."

B59. "Illinois Festival - Enormous and Active." New York Herald Tribune (April 5, 1953), IV, p.5. Reprinted In: Bulletin of the American Composers Alliance v.3, no.2 (Summer 1953), p.17.

A review of activities at the Illinois Festival at the University of Illinois at Champaign-Urbana. Carter presented a lecture "on the changes in the American musical scene as [Carter] had witnessed them." The evening was also devoted to Carter's works.

B60. "In Memoria di Stefan Wolpe, 1902-1972." See: "In Memoriam: Stefan Wolpe" B62.

B61. "In Memoriam Paul Fromm." Ovation v.8, no.11 (December 1987), p.18.

Printed remarks originally made at Paul Fromm's memorial service on October 4, 1987. Carter's Double Concerto and Concerto for Orchestra was commissioned by Fromm.

B62. "In Memoriam: Stefan Wolpe." Perspectives of New Music v.11, no.1 (Fall/Winter 1972), p.3-10. Reprinted as: "Stefan Wolpe (1902-1972) in Memoriam," In: Tempo no.102 (1972), p.17-18. Reprinted with revisions as: "Stefan Wolpe (1902-1972)," In: Proceedings of the American Academy of Arts and Letters and the National Institute of Arts and Letters

2nd series, no.23 (1973), p.115-117. Reprinted In: Stone, p.318-320.
Reprinted as: "In Memoria di Stefan Wolpe, 1902-1972," In: Restagno,
p.212-213.

A tribute to Stefan Wolpe upon his death. Carter describes Wolpe by saying:
"comet-like radiance, conviction, fervent intensity, penetrating thought on
many levels of seriousness and humor, combined with breath-taking
adventurousness and originality, marked the inner and outer life of Stefan
Wolpe, as they do his compositions. Inspiring to those who knew him, these
inspiring qualities reached many more through his music. A man, a musician,
for whom everyone who came close could not help but feel admiration and
affection." A "letter to the editor" by Stefan Bauer-Mengelberg appeared in
Tempo following the article's publication. (See: C9)

B63.   "In Memory of Richard Franko Goldman." See: "Foreword" B49.

B64.   "In the Theatre." Modern Music v.15, no.1 (November/December 1937),
        p.51-53. Reprinted In: Stone, p.17-19.

Review of the Salzburg Opera Guild's first visit to the United States. Their
repertoire included Milhaud's Le Pauvre Matelot, Monteverdi's Coronation of
Poppea, Mozart's Cosi fan Tutte, Ibert's Angelique, and Rossini's Matrimonial
Market.

B65.   "International Music Congress Forum."   Music and Artists v.2, no.1
        (February/March 1969), p.23-29.

A transcript of a panel discussion which occurred at the International Music
Congress session on September 9-16, 1968, entitled "Music and
Communication." The topic of the discussion in which Elliott Carter
participated, was "The sounds of things to come: the attitude of youth, and
the relationships of composer, performer and the changing audience."

B66.   "An Interview with Elliott Carter." Academy v.2, no.1 (July 1979).

A five question interview by George Gelles focusing on influences on Carter's
music and a discussion of his musical development, public support for modern
music, and the training of new composers.

B67.   "An Interview with Elliott Carter." Edited by J.W. Bernard. Perspectives of
        New Music v.28, no.2 (1990), p.180-214.

B68.   "Introduction." In: Mademoiselle: Conversations with Nadia Boulanger.
        Translated by Robyn Marsack. Manchester: Carcanet Press Ltd., 1985.
        (First published in France without Carter's introduction as Mademoiselle:
        Entretiens avec Nadia Boulanger by Van de Velde, 1980.)

An introduction written for a biography of Carter's teacher.

B69.   "Ives Oggi: Il suo Mondo e la sua Sfida e Sistenziale." See: "Ives Today: His Vision and Challenge" B70.

B70.   "Ives Today: His vision and Challenge."   Modern Music v.21, no.4 (May/June 1944), p.199-202. Reprinted In: Stone, p.98-102. Reprinted as: "Ives Oggi: Il suo Mondo e la sua Sfida e Sistenziale," In: Restagno, p.115-118.

Carter discusses Ives' philosophy of musical expression and examines the role of the musician and listener, and states that Ives "believes that composers should be free always to follow their highest instincts.   Difficulty of performance is the performer's problem, not his."

B71.   "Late Winter: New York, 1937." Modern Music v.14, no.3 (March/April 1937), p.147-154. Reprinted In: Stone, p.5-10. Reprinted as: "Fine Inverno, New York, 1937," In: Restagno, p.81-85.

Review of music by 25 composers performed in New York during early 1937.

B72.   "Letter from Europe." Perspectives of New Music v.1, no.2 (Spring 1963), p.195-205. Reprinted In: Stone, p.219-230.

Discussion of European annual festivals and the various musical styles that are reflected in them.

B73.   "Letter to the Editor." Journal of Music Theory v.7, no.2 (Winter 1963), p.270-273.

Written in hopes to standardize modern musical notation. Carter proposes the use of Renée Longy-Miquelle's book: Principles of Music Theory. (Boston: Schirmer Music Company, 1925 & 1952) as a standard. A response follows by Gardner Read. (See: C198)

B74.   "Letters: Brickbats and a Bouquet for Sir John." Musical America v.84, no.7 (September 1964), p.4.

A letter to the editor in response to an interview by Michael Brozen entitled "Quote-Unquote: Sir John Barbirolli" which appeared previously in Musical America (July 1964, p.30). Carter responds by saying "Contemporary composers are very lucky that Sir John Barbirolli has taken the stand he has and will avoid murdering their music in [the] future by giving them ill-digested, uninterested performances out of a sense of 'duty.'"

B75.   "La Mia Ammirazione per Roger Sessions." See: "Roger Sessions Admired" B106.

B76.   "The Milieu of the American Composer." Perspectives of New Music v.1
        (Fall 1962-Spring 1963), p.149-151. Reprinted In: High Fidelity/Musical
        America v.27, no.9 (September 1977), p.MA16, 27. Reprinted In: Stone,
        p.216-218.

        Carter examines the existence of experimentation in American music in
        contrast to the European tradition. "It is by carrying on the European tradition
        and by following the methods of some of its experiments in the different
        context of his own experience that our composer affirms his identity and the
        identity of American music."

B77.   "More about Balanchine." Modern Music v.14, no.4 (May/June 1937), p.237-
        239. Reprinted In: Stone, p.14-15.

        Review of George Balanchine's choreography in the ballets: "Card Party,"
        "Apollon Musagete," and "Apollon."

B78.   "Music and the Time Screen." In: Current Thought in Musicology. Edited
        by John W. Grubbs. Austin: University of Texas Press, 1976, p.63-88.
        Reprinted In: Stone, p.343-365. Reprinted as: "La Musica e lo Schermo
        del Tempo," In: Restagno, p.235-257.

        Using examples from his own music, Carter describes the nature of time
        within music.

B79.   "Music as a Liberal Art." Modern Music v.22, no.1 (November 1944), p.12-
        6. Reprinted In: Stone, p.102-106. Reprinted as: "La Musica come Arte
        Liberale," In: Restagno, p.119-122.

        A discussion of a better way to teach music at the university level. Carter
        proposes less emphasis on a chronology of music in favor of an integrated
        program bringing together all fields of study, thus interrelating music with
        physics, philosophy and literature, resulting in discussions of aesthetic and
        philosophical questions.

B80.   "Music of the 20th Century." In: Encyclopedia Britannica. Chicago:
        Encyclopedia Britannica, 1953. Vol. XVI. p.16-18. Reprinted in several
        succeeding editions.

        A typical encyclopedia entry regarding music of the twentieth century.

B81.   "La Musica Americana Sulla Scena New Yorchese, 1940." See: "American
        Music on the New York Scene" B5.

B82.   "La Musica come Arte Liberale." See: "Music as a Liberal Art" B79.

B83.   "La Musica e lo Schermo del Tempo." See: "Music and the Time Screen"
        B78.

B84.   "Musical Reactions-Bold and Otherwise."   Modern Music v.15, no.3
         (March/April 1938), p.199. Reprinted In: Stone, p.27.

         A Review of Deems Taylor's book: Of Men and Music. Carter writes that
         the book reveals "[d]efinite ideas on important questions in music. . . . On
         these he is very worth reading. . . . When he comes to the subject of
         'modern music,' he hedges. . . . [H]e can boldly take both sides of the
         fence in alternate chapters. After the season of 1926-7, Taylor seems to have
         ceased experiencing contemporary music as anything vital enough to write
         about in detail."

B85.   "La Musique aux Etats-Unis." Synthèses v.9, no.96 (May 1954), p.206-211.

         Discusses the history of American music of the previous fifty years. Carter
         tries to convince his European audience that American music reflects the
         freedom, spirit of adventure, enthusiasm, moral character, and diversity of the
         United States. Carter examines the diffusion of music to the American public
         due mainly to the advent of radio. He argues that new musical works by
         relatively unknown composers receive a cautious welcome from orchestras,
         radio stations and the like, because the public's dislike could result in
         economic ruin. Consequently, many new American composers study and
         experiment in the European arena with chamber music. Carter explains that
         American music was founded on quality performances and compositions rather
         than by application of a nationalistic dogma as in the European examples of
         rich folklore traditions. "By nature," Carter claims, "the American musical
         world is essentially eclectic: music and musicians or their ancestors originated
         from other countries with established [musical] traditions." (In French)

B86.   "New Compositions." Saturday Review v.27, no.4 (January 22, 1944), p.32-
         33.

         Reviews recent Western music published in the United States. The musical
         trends have changed from the "portrayal of new feelings, using all kinds of
         novel devices with apparent disregard for what audiences thought" prevalent
         between 1910 and 1930 toward "clear, intelligible patterns for definite
         audiences and performing groups." Carter uses several specific compositions
         to support his position.

B87.   "New Publications of Music." Saturday Review v.29, no.4 (January 26,
         1946), p.34, 36, 38. Reprinted In: Stone, p.111-116.

         Carter looks at new compositions in an attempt to determine what the post-war
         trends will become.

B88.   "New York Season (Continued)." Modern Music v.14, no.2
         (January/February 1937), p.90-92. Reprinted In: Stone, p.3-5.

Elliott Carter's first writing for Modern Music, actually a continuation of an article by a different reviewer. A review of music performed in New York during early 1937. Performances by the following composers are reviewed: James, Fuleihan, Weinberger, Ducasse, Clementi, Foote, MacDowell, Milhaud, Honegger.

B89.   "The New York Season Opens."   Modern Music v.17, no.1 (November/December 1939), p.34-8. Reprinted In: Stone, p.64-68.

Carter explains why Sibelius' music, though in his words "flat," is so popular. Carter then reviews Frederick Jacobi's Violin Concerto, two works by Mario Castelnuovo-Tedesco and the combined upcoming concert by the Composers' Forum Laboratory, the Music Division of the Library of Congress, and the Juilliard School.

B90.   "O Fair World of Music!" Modern Music v.16, no.4 (May/June 1939), p.238-242. Reprinted In: Stone, p.55-58. Reprinted as: "O Meravigioso Mondo della Musica!" In: Restagno, p.100-103.

Review of music at the 1939 New York World's Fair. "At every crossroads there is a loudspeaker dispensing [music] . . . Such soupy, amplified music always evokes for me the image of some huge Walt Disney monster pouring out his soul in a slightly inarticulate voice, a ludicrous but inevitable trumpet of doom. This sentimental gargantua is what we now accept as the expression of jollity and merriment." Carter also reviews the music used in the exhibits. "There is . . . quite a bit that is interesting which you can stumble on by poking about in the stucco and plaster."

B91.   "O Meravigioso Mondo della Musical!" See: "O Fair World of Music!" B90.

B92.   "On Edgard Varèse." In: The New Worlds of Edgard Varèse: A Symposium. Edited by Sherman Van Solemka. New York: Brooklyn College, 1979. p.1-7. Reprinted as: "Su Edgard Varèse," In: Restagno, p.255-260.

This article was based on an article read over the transatlantic telephone on October 29, 1975, over Radio-France (ORTF). Carter discussed Varèse's use of rhythm as the primary cohesive element in his compositions.

B93.   "Once Again Swing; Also 'American Music.'" Modern Music v.16, no.2 (January/February 1939), p.99-103. Reprinted In: Stone, p.43-47.

Review of the swing style and the amazement of classical composers of its continued popularity. Carter reports on a recent "fascinating" concert at Carnegie Hall tracing the development of swing from African records through Count Basie. Carter also points out that swing will not to be adopted into classical music until "a serious composer with artistic perspective has been able to stylize and make it express his personal, creative attitude toward

American life." Carter comments on recent letters and articles appearing in the New York Sunday Times concerning Barber's Adagio for Strings and whether American composers should be "reactionary" or "modern." Also included are reviews of premieres of Copland's El Salon Mexico which "is a milestone in Copland's development for it represents a change from the introspective attitude previously held." In addition, Carter felt the critics neglected to adequately review Outdoor Overture.

B94.   "Opening   Notes: New   York."   Modern   Music   v.15,   no.1
        (November/December 1937), p.36-37. Reprinted In: Stone, p.16-17.

Review of two premieres performed by the New York Philharmonic during the beginning of the 1937/38 season. Bela Bartok's Music for Strings, Percussion and Celesta and Gardner Reed's Symphony in A Minor. The fall concert series at the Composers' Forum Laboratory is also discussed.

B95.   "Orchestras and Audiences: Winter, 1938." Modern Music v.15, no.3
        (March/April 1938), p.167-171. Reprinted In: Stone, p.28-31.

Carter starts by detailing two types of music listeners: the passive and active. The passive listener "give[s] himself up to an evening of reminiscence or revery after having checked his conscious, critical self at the door with his hat." The active listener is more "objective" and "enthusiastic." "He is eager for new ideas and new feelings. When hearing familiar works he always re-evaluates his previous impressions. The style, no matter how difficult or unusual, does not prevent him from trying to find what the music is all about." Carter continues by examining recent performances, looking at how individuals listen to and receive new music.

B96.   "Parla un Compositore Americano." See: "Shop Talk by an American
        Composer" B111.

B97.   "Un Paso Adelante." Buenos Aires Musical 14 special number (December
        1959), p.63-67. Reprinted as: "A Further Step," In: The American
        Composer Speaks: A Historical Anthology, 1770-1965. Edited by Gilbert
        Chase. Baton Rouge, LA: Louisiana State University Press, 1966, p.245-
        254. Reprinted In: Stone, p.185-191. Reprinted as: "Un Altro Passo
        Avanti (1958)," In: Restagno, p.174-180.

Discussion of the "new principles" of musical compositions. "But today . . . the techniques of continuity and contrast . . . [and] the various kinds of cause and effect patterns . . . occupy the attention of composers more than harmony or other matters, all of which now become simply details in a larger kind of concern."

B97a.   "Pastoral." In: New Music v.18, no.3 (April 1945)

Carter's score is printed in full. (See: W57)

B98.   "Per Pierre, In Occasione dei Suoi Sessant' Anni." See: "For Pierre on His
        Sixtieth" B48.

B99.   "*Piano Concerto.*" Boston Symphony Orchestra Program Notes 86th season
        (January 6, 1967), p.792, 794, 796, 798, 800, 802-804, 806-808.

        Program notes for the premiere performance of Carter's *Piano Concerto*
        performed by the Boston Symphony Orchestra.

B100.   "Piston." See: "Walter Piston" B128.

B101.   "Il Punto di Vista del Compositore di Musica per Orchestra." See: "Elliott
        Carter" B36.

B102.   "Recent Festival in Rochester." Modern Music v.15, no.4 (May/June 1938),
        p.241-243. Reprinted In: Stone, p.31-33.

        Review of the eighth annual Eastman School Festival of American Works.
        Performances of the following composers' works are reviewed: David
        Diamond, Vladimir Ussachevsky, Charles Vardell, Aaron Copland, Bernard
        Rogers, Burril Phillips, and Kay Swift.

B103.   "Reel Vs. Real." Newsletter of the American Symphony League v.11, no.5/6
        (July 1960), p.8-10.

        Transcript of a lecture Carter gave at the League's Annual Composers'
        luncheon. Carter, speaking about the current state of electronic music, stresses
        the need for composers to write music of high quality.

B104.   "Reminiscences on Music."   Musical Newsletter (January 1972), p.3-6.
        Reprinted from: Flawed Words and Stubborn Sounds. Edited by Allen
        Edwards.

        In this article Carter discusses Nadia Boulanger and her influences on his
        musical training and the affect this training had on his musical career.

B105.   "The Rhythmic Basis of American Music." The Score and I.M.A. Magazine
        v.12 (June 1955), p.27-32. Reprinted In: Stone, p.160-166. Reprinted as:
        "Le Basi Ritmiche della Musica," In: Restagno, p.151-156.

        Carter explores the influence of jazz on the rhythmic techniques of American
        music. Carter suggests that the music of American composers has "lost its
        original freshness; the techniques have become shopworn, the performances
        routine and dull."   Carter looks at the rhythmic technique of the four
        composers who helped to establish these techniques in the early stages of the
        contemporary movement in America[:]" Roy Harris, Aaron Copland, Roger
        Sessions and Charles Ives.

B106.   "Roger Sessions Admired." Perspectives of New Music v.23, no.2
        (Spring/Summer 1985), p.120-122. Reprinted as: "La Mia Ammirazione
        per Roger Sessions," In: Restagno, p.263-265.

        One of several articles written under the general title: "In memoriam: Roger
        Sessions." Carter's article reveals not only a friendship, but also a sense of
        loss for an end to new music by Sessions.

B107.   "Scores for Graham; Festival at Columbia." Modern Music v.23, no.1
        (Winter 1946), p.53-55. Reprinted In: Stone, p.116-118.

        A Review of recent performances. Carter states that the dances to Copland's
        Appalachian Spring and Hindemith's Hérodiade presented by Martha Graham
        in her recent New York Season "are the most completely integrated and
        carefully conceived scores that have yet been written for her." Chavez's Dark
        Meadow also presented by Graham "returns to the older modern dance idiom
        with an increased sense of projection that makes it one of her [Graham's] most
        perfectly realized works in this style." Carter also reviews one of a series of
        annual festivals of American music which opened the previous Spring at
        Columbia University and was excellently performed by the Walden Quartet.

B108.   "Season of Hindemith and Americans." Modern Music v.16, no.4 (May/June
        1939), p.249-254. Reprinted In: Stone, p.60-63.

        Carter comments on the recent increase of performances of Hindemith's
        compositions. Carter reviews the All-American Concert at Carnegie Hall
        which was devoted to the works of Guggenheim Fellows. Other concerts
        reviewed include the New School Concerts, the Juilliard Alumni Concerts, the
        Third League of Composers' Concert which "dispelled any lingering
        impression that young Americans today show less promise than the preceding
        generation."

B109.   "Season's End in New York." Modern Music v.14, no.4 (May/June 1937),
        p.215-217. Reprinted In: Stone, p.11-13. Reprinted as: "La Chiusura
        della Stagione 1937 a New York," In: Restagno, p.86-88.

        Review of music performed in New York during the close of the 1937 season.
        Performances of the following composers are reviewed: Hindemith,
        Stravinsky, Sessions, Copland, Honegger, Straus, Szymanowski, Kodaly,
        Lieberson, and Citkowitz.

B110.   "Season's End: New York, Spring, 1938." Modern Music v.15, no.4
        (May/June 1938), p.228-233. Reprinted In: Stone, p.34-38. Reprinted as:
        "La Chiusura della New York Primavera, 1938," In: Restagno, p.89-92.

        Carter discusses the role and influence of a music critic. "His obvious
        function is to point out what works are important, which creators are
        influencing the contemporary scene. . . . Unfortunately music critics in the

daily press pay no attention to that important phase of their work." The critic "can, and he frequently does, condemn every new work as it appears. . . . The critic need make no effort to understand, or even to be literate in his condemnation." Carter continues by reviewing recent performances of modern composers.

B111.   "Shop Talk by an American Composer." Musical Quarterly v.46, no.2 (April 1960), p.189-201.   Reprinted In: Contemporary Composers on Contemporary Music. Edited by Elliott Schwartz and Barney Childs. New York: Holt, Rinehart and Winston, 1967.   p.261-273.   Reprinted In: Problems of Modern Music. Edited by Paul Henry Lang. New York: W.W. Norton, 1962.   p.51-63.   Reprinted In: Stone, p.199-211. Reprinted as: "Parla un Compositore Americano," In: Restagno, p.185-195.

An Interview with Carter regarding his musical style, and in particular, his rhythmic procedures.

B112.   "Sixty Staves to Read."   New York Times (January 24, 1960), II, p.9:7. Reprinted In: Stone, p.197-198.   Reprinted as: "IGNM-Jury vor Neuen Problemen," In: Melos v.27, no.6 (June 1960), p.165-166.

Details criteria and procedures for scoring winning compositions at the 34th annual I.S.C.M. Festival in Cologne of which Carter was one of the judges. The winners are also announced.

B113.   Sketches and Scores in Manuscript: A Selection of Manuscripts and Other Pertinent Material from the Americana Collection of the Music Division, the New York Public Library, on Exhibition December 1973 through February 1974 in the Vincent Astor Gallery, Library and Museum of the Performing Arts, The New York Public Library at Lincoln Center. NY: New York Public Library and Readex Books, 1973.

An exhibition catalog for the exhibit on Elliott Carter which includes 118 entries highlighting photographs, musical sketches and manuscripts.   Also included is a works list detailing publication information, first performance, awards and commissions, a bibliography and a discography.

B114.   "The Sleeping Beauty."   Modern Music v.14, no.3 (March/April 1937), p.175-176. Reprinted In: Stone, p.10-11.

Review of Tchaikovsky's American premiere of Sleeping Beauty choreographed by Catherine Littlefield.

B115.   Stefan Wolpe (1902-1972) in Memoriam."   See: "In Memoriam: Stefen Wolpe" B62.

B116.   "[Stravinsky: a Composer's Memorial]." Perspectives of New Music v.9, no.2 and v.10, no.1 (Spring/Summer 1971, Fall/Winter 1971), p.1-6. Reprinted In: Stone, p.301-306.

A special double issue entitled: "Stravinsky: a Composer's Memorial." The issue includes tributes to Stravinsky upon his death by many composers including Elliott Carter.

B117.   "Stravinsky and Other Moderns in 1940." Modern Music v.17, no.3 (March/April 1940), p.164-70. Reprinted In: Stone, p.74-81. Reprinted as: "Stravinsky e Altri Moderni nel 1940," In: Restagno, p.109-114.

Review of recent performances of Igor Stravinsky's music inspired by his presence in America.   A brief review of recent ballets including Saroyan's Great American Goof for which Henry Brant wrote the music.   Carter describes it as having "tact and ingenuity." Carter reviews the Contemporary Concerts organized by Mark Brunswick, Roger Sessions and Edvard Steuermann and states: "Here, we have a rare opportunity to hear extradinary performances of little known works of the past together with many of the 'learned,' serious pieces of the last thirty years." Other reviews include music by Walter Piston, Quincy Porter, Douglas Moore, Henry Cowell, Paul Creston, William Schuman, Charles Ives, Nikolai Lopatnikoff, Alexander Von Zemlinsky, Karol Rathaus, Paul Dessau, and Stefan Wolpe.

B118.   "Stravinsky e Altri Moderni nel 1940." See: "Stravinsky and Other Moderns in 1940" B117.

B119.   "Su Edgard Varèse." See: "On Edgard Varèse" B92.

B120.   "Symfoni för Tre Orkestrar." Nutida Musik v.31, no.3 (1987/88), p.35-36.

A brief description of Carter's work A Symphony of Three Orchestras.   (In Swedish)

B120a.   "Tarantella." In: Words and Music: The Composer's View. Edited by Lawrence Berman.   Cambridge, MA: Music Department of Harvard University, 1972.

Carter's score is printed in full. (See: W29)

B121.   "Theatre and Films." Modern Music v.20, no.4 (May/June 1943), p.282-284. Reprinted In: Stone, p.93-95.

Review of theatrical performances and films including: A Tree on the Plains by Paul Horgan and Ernst Bacon, The Wind Remains by Paul Bowles, The Human Comedy by Roy Webb, Mission to Moscow by Max Steiner and the music to the film Desert Victory.

B122.   "Theatre and Films." Modern Music v.21, no.1 (November/December 1943), p.50-3. Reprinted In: Stone, p.95-98.

Review of theatrical performances and films including: One Touch of Venus by Kurt Weill, The Merry Widow by Franz Lehár, Carmen Jones by Russell Bennett and Oscar Hammerstein II, North Star by Aaron Copland, Flesh and Fantasy by Alexandre Tansman, Constant Nymph by Eric Korngold and The Great Mr. Handel.

B123.   "The Time Dimension in Music." Music Journal v.23, no.8 (November 1965), p.29-30. Reprinted In: Boston Symphony Orchestra Program Notes (January 6, 1967), p.800-808. Reprinted In: Stone, p.243-247.

Based on a lecture given at the University of Texas at Austin, Carter examines his own use of rhythmic procedures through examples from his music. Carter also discusses how current composers were influenced by the "great musical revolutions brought about by Schoenberg and Stravinsky" with regard to the "basic dimensions of music: pitch, duration, volume, and timbre."

B124.   "To Think of Milton Babbitt." Perspectives of New Music v.14, no.2 and v.15, no.1 (Spring/Summer-Fall/Winter 1976), p.29-31.

Explains the acoustical and "live-performance" problems which are the reasons why Milton's works have not been widely performed nor appreciated.

B125.   "Vacation Novelties: New York." Modern Music v.15, no.2 (January/February 1938), p.96-103. Reprinted In: Stone, p.21-22.

Carter emphasizes that though some American music is amateurish and perhaps of poor quality, there is a wealth of excellent American music which is being overlooked. Carter then reviews recent compositions and performances of American composers.

B125a.   "Variationer for Orkester." Nutida Musik 4 (1960/61), p.14-16.

(In Swedish)

B126.   "Vassar Choir Concert Features Belgian Music." New York Herald Tribune (March 15, 1945), p.17:4.

Review of a concert including early Belgian music performed by organist Kathleen Pearson, harpsichordist Ralph Kirkpatrick, and the Vassar College Choir, E. Harold Geer directing.

B127.   "Wallingford Riegger." American Composers Alliance Bulletin v.2, no.1 (February 1952), p.3-5. Reprinted In: Stone, p.158-159.

A discussion of why Riegger is, at the time of the article, such a little known composer and why his works have recently been revived. Carter examines reviews of first performances and more recent performances of Reigger's Symphony No. 3, Study in Sonority and Dichotomy to show how Riegger's music was not understood.

B128.   "Walter Piston."   Musical Quarterly v.32, no.3 (July 1946), p.354-375. Reprinted In: Stone, p.121-140.   Condensed version reprinted as: "Piston," In: The Book of Modern Composers.   2nd ed. New York: Knopf, 1950, p.498-508.   Condensed version reprinted as: "Walter Piston," In: Restagno, p.127-144.

A summary of Walter Piston's life, musical genius and career including an analysis of his musical tendencies with examples.   A list of his works follows the article.

B129.   "Was ist Amerikanische Musik?" Österreichische Musik Zeitschrift v.31, no.10 (October 1976), p.468-470.

"An issue devoted entirely to twentieth century American musical life: contemporary music, composers and their working conditions, musicological activities, publishing, and recording of music."   (RILM Abstracts 1976, #8657)

B130.   "What's New in Music?" Saturday Review v.28, no.3 (January 20, 1945), p.13-14, 34.

Carter comments on various new and old compositions recently published by a strengthing American publishing market.

B131.   "With the Dancers."   Modern Music v.15, no.1 (November/December 1937), p.55-56. Reprinted In: Stone, p.19-20.

Carter reviews new dance performances by the Catherine Littlefield and the Russian Ballet.   Performances include Poulenc's Aubade, a miniature Fantastic Symphony entitled Poème to Ravel's Pavane, and a miniature Choreartium based on music by Bach; Handel's Gods Go A-Begging, Francesca da Rimini by choreographer Lichine; and Cog d'Or by choreographer Nathalia Goncharova.

B132.   "With the Dancers."   Modern Music v.15, no.2 (January/February 1938), p.118-122. Reprinted In: Stone, p.23-26.

Review of the Dance International which was held in December 1938.   Much of the review is devoted to the "Modern Dance" evening of the festival. Dancers featured included Ruth St. Denis, Martha Graham, Doris Humphrey,

Charles Weidman, Helen Tamiris, Hanya Holm and their groups. Carter writes in objection to their dance style which "Misrepresent[s] our contemporary American life to us."

B133.   The Writings of Elliott Carter: An American Composer Looks at Modern Music." Edited by Else and Kurt Stone. Bloomington, IN: Indiana University Press, 1977.

Selected writings by Carter are reproduced in the book. Roughly, the first half of the book includes reviews and articles originally appearing in Modern Music. The second half includes articles from numerous sources ranging from program notes and record sleeves to full discourses. The book is arranged in chronological order, thus giving insight into the development of Carter as a music critic and composer. (For a review of the book, see: C33)

Bibliography of Material About Carter

Included here are articles, books, and films about Elliott Carter. Master's theses and doctoral dissertations are also included. Due to the difficulty in obtaining copies of theses and dissertations to examine, I have elected to use abbreviated reviews which already exist. The citations follow the review. Common indexing sources used throughout this section are DAI (Dissertation Abstracts International) and MAI (Masters Abstracts International). The dissertation titles and abstracts contained here are published with permission of University Microfilms, Inc., publishers of <u>Dissertation Abstracts International</u> and may not be reproduced without their prior permission. Copies of the dissertations may be obtained by addressing your request to: University Microfilms, Inc., 300 North Zeeb Road, Ann Arbor, Michigan 48106 or by telephoning (toll-free) 1-800-521-3042.

C1.   Adams, Daniel Clifford. <u>Striking Implements and Surface Specification in Unaccompanied Multiple Percussion Solos: Its Compositional Significance</u>. D.M.A. diss., University of Illinois at Urbana-Champaign, 1985.

"An examination of how the composers' written specifications contribute to the structure of selected multiple percussion solos with regard to striking implements and surface areas. The subsequent analytical chapter consists of comprehensive analyses of, and comparisons between, three virtuosic multiple percussion solos:" *Moto Perpetuo* (Elliott Carter); Janissary Music (Charles Wuorinen); Touch and Go (Herbert Brün)." (DAI v.46, no.11, p.3183 A)

C2.   Altenbernd, Nicholas. <u>Form and Rhythm in the Music of Elliott Carter (1946-52)</u>. M.A. thesis, Cornell University, 1971.

C3.   Anderson, Bruce Clarke. <u>The Solo Piano Music of Elliott Carter: A Performance Guide</u>. Ph.D. diss., New York University, 1988.

The "study begins with . . . [a] presentation of his training, influences, musical values and stylistic evolution[; this] provides a larger context in which to view the solo piano works." The following chapters "focus on analysis of

. . . the solo piano works: *Piano Sonata* (1945-46), *Piano Concerto* (1965) and *Night Fantasies* (1980). Analyses of the works are based upon a modified version of Jan La Rue's method of style analysis and David Schiff's presentation of theoretical principles in Carter's music. . . . The two analytical procedures were used to identify stylistic characteristics related to performance problems rather than to develop extensive analyses of musical form and content." (DAI v.49, no.9, p.2439 A)

C4.   Archibald, Bruce. "Reviews of Records: *Double Concerto* for Harpsichord and Piano with Two Chamber Orchestras . . . [and] *Duo for Violin and Piano.*" Musical Quarterly v.63, no.2 (April 1977), p.287-289.

A review of a recent Nonesuch recording. The article is particularly important for its historical discographical information concerning recordings of the two works. (See: D17, D18)

C5.   Arlton, Dean Luther. American Piano Sonatas of the Twentieth Century: Selective Analyses and Annotated Index. Ed.D. diss., Columbia University, 1968.

After discussing the history and development of the American piano sonata, Arlton's dissertation provides analyses of piano sonatas of seven composers. Carter's *Piano Sonata* consumes 62 pages.

C6.   Bakker, Anne J. Elliott Carter: The Making of the Metrical Modulation Concept. M.M. thesis, Virginia Commonwealth University, 1976.

C7.   Bals, Karen Elizabeth. The American Piano Concerto in the Mid-Twentieth Century. D.M.A. diss., University of Kansas, 1982.

"Chapters III and IV, which constitute the main body of the paper, examine the piano concerto in America from 1940 to 1970." Carter's *Piano Concerto* is among eight concertos covered in depth. (DAI v.43, no.8, p.2485 A)

C8.   Barnes, Marsha Korth. Aspects of Pitch Structure in Elliott Carter's *Sonata for Cello and Piano, 1948*. M.M. thesis, University of Maryland, 1975.

C9.   Bauer-Mengelberg, Stefan. "Letter to the Editor." Tempo no.103 (December 1972), p.63-64.

A letter to the editor citing inaccuracies in Carter's article entitled "In Memoriam: Stefan Wolpe." (See: B62) Bauer-Mengelberg states that Carter's speculative comment regarding Stefan Wolpe's performance ordeal and the onset of Parkinson's disease was flawed in terms of chronological events and medical inaccuracies.

C10.   Beckstrom, Robert Allen. Volume I. Analysis of Elliott Carter's *Variations*
        for Orchestra (1955). Volume II. Concerto for Clarinet and Winds.
        [original composition]. Ph.D. diss., University of California, Los Angeles,
        1983.

        "Volume 1. Elliott Carter's *Variations for Orchestra* (1955) is examined both
        as an outgrowth of several historical trends, and as a work built from its own
        internal characteristics.   The historical discussion includes an overview of
        variations as a compositional premise.   It also considers the issue of block
        structuring found in music of this century.   The analysis concentrates on the
        structural properties of *Variations for Orchestra*, its approach to variation
        technique, and its pitch organization." (DAI v.45, no.5, p.1233 A)

C11.   Below, Robert. "Elliott Carter's *Piano Sonata*: An Important Contribution
        to Piano Literature." Music Review v.34, nos.3-4 (August/November
        1973), p.282-293.

        Below examines the "pitch relations and their role in [the] structure" of the
        sonata.

C12.   Belt, Byron. "Carter Quartet: Dazzling Debut." Newark Star-Ledger
        (January 24, 1973).

        Review of the premiere of Carter's *String Quartet No. 3* performed by the
        Juilliard String Quartet. "The rhythmic, harmonic and melodic complexities
        are tremendous, and yet they never seem to stand in the way of music that is
        intense, emotional and sonically exciting."

C13.   Berger, Arthur. "Ballet Society: Dance Program Presented with 3 New
        Scores." New York Herald Tribune (March 28, 1947), p.20:2.

        Review of three productions performed by the Ballet Society at the Central
        High School of Needle Trades on March 26 including the premiere of Carter's
        The Minotaur.

C14.   ----------. "Concert and Recital: Bernard Greenhouse." New York Herald
        Tribune (February 28, 1950), p.18:6.

        Review of a concert of cello music performed by Bernard Greenhouse on
        February 27, 1950. Included in the concert was the premiere of Carter's
        Sonata for Violoncello and Piano.

C15.   Berger, Melvin. "Elliott Carter." In: Guide to Chamber Music. New York:
        Dodd, Mead & Co., 1985. p.123-130.

        A quick look at five significant works by Carter including *Eight Etudes and
        a Fantasy*, *String Quartets Nos. 1, 2 and 3* and *Brass Quintet*.

C16.   Bernard, Jonathan W. "The Evolution of Elliott Carter's Rhythmic Practice."
        Perspectives of New Music v.26, no.2 (Summer 1988), p.164-203.

        A detailed examination of Carter's rhythmic practices including metrical
        modulation. Carter's *Sonata for Violoncello and Piano* and *String Quartet No.
        1, and No. 2* and his *Double Concerto* are examined in detail.

C17.   ----------. "Spatial Sets in Recent Music of Elliott Carter." Music Analysis
        v.2, no.1 (March 1983), p.5-34.

        Carter's 'Harmony book' ("a tabulation of pitch relations"), compiled between
        1963 and 1967, now housed in the Carter collection at the New York Public
        Library, reveals that "Carter began to compose with set-like materials in
        mind." In light of this book, Bernard looks at Carter's *Piano Concerto,
        Concerto for Orchestra, Brass Quintet* and *String Quartet No. 3* in order to
        reveal the extent of Carter's use of spatial sets. (See: A7)

C18.   Blyth, Alan. "Elliott Carter on Musical Vocabulary." The Times (London)
        (January 10, 1968), p.7:4.

        Carter's musical style is examined and compared to that of his contemporaries.

C19.   Borders, Barbara A. Elliott Carter's Double Concerto for Harpsichord and
        Piano with Two Chamber Orchestras (1961). M.M. thesis, University of
        Kansas, 1973.

C20.   Boretz, Benjamin. "Music." The Nation v.204, no.14 (April 3, 1967), p.445-
        446.

        A review of Carter's *Piano Concerto* performed by Jacob Lateiner and the
        Boston Symphony Orchestra. "[T]his Concerto has discovered new paths of
        perception, and new possibilities of coherent articulation under conditions of
        unprecedented complexity through structural 'dramatization' of music-relational
        situations."

C21.   Boykan, Martin. "Elliott Carter and Postwar Composers." Perspectives of
        New Music v.2, no.2 (Spring/Summer 1964), p.125-128. Reprinted In:
        Perspectives on American Composers. Edited by Benjamin Boretz and
        Edward T. Cone. New York: W.W. Norton, 1971. p.213-216.

        Details how Carter's *String Quartet No. 1*'s success was not only a result of
        its quality, but because "this quartet was the kind of work that was very much
        needed and desired."

C22.   "Brandeis Presents Awards in the Arts." New York Times (March 29, 1965),
        p.43:1.

Announcement of Carter being conferred a 1965 Creative Arts Awards Medal by Brandeis University. The Award carried a $1,000 stipend.

C23.   Brandt, William E.   "The Music of Elliott Carter: Simultaneity and Complexity." Music Educators Journal v.60, no.9 (May 1974), p.24-32. Reprinted as: "The Music of Elliott Carter," In: Breaking the Sound Barrier: A Critical Anthology of the New Music." Edited by Gregory Battcock. New York: Dutton, 1981. p.221-234.

Written as the sixth feature article of the Journal's bicentennial series "Sounds of America."   Describes certain aesthetic traits of Elliott Carter which go against popular trends of the time. Also examined are his use of "instrumental characterization," "strata," and "metrical modulation."

C24.   Breedon, Daniel Franklin.   An Investigation of the Influence of the Metaphysics of Alfred North Whitehead upon the Formal-Dramatic Compositional Procedures of Elliott Carter. D.M.A. diss., University of Washington, 1975.

"This paper is an investigation of the influence of Alfred North Whitehead's metaphysics upon Elliott Carter's formal-dramatic compositional procedures, and an illustration of the usefulness of this philosophy in formally analyzing Carter's work." (DAI v.37, no.2, p.678-679 A)

C25.   "Calder and Carter Win Awards in Art." New York Times (January 24, 1971), p.66:4.

Carter named recipient of Gold Medal Award by the National Institute of Arts and Sciences.

C26.   Calta, Louis. "Muriel Spark Calls for New Art Forms." New York Times (May 27, 1970), p.40:1.

Carter named one of three inducted into the Academy of Arts and Letters and given a $3,000 grant.

C27.   "Carter Composition in World Premiere." New York Times (February 27, 1953), p.17:2.

Review of the premiere performance of Carter's String Quartet No. 1 on February 26 by the Walden Quartet.

C28.   "Carter, Elliott Cook, Jr." In: American Composers: A Biographical Dictionary." By David Ewen. New York: G.P. Putnams Sons, 1982. p.110-114.

A comprehensive chronology and biography of Carter's musical career.

C29.   "Carter, Foss and Poulenc Works Get Music Critics Circle Awards." New York Times (April 19, 1961), p.34:1.

Announcement of Carter's *String Quartet No. 2* winning the Music Critics Circle Award for the best new works for the period January 1960-April 1961.

C30.   "Carter Quartet Wins Belgian Contest." Musical America v.73, no.13 (November 1, 1953), p.27.

Announcement of Carter winning first place in the Concours International de Composition pour Quatuor à Cordes in Liège, Belgium for his *String Quartet No. 1*.

C31.   "Carter Vogue." Time v.105, no.6 (February 10, 1975), p.65.

A review of Carter's *String Quartets Nos. 1, 2 and 3* recently performed by the Composer's String Quartet. This was the first concert in which more than one of Carter's quartets were performed. The article continues by depicting Carter as a leader with no teacher.

C32.   "Carter Work Wins UNESCO Music Prize." New York Times (May 20, 1961), p.13:4.

Announcement that Carter's *String Quartet No. 2* was selected by UNESCO as the outstanding musical work of 1961.

C33.   Clements, Andrew. "Elliott Carter Views American Music." Music and Musicians v.27, no.7 (March 1978), p.32-34.

More than a review for Else and Kurt Stone's book, The Writings of Elliott Carter (See: B133), this article chronicles Carter's career as a music critic.

C34.   Cogan, Robert and Pozzi Escot. "Elliott Carter: *Second String Quartet*, Introduction." In: Sonic Design. Englewood Cliffs, N.J.: Prentice-Hall, 1976. p.59-70.

An introduction to Carter's *String Quartet No. 2*. The work is examined with special regard to spatial design.

C35.   Cohn, Arthur. "Elliott Carter's *Piano Concerto*." The American Record Guide v.34, no.10 (June 1968), p.936-937, 945.

A review of Carter's *Piano Concerto* upon the release of the live recording of the premiere performed by Jacob Lateiner and the Boston Symphony Orchestra. (See: D77)

C36.   ----------. "His Own Man -- The Music of Elliott Carter." The American Record Guide v.37, no.11 (July 1971), p.756-759.

Review of Carter's *String Quartets Nos. 1 and 2* (See: D111, D115), *Variations for Orchestra* (See: D153) and *Double Concerto* (See: D16) upon release of two new recordings.

C37.   "Committee Chosen for Hopkins Center." New York Times (May 27, 1962), p.96:2.

Announcement that Elliott Carter is among sixteen men to serve on the music advisory committee for the new Hopkins Center of Music, Drama and Art at Dartmouth University.

C38.   *"Concerto for Orchestra."* Philharmonic Symphony Society of New York Program Notes (February 5, 1970), p.F,H.

Program notes from the premiere performance of Carter's *Concerto for Orchestra* which include Carter's own description of the work along with biographical information and Charles Ives' letter of recommendation for Carter's admittance to Harvard University.

C39.   Coonrod, Michael McGill. Aspects of Form in Selected String Quartets of the Twentieth Century. D.M.A. diss., Peabody Institute of the Johns Hopkins University, Peabody Conservatory of Music, 1984.

"This dissertation presents the compositional ideas in selected string quartets written in the twentieth century. [T]he main text analyzes the general styles and methods of organizing pitch, harmony, rhythm, texture, and overall shape in [six works including] the *Third Quartet* (1971) by Elliott Carter . . ." (DAI v.45, no.5, p.1233 A)

C40.   Copland, Aaron. "Presentation to Elliott C. Carter of the Gold Medal for Music." Proceedings of the American Academy of Arts and Letters and the National Institute of Arts and Letters 2nd series, no.22 (1972), p.32-33.

Presentation of the Institute's 1971 Gold Medal for Music to Elliott Carter who is described as having "gradually produced a body of work so original in conception and so imaginative in execution that we can proudly point to it as among the finest examples of musical creation that we in America have -- or that any other country has."

C41.   Cowell, Henry. "Current Chronicle: United States: New York." Musical Quarterly v.38, no.4 (October 1952), p.595-600.

Review of a concert of percussion music composed between 1926 and 1952 presented by the Junior Council of the Museum of Modern Art on May 6. Among the pieces performed was the premiere of Carter's *Suite for Timpani* (1950) performed by Al Howard.

C42.   Cundiff, Morgan. "A Guide to Elliott Carter Research Materials at the Library of Congress Music Division." In: The Musical Languages of Elliott Carter. By Charles Rosen. (See: C206, A6)

C43.   Daniel, Oliver. "Carter and Shapero." Saturday Review v.43 (December 17, 1960), p.43.

Review of Carter's *Sonata for Flute, Oboe, Violoncello, and Harpsichord* and a comparison of Carter's musical style to that of Harold Shapero upon the release of a Columbia recording of Carter's work and Shapero's *String Quartet No. 1*. (See: D98)

C44.   Danner, Gregory Guy. Theoretical Constructs for the Analysis of Acoustic Dissonance Fluctuation [with] Music for Nineteen Players [original composition]. Ph.D. diss., Washington University, 1984.

Examines "recent research in acoustical theories of dissonance and . . . outline[s] methods of applying this research in musical analysis.   Part 2 presents a model analysis of acoustic dissonance fluctuation in . . . Elliott Carter's *Canon for 3* (1971)." (DAI v.45, no.5, p.1234 A)

C45.   ----------. "The Use of Acoustic Measures of Dissonance to Characterize Pitch-Class Sets." Music Perception v.3, no.1 (Fall 1985), p.103-122.

"Recent scholarship in acoustics has provided a mathematical model for the approximation of what has been termed 'acoustic dissonance,' or 'roughness' in the interaction of two or more simultaneously sounded complex tones." "This article provides an overview of the acoustical theory, its application in profiling pitch-class sets, and a representative musical analysis." Carter's *Canon for 3* is used as a model.

C46.   Darter, Thomas Eugene. Elliott Carter's *String Quartet No. 1*. M.F.A. diss., Cornell University, 1972.

C47.   Davis, Peter G. "Speculum Musicae Celebrates Elliott Carter at 70." New York Times (December 11, 1978), III, p.18:4.

Concert honoring Carter on his 70th birthday presented by Speculum Musicae in Alice Tully Hall which included the premiere of Carter's *Syringa*. "Confronted with so many areas of activity, a listener can only surrender himself to the poetical/musical images on a sensual level, if he can, awaiting further enlightenment from repeated hearings."

C48.   DeLio, Thomas. "Spatial Design in Elliott Carter's *Canon for 3*." Indiana Theory Review v.4, no.1 (Fall 1980), p.1-12.

An analysis of the "unique and complex spatial design" employed by Carter in his *Canon for 3*.

C49.   Derby, Richard. "Carter's *Duo for Violin and Piano.*" Perspectives of New Music v.20, no.1-2 (Fall/Winter 1981-Spring/Summer 1982), p.149-168.

The "continuous interaction and opposition of the two instruments and their personalities" are analyzed as well as Carter's use of a "fixed octave scheme" with regard to rhythm and harmony.

C50.   Detweiler, Greg Jeffrey. The Choral Music of Elliott Carter. D.M.A. diss., University of Illinois at Urbana-Champaign, 1985.

Presents "analyses of the choral works which will allow fellow conductors to have a firmer musical grasp of these scores . . . to obtain better performances . . . [T]he first portion of the paper is occupied with analysis of his early life experiences and the impact of the musio-historical setting in which he wrote. The remaining chapters contain detailed descriptive analyses of the seven choral pieces." (DAI v.46, no.11, p.3185 A)

C51.   Diether, Jack. "Fromm Concert." Musical America v.81, no.10 (October 1961), p.29.

Review of the premiere performance of Carter's *Double Concerto* performed by Ralph Kirkpatrick and Charles Rosen. "This concerto is of extreme rhythmic and textural complexity, demanding much rehearing, and these factors, possibly combined with under-rehearsal, produced an effect of chaos and structural confusion at first, dominated by a proliferation of small background explosions."

C52.   Driver, Christopher. "Elliott Carter is a Composer Deeply Respected but . . ." Guardian (August 25, 1975), p.6:1.

In light of the British premiere of Carter's *String Quartet No. 3*, a comparison of Carter's popularity in Britain to that in the United States follows. An historical glimpse of the composition and performance of Carter's string quartets is also provided.

C53.   Driver, Paul. "Modernist Appeals to the Mind." The Times (London) (March 18, 1990), E, p.5:1.

A look at the difficulty to both comprehend and perform Carter's music.

C54.   ----------. "'*Triple Duo*' and 'Image, Reflection, Shadow'." Tempo no.146 (September 1983), p.53-55.

A review of the premiere of Carter's *Triple Duo* by the Fires of London in which Driver describes the instrumentation as "a pure explosion of 'joie de la musique', fluent, volatile, instrumentally idiomatic and characterized as never before."

C55.   *"Duo for Violin and Piano* (1974)." Philharmonic Symphony Society of New
         York Program Notes (March 21, 1975)

         Program notes from the premiere performance of Carter's work performed by
         Paul Zukofsky and Gilbert Kalish.

C56.   Elliott Carter: A 70th-Birthday Tribute. London: G. Schirmer Ltd., 1978.

         A 15 page tribute to Carter's 70th birthday. Outlines Carter's importance and
         influence as a composer and includes a detailed list of works.

C57.   "Elliott Carter to Get Handel Medallion from Mayor." New York Times
         (December 11, 1978), III, p.16:5.

         Announcement that Carter is the recipient of New York City's highest cultural
         award; the 1978 Handel Medallion presented by Mayor Koch.

C58.   "Elliott Carter Wins Prize for Orchestral Works." New York Times
         (February 27, 1981), II, p.7:1.

         Announcement of Carter's winning the 1981 Ernst von Siemens Musik-Pries
         for his orchestral works.

C59.   "Ensemble Offers Sonata by Carter." New York Times (November 11, 1953),
         p.35:6.

         Review of a concert held November 10th, 1953, by the Harpsichord Quartet
         which contained the premiere of Carter's *Sonata for Flute, Oboe, Violoncello
         and Harpsichord.*

C60.   Epstein, Helen. "Music." New York Times (November 17, 1974), II,
         p.19:1.

         Epstein discusses brass ensemble playing with a short history of the American
         Brass Quintet. Elliott Carter and Virgil Thomson briefly comment on the
         article and their brass quintets commissioned by the ABQ.

C61.   Ericson, Raymond. "Concert: Carter *Duo* in Premiere." New York Times
         (March 23, 1975), p.48:6.

         Review of the premiere of Carter's *Duo for Violin and Piano* performed by
         Paul Zukofsky and Gilbert Kalish. "Carter observed that he was using the
         contrasting acoustical properties of the violin and piano as a spring board."

C62.   ----------. "Carter on the Record." New York Times (February 1, 1970), II,
         p.23:1.

Review of an upcoming concert by the New York Philharmonic featuring the premiere of Carter's *Concerto for Orchestra* conducted by Leonard Bernstein. Ericson also previews a new production of Carter's ballet, *The Minotaur*, revived by the Boston Ballet Company and the Boston University Symphony Orchestra.

C63.   ----------. "Music: Ewald's Quintet No.3 Revived." New York Times (January 15, 1975), p.52:1.

Review of a concert by the American Brass Quintet on January 13, 1975, in the second of four concerts. Among the compositions performed were Carter's *Brass Quintet* and the premiere of his *Fantasy about Purcell's 'Fantasia upon One Note'*.

C64.   Ewen, David. "Carter, Elliott, 1908-." In: American Composers Today: A Biographical and Critical Guide. New York: H.W. Wilson, 1949. p.48-50.

A biographical sketch of Carter including his personal musical career and his rise to prominence.

C65.   ----------. "Elliott Carter, 1908-." In: World of 20th Century Music. New York: Prentice Hall, 1968. p.145-150.

A biographical sketch highlighting five of Carter's works: *String Quartets Nos. 1 and 2, Variations for Orchestra, Double Concerto,* and *Piano Concerto*.

C65a.   ----------. "Carter, Elliott Cook, Jr." In: American Composers: A Biographical Dictionary. New York: G.P. Putnam's Sons, 1982. p.110-114.

Comprehensive chronology and biography of Carter's musical career.

C66.   Eyer, Ronald. "New Music at Museum." New York Herald Tribune (September 7, 1961), p.14:4.

Review of a concert held on September 6th in honor of the Eighth Congress of the International Society for Musicology being held in New York. The premiere of Carter's *Double Concerto* was among the pieces performed by Ralph Kirkpatrick and Charles Rosen. "[T]he concerto is wide-open, free-striding music that often had the fragrance of outdoors about it . . . It is a provocative piece with one major flaw . . . that is the role in which the harpsichord found itself. The sound of the instrument is basically too thin to play a leading role in a loud and frequently percussive ensemble."

C67.   ----------. "Works for Tape Recorder Played in Stokowski Concerts." Musical America v.72, no.14 (November 15, 1952), p.8.

Review of two concerts of contemporary music including the premiere of Carter's *Eight Etudes and a Fantasy* performed by members of the New York Woodwind Quintet. "These would be engrossing essays for anyone studying instrumentation. They are a tour de force of virtually the whole school of flute, clarinet, oboe, and bassoon playing. They explore every nook and cranny of tonguing, range, attack, dynamics, fingering, coloristic effects, and ensemble possibilities."

C68.   "Festival of String Quartets: Prize Awarded to an American Composer." The Times (London) (September 29, 1953), B, p.9:3.

Report from the Liège International String Quartet Festival which announced Carter as the 1953 recipient of first prize for his *Chronometros (String Quartet No. 1)*.

C69.   Gass, Glenn. "Elliott Carter's *Second String Quartet*: Aspects of Time and Rhythm." Indiana Theory Review v.4, no.3 (Spring 1981), p.12-23.

An analysis of Carter's composition. Gass examines the unique character given each instrument which, when juxtaposed, serves as the basis of the composition. In addition, Carter's use of time and rhythm, which anticipate 'metric modulation' are discussed.

C70.   Geertsema, Anita. The Correlation Between the Aesthetic Writings of Elliott Carter and his *Second String Quartet*. M.MUS. thesis, University of South Africa, 1980.

"[A] broad outline of Elliott Carter's most important aesthetic concepts as put forward in his writings, and [an investigation into] the correlation between his aesthetic writings and the contents of his *String Quartet No. 2*. The relevant parameters and techniques analyzed were duration, pitch, texture, timbre, space, instrumental characterization, stratification and simultaneous sound layers." (MAI v.19, no.4, p.330)

C71.   ----------. The Tonal Chamber Music of Elliott Carter. D.MUS. diss., University of South Africa, 1989.

"This study investigates the elements of sound, harmony, melody, rhythm and growth of the selected chamber works in order to trace the evolution of Carter's style." (DAI v.50, no.9, p.2695 A)

C72.   Geissler, Fredrick Dietzmann. Part 1: Variations on a Modern American Trumpet Tune for Solo Trumpet and Concert Band. [original composition]. Part 2: Considerations of Tempo as a Structural Basis in Selected Orchestral Works of Elliott Carter. D.M.A. diss., Cornell University, 1974.

"This thesis surveys the orchestral music of Elliott Carter as well as his chamber music from the *Piano Sonata* to the present with particular interest in the area of tempo and speed." Works discussed include: *Holiday Overture, Sonata for Violoncello and Piano, Eight Etudes and a Fantasy, Sonata for Flute, Oboe and Harpsichord, String Quartet No. 1, Variations for Orchestra, Double Concerto, Piano Concerto, Concerto for Orchestra.* Included is a "bibliography of bibliographies on Carter, a bibliography of writings on Carter and his music, a chronological list of Carter's own writings and a chronological list of his compositions." (DAI v.35, no.5, p.3036 A)

C73.   Glock, William. Elliott Carter: A Birthday Tribute. London: Associated Music Publishers/Schirmer, 1978.

A birthday tribute upon Carter's 70th birthday. Included is a works list. "If you had to single out Carter's most characteristic gift, it would surely be the sheer power of invention which has unfailingly carried him through the grandest structures with a momentum and purposefulness equal to any composer this century."

C74.   ----------. Laudatio auf Elliott Carter: Ernst-von-Siemens-Musikpreis, 1981. Zug (Schweiz): Ernst-von-Siemens-Stiftung, 1981.

(In German)

C75.   ----------. "A Note on Elliott Carter." The Score and I.M.A. Magazine no. 12 (June 1955), p.47-52.

An examination of Carter's use of "metrical modulation" as Glock has now coined in his *Piano Sonata, Sonata for Violoncello and Piano*, and *String Quartet No. 1.*

C76.   Godfrey, Daniel. "A Unique Vision of Musical Time -- Carter's *String Quartet No. 3.*" Sonus v.8, no.1 (Fall 1987), p.40-59.

An examination of Carter's use and the interrelation-ship between 'musical time,' 'metric modulation,' and the 'projecting of instrumental personalities' in his *String Quartet No. 3.*

C77.   Goldman, Richard Franko. "Current Chronicle: United States: New York." Musical Quarterly v.37, no.1 (January 1951), p.83-89. Reprinted In: Goldman. p.69-74. (See: C81)

A review and analysis of Carter's *Piano Sonata* in light of a recent performance of his *Sonata for Violoncello and Piano.*

C78.   ----------. "Current Chronicle: United States: New York." Musical Quarterly v.46, no.3 (July 1960), p.361-367. Reprinted In: Goldman. p.119-122. (See: C81)

A brief review and general analysis of Carter's *String Quartet No. 2*.

C79.   ----------. "Current Chronicle: United States: New York." Musical Quarterly v.48, no.1 (January 1962), p.93-99. Reprinted In: Goldman. p.135-141. (See: C81)

A review of the concert sponsored by the Eighth Congress of the International Society of Musicology including Carter's *Double Concerto*. Goldman reviews the work and looks at its importance in Carter's development as a composer.

C80.   ----------. "The Music of Elliott Carter." Musical Quarterly v.43, no.2 (April 1957), p.151-170. Reprinted In: Goldman. p.33-47. (See: C81)

Goldman describes Carter and his music as representing "what is perhaps the most significant American development of the last ten years." Goldman lists Carter's compositions to date and reviews their place in Carter's musical development and the musical world.

C81.   ----------. Selected Essays and Reviews, 1948-1968. Edited by Dorothy Klotzman. I.S.A.M. Monographs. New York: Brooklyn College and the Institute for Studies in American Music, 1980.

Contains reprints of articles written by Goldman. Four articles are about Carter. (See: C77-C80)

C82.   Grau, Irene Rosenberg. Compositional Techniques Employed in the First Movement of Elliott Carter's *Piano Concerto*. Ph.D. diss., Michigan State University, 1973.

"The present study investigates the compositional aspects of the first movement of the two-movement concerto. An analysis in depth has been made of form, melody, harmony, density, dynamics, rhythmic activity and rhythmic character, tempo, meter, and metrical modulation, and interpretation and articulation markings." (DAI v.34, no.10, p.6685 A)

C83.   Griffith, Paul. "Tippett, Elliott Carter, Bath Festival." The Times (London) (June 3, 1980), p.11:1.

Review of the Bath Festival including the world premiere of Carter's *Night Fantasies* performed by Ursula Oppens. "As is often in Carter's music, the surface is packed with precisely-figured detail, while underneath there is a heaving, organic feeling and this makes for formidable difficulty of execution."

C84.   Haberkorn, Michael H. A Study and Performance of the *Piano Sonatas* of Samuel Barber, Elliott Carter, and Aaron Copland. Ed.D diss., Columbia University Teachers College, 1979.

C85.   Hailey, Foster. "'Fiorello!' Is Pulitzer Play; 'Advise and Consent' Wins."
       New York Times (May 3, 1960), p.1:3.

       Announcement of Carter's winning the 1960 Pulitzer Prize for his *String
       Quartet No. 2.*

C86.   Hamburg, Jeff. "I Have Nothing to Say." Key Notes v.23 (1986), p.41-49.

       Contrasts American and Dutch musical philosophies and the role of their social
       and political statements toward music. Carter's *String Quartet No. 3* is
       compared to other compositions including: Louis Andriessen's De Tijd, Joël
       Bons' Tour, Paul Termos' Carrara, Guus Janssen's Octet, Diderik Wagenaar's
       Limiet with regard to the simplicity of 'points of departure' and that "metrical
       progress of the composition is clear so that the process of the piece also
       becomes clear."

C87.   Hamilton, David. "Carter's Virtuoso Concerto." High Fidelity v.20, no.5
       (May 1970), p.22.

       A review of the premiere performance of Carter's *Piano Concerto* by Jacob
       Lateiner and the Boston Symphony Orchestra. The article appears under the
       column "Behind the scenes: Reports from the International Recording
       Centers."

C88.   ----------. "Elliott Carter, Early and Late." High Fidelity v.33, no.9
       (September 1983), p.69-70, 113.

       Detailed review of four recordings containing seven of Carter's recent
       compositions. (See: D10, D51, D68, D88, D93, D131, D135)

C89.   ----------. "Elliott Carter's Contributions to the American Bicentennial." High
       Fidelity/Musical America v.31, no.8 (August 1981), p.52, 55.

       Review of a recording of Carter's *A Symphony of Three Orchestras* and *A
       Mirror on Which to Dwell.* "[T]his disc couples two remarkably different
       realizations of Elliott Carter's central vision of musical diversity."
       (See: D60, D134)

C90.   ----------. "In Carter's *String Quartets*, Difficulty Can Hold Delight." New
       York Times (October 6, 1991), p.31, 43.

       In celebration of 45 years of existence, the Juilliard Quartet gears up to play
       Carter's four quartets. An analysis of Carter's music and his *String Quartets*
       in particular follows.

C91.   ----------. "Music." The Nation v.210, no.8 (March 2, 1970), p.253-254.

Review of Carter's *Concerto for Orchestra.* "With each successive work, Carter's language seems to increase in flexibility."

C92.   ----------. "Music." The Nation v.216, no.8 (February 19, 1973), p.250-252.

Review of the premiere of Carter's *String Quartet No. 3* held 27 days earlier and performed by the Juilliard String Quartet. Carter's quartet is "a fresh and arresting conception of the internal dynamics of the medium, couched in a language and form that, although complex, are still convincing to the ear."

C93.   ----------. "Music." The Nation v.220 (January 11, 1975), p.27-28.

A review of Carter's *Brass Quintet* given its premiere nearly one month before by the American Brass Quintet. Hamilton states the "long-range contrast between the ensemble's solemn, elegiac potential and its more raucous manifestations enables the work to embrace the entire range of brass's expressive capability."

C94.   ----------. "The Unique Imagination of Elliott Carter." High Fidelity Magazine v.24, no.7 (July 1974), p.73-75.

A review of Carter's *String Quartet No. 3* upon release of the Columbia recording. "The Juilliard's awe-inspiring recording permits in-depth exploration of the third string quartet -- and a fresh outlook on the second." (See: D116, D120)

C95.   Harmon, Carter. "Goldman's Work Introduced Here: NAACC Offers Piece in Concert at Times Hall -- Dahl and Ruggles Music on Bill." New York Times (February 28, 1949), III, p.16:5.

Review of a concert at the National Association of American Composers and Conductors. Among the works performed was the premiere of Carter's *Woodwind Quintet* performed by Martin Orenstein, David Abosch, Louis Paul, Pinson Bobo, and Mark Popkin. "Elliott Carter's *Quintet for Winds* (1948) was an attractive piece which had profile and made telling use of woodwind textures."

C96.   Harris, Jane Duff. Compositional Process in the String Quartets of Elliott Carter. Ph.D. diss., Case Western Reserve University, 1983.

"It is the aim of this dissertation to trace the development of the compositional process of Elliott Carter. This is accomplished through the study of his writings and his [*String Quartets Nos. 1, 2, 3*]. The string quartets were chosen because they span twenty years of Carter's compositional career (1951-1971) and are reasonably representative thereof. The discussion of compositional process is based upon three concerns which Carter mentions in his article 'A Further Step' (1958). These are discourse, time and texture." (DAI v.44, no.11, p.3200 A)

C97. Harrison, Jay. "Concert and Recital: American Composers Alliance." New York Herald Tribune (October 29, 1952), p.26:5.

Review of a concert held on October 28th and sponsored by the American Composers Alliance including Carter's *Eight Etudes and a Fantasy* for woodwind quartet performed by members of the New York Woodwind Quintet.

C98. Harvey, David. "Elliott Carter: *A Symphony of Three Orchestras, A Mirror on Which to Dwell.*" Tempo no.143 (December 1982), p.30-31.

A review of a recording of Carter's *A Symphony of Three Orchestras* and *A Mirror on Which to Dwell*. Harvey questions the importance of Schiff's "tonic register positions of intervals" in Carter's *A Symphony of Three Orchestras* (See: D60, D134). A reply by David Schiff followed as a letter to the editor (See: C223).

C98a. ----------. The Later Music of Elliott Carter: A Study in Music Theory and Analysis. New York: Garland Publishing, Inc., 1989. Originally written as a Ph.D. diss. in 1986 for Worcester College, Oxford.

This is an "extended critical analysis" of Carter's music with substantial musical examples. Carter's *String Quartet No. 2, Double Concerto* and *Concerto for Orchestra* receive full chapter analysis.

C99. Headrick, Samuel Philip. Thematic Elements in the Variations Movement of Elliott Carter's *String Quartet Number One* [with] Divertimento [original composition]. Ph.D. diss., The University of Rochester, Eastman School of Music, 1981.

"This research paper is a study of the principle thematic elements in the 'Variations' movement of Elliott Carter's *String Quartet No. 1*. Although the final movement is entitled Variations, it does not use traditional variation form. In his program notes, Elliott Carter states that the Variations movement consists of 'a series of different themes repeated faster at each successive recurrence, some reaching their speed vanishing point sooner than others.' Specifically, this movement has three main themes and many subsidiary themes and motives." (DAI v.42, no.3, p.907 A)

C100. Heaton Roger. Elliott Carter's *Third String Quartet*: An Analysis of Pitch and Form. M.Mus thesis, King's College, 1979.

C101. ----------. "*In Sleep, In Thunder.*" Tempo no.144 (March 1983), p.28-9.

Review of the first performance by Martyn Hill and the London Sinfonietta. Heaton calls "the new work . . . fluent and subtle in its detailed character."

C102.   Hellqvist, Per-Anders.   "Elliott Carter."   Nutida Music v.26, no.3 (1982-1983), p.21-23.

(In Swedish)

C103.   Henahan, Donal.   "Carter's '*A Mirror*' Given Premiere by a New Group."   New York Times (February 26, 1976), p.22:7.

Review of the premiere performance of Carter's *A Mirror on Which to Dwell* performed by Susan Davenny Wyner and the Speculum Musicae. "The first thing that struck one about the Carter song cycle was its directness and accessibility."

C104.   ----------.   "Concert: Retrospective of Carter and Babbitt Given."   New York Times (December 18, 1974), p.57:1.

Review of a concert held December 16th with music by Babbitt and Carter performed by the Group for Contemporary Music.   Among the pieces performed were Carter's *Pieces for Four Timpani*, and *String Quartet No. 2*.

C105.   ----------.   Métier of Modern Dance."   New York Times (May 18, 1988), III, p.17:1.

Review of performances of the Da Capo Chamber Players including the premiere of Carter's *Enchanted Preludes*.   The piece [seemed oddly earthbound, consisting of about six minutes of prosaic interplay between flute and cello."

C106.   ----------.   "Music: A Difficult Work."   New York Times (January 25, 1973), p.54:3.

Review of the premiere performance of Carter's *String Quartet No. 3* performed by the Juilliard Quartet on January 23.

C107.   ----------.   "Music: For Elliott Carter."   New York Times (November 1, 1974), p.26:1.

Review of a Composer's Showcase Series concert held on October 30th entitled "An Evening with Elliott Carter." Compositions performed included: *String Quartet No. 3*, *Sonata for Violoncello and Piano*, and *Double Concerto*.

C108.   ----------.   "New Music Series Dips into the Old, Too."   New York Times (January 24, 1972), p.22:1.

Review of a concert on January 23rd at Lincoln Center as part of the series "New and Newer Music." Among compositions performed include Carter's *Double Concerto* and the premiere of Carter's *Canon for 3* performed by Joel Timm, Allen Blustein, and James Stubb.

C109.   ----------. "What Does Today's Music Owe to This Quartet." New York
         Times (December 4, 1983), II, p.1:1.

         Discusses the effects Anton Webern, Edgard Varèse, Olivier Messiaen and
         Elliott Carter have had on other musicians.

C110.   ----------. "Why Must New York Wait for New Music?" New York Times
         (March 9, 1975), II, p.21:1.

         Exposes the delayed premiere performances of new music for New York
         audiences including Elliott Carter's *Piano Concerto*.

C111.   Henderson, Robert. "Elliott Carter." Music and Musicians v.14, no.5
         (January 1966), p.20-23.

         Henderson gives a very brief history of Carter's musical background and
         examines some of the more complex modulations of the *Piano Sonata, Cello
         Sonata*, and the *String Quartet No. 2*.

C112.   Heyworth, Peter. "Carter's Characters." The Observer (London) (June 8,
         1980), p.30:1.

         Review of various performances including the world premiere of Carter's
         Night Fantasies at the Bath Festival performed by Ursula Oppens. "Carter has
         a way of defying expectation: he never develops his ideas as one might
         anticipate. His musical thinking is wholly free of cliché and convention."

C113.   ----------. "Indian Summer." The Observer (London) (June 26, 1988), p.41:1.

         Review of various performances including the world premiere of Carter's
         Oboe Concerto performed by Heinz Holliger and the Collegium Musicum.
         "Not since his early populist days has Carter composed music of such telling
         directness."   .

C114.   "Institute of Arts Adds 13 Members." New York Times (February 7, 1956),
         p.38:4.

         Carter named as a member of the National Institute of Arts and Letters.

C115.   Jenny, Jack David. Part I. Elliott Carter: The Manipulation of Musical
         Time. Part II. Matrix: Structure for Orchestra [original composition].
         D.M.A. diss., Ohio State University, 1979.

         "Discusses the manipulation of musical time as put forth by Elliott Carter and
         how such manipulations affect our perception and our response to music. A
         detailed time graph of Carter's *String Quartet No. 3* is appended to the
         document." (DAI v.40, no.10, p.5242 A)

C116.   ----------. "A Prestigious German Award for Elliott Carter." Symphony
Magazine v.32, no.3 (June/July 1981), p.113-114.

Highlights Carter's orchestral achievements, particularly in Europe, in light of
his recent receipt of the prestigious Ernst von Siemens Musik-Pries on April
8, 1981.

C117.   Johnson, Lilla. The 'Kenner und Liebhaber' Fantasias of Carl Phillip
Emanuel Bach and Selected Fantasias of Wolfgang Amadeus Mozart: A
Comparative Study. II. Franz Liszt's Piano Style as Reflected in the 'B
Minor Sonata' and the Fantasia Quasi Sonata 'Après une Lecture du Dante'.
Rhythmic Techniques in Twentieth Century Music Including Those
Employed in the Piano Sonatas of Elliott Carter and Leon Kirchner.
D.Mus. diss., Northwestern University, 1973.

C118.   Johnston, Robert. "Elliott Carter's Imagery Drawn from Modern Life."
Music Magazine v.8, no.5 (November/December 1985), p.12-14, 33.

An interview with Elliott Carter focusing on contemporary composers and the
modern music audience and highlighting the musical education and early career
of Carter.

C119.   Jones, Allan Clive. "Elliott Carter and the Music of Change." Classical
Guitar v.3, no.3 (November 1984), p.23-25.

This brief article highlights the musical background and career of Elliott Carter
with particular attention to the treatment of the guitar in Carter's compositions,
primarily Changes.

C120.   Jones, Patricia. "Rutgers University: Elliott Carter Lectures." Current
Musicology v.20 (1975), p.9-10.

Jones' article is among eleven such reviews of conferences, lectures, seminars,
colloquiums, and performances generally entitled: Reports from the domestic
corresponding editors." Jones' article reviews Carter's recent series of
lectures at Rutgers University where Carter discussed his String Quartet No.3
to a seminar class in musical analysis under the direction of Robert Moevs.

C121.   Jones, Thomas W. An Analysis of Elliott Carter's String Quartet No.3. M.
Music Theory thesis, Northwestern University, 1979.

Carter's String Quartet No. 3 is examined with regard to form, rhythm,
instrumental writing, overall tension-relaxation profile and pitch organization.
Use is made of Elliott Carter's sketches and notes at the Library of Performing
Arts, Lincoln Center, to illustrate his methods of pitch selection. A
comparison of Carter's compositional methods is made to other twentieth
century composers. (See: A8)

C122.   Kastendieck, Miles.   "Carter, Schuman Works Receive World Premieres."
        Christian Science Monitor v.62, no.65 (February 11, 1970), I, p.6:2.
        Reprinted as: "N.Y. Philharmonic: Back to Back," In: American Musical
        Digest v.1, no.5 (1970), p.25.

        Review of the premiere of Carter's *Concerto for Orchestra* performed by the
        New York Philharmonic Orchestra. "The listener . . . waits vainly for the
        'poetry,' for he experiences only a keenly studied acoustical impressionism,
        somewhat meaningless as only intellectually conceived sound."

C123.   ----------.   "Greenhouse Near Top Rank."   New York Journal American
        (February 28, 1950), p.13:1.

        Review of a concert including the premiere of Carter's *Sonata for Violoncello
        and Piano* performed by Bernard Greenhouse and Anthony Makas. "It is
        neatly-fashioned, fresh-sounding music but somewhat austere even to the point
        of grimness. Strongly rhythmic and sometimes strange in its melodic contours
        the sonata balances intellectual concept with folkish touches. The audience
        indicated definite approval in its applause."

C124.   Keith, Nancy Alton.   A Comparative Analysis of the Fugue in the Twentieth-
        Century American Piano Sonata.   M.M. thesis, University of Cincinnati,
        1987.

        "A comparative, parametric analysis of three fugues within the twentieth-
        century American piano sonata, found in Samuel Barber's 'Piano Sonata' Op.
        26 (1949), Elliott Carter's *Piano Sonata* (1946), and Paul Hindemith's 'Third
        Piano Sonata' (1936). The objective is . . . to compare and contrast the
        composer's handling of the fugue procedure, and to examine each composer's
        fugue technique as it relates to and reflects his overall style." (MAI v.26,
        no.2, p.171)

C125.   Kenyon,   Nicholas.   "Concerts: Exhausting,   Stimulating   Mix:
        Sinfonietta/Knussen: St. Johns." The Times (London) (October 27, 1982),
        p.9:1.

        Review of the premiere of Carter's *In Sleep, In Thunder* performed by the
        London Sinfonietta and Martyn Hill. In this work "Carter can shift from
        passion to coolness, from violent activity to sudden repose, without the
        slightest suspicion of incoherence."

C126.   Kerman, Joseph.   "American Music: The Columbian Series." Hudson
        Review v.11, no.3 (Autumn 1958), p.420-430.

        An analysis of Carter's *String Quartet No. 1* with regard to speed. "Carter
        experiments in an area that has been neglected as a serious musical resource
        . . . he works with different speeds simultaneously and successively."
        Kerman then compares Carter's quartet with Rogers Sessions' Second Quartet.

"Sessions is as strained, unwieldy, thick, and 'unmusical' as Carter. The difference is that Carter is perfectly glad to have it at that, whereas Sessions is determined to transmute the notes into passion . . .

C127.   Kies, Christopher R. A Discussion of the Harmonic Organization in the First Movement of Elliott Carter's Sonata for Violoncello and Piano in Light of Certain Developments in 19th and Early 20th Century Music. Ph.D. diss., Brandeis University, 1984.

"Examine[s] the technical means and musical effects of the harmonic organization, operating in tandem with other musical aspects, of the first movement of Carter's Sonata for Violoncello and Piano (1948). The result of the investigation shows that, in many important respects, the origins of Carter's approach to composition can be found in works as early as those of the late 18th century. It is clear, furthermore, that Carter is the heir to certain traditions of harmonic organization, involving the use of unordered pitch-class collections, and developed specifically by composers such as Liszt, Debussy, Griffes and Scriabin since the breakdown of traditional tonality." (DAI v.47, no.2, p.342 A)

C128.   "Knusson [sic] and the BBCSO." Musical Opinion v.113, no.1345 (January 1990), p.23.

Review of a concert including the premiere of Carter's Three Occasions for Orchestra performed by Oliver Knussen and the BBC Symphony Orchestra. "Three Occasions demonstrates the range the composer has been able to achieve using his large repertoire of chords based on various intervals, allied to the complex patterns of metrical modulation he has built up during his long career."

C129.   Koegler, Horst. "Begegnungen mit Elliott Carter." Melos v.26 (September 1959), p.256-258.

(In German)

C130.   ----------. "Salzburg." Musical Courier v.157, no.7 (June 1958), p.14-15.

Outlines Carter's participation in the 55th session of the Salzburg Seminar in American Studies in which he gave lectures, led seminars and analyzed his own Piano Sonata and Sonata for Violoncello and Piano.

C131.   Kolodin, Irving. "Carter's Symphony; Beethoven by Maazel." Saturday Review v.4, no.13 (April 2, 1977), p.37-38.

A review of two concerts including the premiere performance of Carter's Symphony of Three Orchestras performed by the New York Philharmonic. Kolodin comments that the Symphony "is a work of stunning authority and imposing imagination."

C132.   ----------. "A New Quartet by Elliott Carter." Saturday Review of Education
          v.1, no.2 (March 1973), p.80.

          A review of the premiere of Carter's *String Quartet No. 3* performed by the
          Juilliard String Quartet.

C133.   Kondracki, Michal. "List z USA." Ruch Muzyczny v.12, no.15 (1968),
          p.17-18.

          (In Polish)

C134.   Kostelanetz, Richard. "The Astounding Success of Elliott Carter." High
          Fidelity v.18, no.5 (May 1968), p.41-45.

          Based on an interview with Carter, Kostelanetz discusses Carter's climb to
          musical acclaim. Glimpses of Carter's lifestyle and compositional beliefs are
          also given.

C135.   ----------. "Elliott Carter (1968)." In: On Innovative Music(ian)s. New
          York: Limelight Eds., 1989. p.85-93.

          Short biographies of many composers including Elliott Carter written as
          reflecting Kostelanetz's long career as a music critic.

C136.   ----------. "Elliott Carter: Effort and Excellence." In: Master Minds:
          Portraits of Contemporary American Artists and Intellectuals. New York:
          Macmillan, 1969. p.289-303.

          Details how Carter has "become one of the most innovative composers in the
          world today."

C137.   Kozinn, Allan. "Elliott Carter's *Changes*." Guitar Review n.57 (Spring
          1984), p.1-4.

          A detailed and in-depth examination of Carter's solo for guitar *Changes* which
          reveals the professional relationship between David Starobin and Elliott Carter.
          Highlighted in this article is Starobin's desire to commission a solo work for
          guitar and the revision process undertaken to produce *Changes*. Also included
          is a brief analysis of the composition.

C138.   ----------. "A Finale at Tanglewood for New-Music Festival." New York
          Times (August 14, 1988), p.60:5.

          Review of a concert including the premiere of Carter's *Remembrance*
          performed by John DiLutis and the Tanglewood Music Center Orchestra.
          "[T]he score is not so much mournful as meditative, but it has warmth and
          heart, elements typically veiled in Mr. Carter's music. It is also less frenetic

than many of the composer's scores, and its themes are stated simply and eloquently by a solo trombone, soulfully played by John DiLutis."

C139.   Kramer, Lawrence. "*Syringa*: John Ashbery and Elliott Carter." In: <u>Beyond Amazement: New Essays on John Ashbery</u>. Edited by David Lehman. Ithaca, NY: Cornell University Press, 1980. p.255-271.

An analysis of Carter's *Syringa* from a literary view. Numerous comparisons are made between Ashbery's poem and Carter's musical setting. Kramer comments that seldomly are "poems that faithfully mirror the intricacy of our inner lives" successfully set to music without losing these inner feelings.

C140.   Krebs, Albin. "Notes on People." <u>New York Times</u> (June 7, 1977), p.29:2.

Sir Georg Solti is asked by a Tokyo reporter if there is any political motive for substituting Elliott Carter's *Variations for Orchestra* for a Charles Ives piece in a Tokyo program of the Chicago Symphony Orchestra.

C141.   Kuchenmeister, Mary Jeanne. <u>Formal and Thematic Relationships in the First String Quartet of Elliott Carter</u>. M.M. thesis, University of Arizona, 1967.

C142.   Kujawsky, Eric. <u>Double-Perspective Movements: Formal Ambiguity and Conducting Issues in Orchestral Works by Schoenberg, Sibelius and Carter</u>. D.M.A. diss., Stanford University, 1985.

"[E]xamines double-perspective movements and the techniques of ambiguity they employ. The principal works discussed and compared are Schoenberg's Chamber Symphony op.9, Sibelius' Symphony No.7, and Carter's *Concerto for Orchestra*. Conducting problems arising from their dual natures are also examined." (DAI v.46, no.8, p.2123-2124 A)

C143.   Lang, Paul Henry. "Music: Juilliard String Quartet." <u>New York Herald Tribune</u> (March 26, 1960), p.8:5.

Review of a concert held March 25, 1960, and performed by the Juilliard String Quartet including the premiere of Carter's *String Quartet No. 2*.

C144.   Larrick, Geary. "*Eight Pieces for Timpani* by Elliott Carter: Analysis." <u>Percussionist</u> v.12, no.1 (Fall 1974), p.12-15.

Larrick discusses the performance employed in four pieces from Carter's composition: 'Recitative,' 'Improvisation,' 'Adagio,' and 'March.'

C145.   ----------. "Elliott Carter and His Timpani Pieces." <u>NACWPI Journal</u> v.36, no.2 (Winter 1987/1988), p.22-25.

In this short article, Larrick discusses metrical modulation in Carter's *Eight Pieces for Timpani*.

C146.   Lee, Jan. "Elliott Carter." Ruch Muzyczny v.28, no.5 (1984), p.22-23.

(In Polish)

C147.   Lees, Eugene. "Carter's *Variations* Fantastically Complex." Louisville Times
(April 23, 1956), I, p.9:2.

A short review of the premiere of Carter's *Variations for Orchestra* performed
by the Louisville Orchestra. Lees states that "chaotic moods come pell-mell
in this work. The music is fiery. Yet the fire lacks warmth. Carter seems
to say the modern man lacks soul."

C148.   Machlis, Joseph. "Elliott Carter (1908-)." In: Introduction to Contemporary
Music. 2nd ed. New York: W.W. Norton, 1980. p.588-596.

Included is short biography of Carter, a person whose "works are not of the
kind that achieve easy popularity. But their sureness of line, profundity of
thought and maturity of workmanship bespeak a musical intellect of the first
order." Machlis continues with a description of Carter's musical style
including an analysis of Carter's *Variations for Orchestra* and *String Quartet
No. 2.*

C149.   Mahder, William Carl. Elliott Carter's *String Quartet No. 1*: An Analysis of
the Adagio. M.M. thesis University of Michigan, 1973.

C150.   Mayer, Martin. "Elliott Carter: Out of the Desert and into the Concert Hall."
New York Times (December 10, 1978), II, p.21:4.

Reveals how the success of Carter's *String Quartet No. 1* provided him with
a national reputation.

C151.   McBean, Bruce Parker. Elliott Carter: *Variations for Orchestra*. M.M.
thesis, University of Michigan, 1963.

C152.   McCormick, Robert M. "*Eight Pieces for Four Timpani* by Elliott Carter:
Analysis." Percussionist v.12, no.1 (Fall 1974), p.7-11.

McCormick looks at Carter's composition with regard to performance
techniques. The movements: 'Canaries,' 'Moto Perpetuo,' and 'March' are
examined closely.

C153.   McElroy, William Wiley. Elliott Carter's *String Quartet No. 1*: A Study of
Heterogeneous Rhythmic Elements. M.M. thesis, Florida State University,
1973.

C154.   McInerney, John. "Paul Jacobs, Piano: Carter *Night Fantasies* (N.Y.
Premiere)." High Fidelity/Musical America v.32, no.3 (March 1982),
p.MA28.

Review of a Paul Jacobs' recital including the New York premiere of Carter's *Night Fantasies*. "Jacobs played this pianistic nightmare with vibrant, tensile strength coupled with great agility. The work sparkled under his fingers, revealing its evanescent qualities with grace."

C155.   McManus, James Michael. Rhetoric and Resistance in the Music of Elliott Carter. D.M.A. diss., University of Illinois at Urbana-Champaign, 1988.

"[I]nvestigate[s] links between surface and deep structures in Elliott Carter's 1980 piece for solo piano, *Night Fantasies*. A specific harmonic structure, comprised of 12-note all-interval chords, was described in detail. At the same time, the rhetoric of the music's surface was investigated, and the roles of fast and slow layers of music in effecting a background/foreground shift were discussed. Carter's ideas about serialism were reviewed in order to understand the composers own aesthetic in the application of abstract ordering systems." (DAI v.50, no.4, p.825 A)

C156.   Mead, Andrew. "Pitch Structure in Elliott Carter's *String Quartet No. 3*." Perspectives of New Music v.22 (Fall/Winter 1983 - Spring/Summer 1984), p.31-60.

Mead offers a "strategy for examining the pitch structure" of Carter's *String Quartet No. 3* using collection classes.

C157.   Meckna, Robert Michael. The Rise of the American Composer-Critic: Aaron Copland, Roger Sessions, Virgil Thomson, and Elliott Carter in the Periodical 'Modern Music', 1924-1946. Ph.D. diss., University of California, Santa Barbara, 1984.

"[E]xamines and assesses music criticism by Aaron Copland, Roger Sessions, Virgil Thomson, and Elliott Carter in the periodical Modern Music, 1924-1946. The most important contributors to a journal founded by the League of Composers as a literary outlet for ideas and opinions about contemporary music." (DAI v.45, no.9, p.2689 A)

C158.   Mellers, Wilfred. "The Pioneer's Energy and the Artist's Order: Elliott Carter." In: Music in a New Found Land: Themes and Developments in the History of American Music. London: Barrie and Rockliff, 1964. p.102-121. (This book has been republished by Alfred Knopf, 1965; Oxford University Press, 1987; and by Faber and Faber, 1987.)

Carter's music is described and analyzed as a compromise between Charles Ives' "desire to make anew the toughness, power, copiousness, triviality and grandeur of the American scene and the American spirit" and Aaron Copland's "attempt to reintegrate, in a kind of musical cubism, the disintegrated fragments of the present."

C159.   Moe, Orin. "The Music of Elliott Carter." College Music Symposium v.22, no.1 (Spring 1982), p.7-31.

Traces the impact of Carter's early vocal works on his later instrumental pieces, namely his *Variations for Orchestra, String Quartet No. 2* and *Double Concerto*. Particular attention is placed on: "lyricism," "a texture of differently and irregularly scanned lines," and "musical inspiration."

C160.   Moevs, Robert. "Elliott Carter: *String Quartets Nos. 2 and 3.*" Musical Quarterly v.61, no.1 (January 1975), p.157-168.

A detailed analysis of Carter's *String Quartet No. 3* upon the release of a Juilliard Quartet recording of Carter's quartets.

C161.   Molotsky, Irvin. "12 Are Named Winners of New U.S. Arts Medal." New York Times (April 18, 1985), III, p.17:2.

Carter, among others, are the first to receive National Medal of Arts Awards for their contribution to American culture.

C162.   Mootz, William. "[Title unknown]." Louisville Courier-Journal (April 1956).

Review of the premiere performance of Carter's *Variations for Orchestra* by the Louisville Orchestra. A full citation could not be found.

C163.   Morgan, Robert P. "Elliott Carter's String Quartets." Musical Newsletter v.4, no.3 (Summer 1974), p.3-11.

A review of Carter's *String Quartets Nos. 1, 2, and 3* upon release of the Juilliard recording of *Quartets 2 and 3*. (See: D116, D120) Morgan compares the similarities and differences in the three quartets and discusses the place of the quartets and their importance among Carter's other compositions. He briefly analyses *Quartet No. 3*.

C164.   Morrison, Richard. "Concert: EIC/Boulez: Albert Hall/Radio 3." The Times (London) (July 27, 1985), p.2:2, p.19:4.

Review of the premiere of Carter's *Penthode* performed by l'Ensemble InterContemporain.

C165.   ----------. "Master of Complexity." The Times (London) (March 8, 1990), p.20:2.

A profile of Carter's more recent and difficult music. The article is written in light of upcoming concerts.

C166.   ----------. "Spurring on the American Outlaw Instinct." The Times (London) (October 6, 1989), p.16:2.

Review of the premiere of Carter's *Anniversary* performed by the BBC Symphony Orchestra and originally written as part of his *Three Occasions for Orchestra*.

C167.   "Music Critics' Circle Votes to Cite Four New Works." New York Times (May 23, 1962), p.37:2.

Announcement of Carter's *Double Concerto* as being the recipient of the Music Critics' Circle Citation for 1961.

C168.   "Music to be Published: Society Selects Works of Carter and [Paul] Fetler for Current Session." New York Times (May 27, 1953).

Society for the Publication of American Music announces publication of Carter's *Sonata for Violoncello and Piano*.

C169.   Nelson, Jon Christopher. Compositional Technique in Elliott Carter's *Penthode*: A Study in Phraseology and Formal Design. Ph.D. diss., Brandeis University, 1991.

C170.   New Grove Twentieth-Century American Masters: Ives, Thomson, Sessions, Cowell, Gershwin, Copland, Carter, Barber, Cage, Bernstein. London: Macmillan, 1988, c1987.

A reprint of the article appearing in the New Grove Dictionary of Music and Musicians with minor corrections and a greatly updated section on Carter's newer works. Includes works from 1960 to 1986 with the latest composition mentioned being his *Oboe Concerto* which is listed as being "in progress."

C171.   "N.Y. Phil.: Carter Premiere." High Fidelity/Musical America v.27, no.6 (June 1977), p.MA32.

Review of Carter's *Symphony of Three Orchestras* being given its premiere performance by the New York Philharmonic. "The Symphony differs from recent works in that the anger and 'battle' seem to have given way to what could be termed an aerated serenity."

C172.   Northcott, Bayan. "Carter in Perspective." The Musical Times v.119, no.1630 (December 1978), p.1039-1041.

Compares Carter's musical style and tendencies to his contemporaries and predecessors thus creating a link of similarities and differences.

C173.   ----------. "Carter's 'Syringa'." no.128 Tempo (March 1979), p.31-32.

Review of the premiere performance by Jan DeGaetani and Thomas Paul. Northcott comments that the "work pursues as seamless and volatile a flow as anything in Carter's output . . . [yet flows] into passages of a quite breathtaking, pan-diatonic beauty."

C174.   ----------. "Elliott Carter." In: The New Grove Dictionary of Music and Musicians. v.3. Edited by Stanley Sadie. New York: Macmillan Press, 1980. p.831-836. Reprinted with minor additions and corrections In: The New Grove Dictionary of American Music. v.1. New York: Macmillan Press, 1986. p.364-372.

C175.   ----------. "Elliott Carter: Continuity and Coherence." Music and Musicians v.20, no.12 (August 1972), p.28-39.

A brief analysis of much of Carter's music with regard to many aspects of musical analysis including: rhythm, notation and harmony. Northcott compares Carter's music to that of other modern and non-modern composers by looking at influences from those composers. As a result, Carter's earlier music is most frequently cited.

C176.   ----------. "Elliott Carter at 80." The Musical Times v.129, no.1750 (December 1988), p.644-647.

Brief examination of Carter's musical output from 1978-1988. Northcott looks at Carter's changing tendencies and places each composition in its historical perspective.

C177.   Pappastavrou, George C. "Carter's *Piano Sonata* and *Night Fantasies*." American Music Teacher v.38, no.2 (November/December 1988), p.18-19.

Review, short analysis and comparison of Carter's two piano solo works.

C178.   Perkins, Francis D. "Sykes Recital: Pianist Gives Carter Sonata First Concert Performance." New York Herald Tribune (March 6, 1947), p.21:6.

Review of a concert held on March 5, 1947 and performed by James Sykes including the premiere of Carter's *Piano Sonata*.

C179.   Peyser, Joan. "Acclaim for a Musical Loner." New York Times (March 2, 1969), II, p.21:1.

An interview with Carter in which he talks about the musician's role in performing modern music, the lack of adequate newspaper coverage of musical events in New York, the problem of orchestras giving commissions when they have never performed the composer's older music, and European composers' refusal to take American composers seriously.

C180.   Pflugradt, William Charles. Elliott Carter and the Variation Process. Ph.D. diss., Indiana University, 1984.

An examination of Carter's variation techniques used in the final portion of *The Minotaur*, the variation movements of the *String Quartet No. 1* and the *Variations for Orchestra*.

C181.   "'*Pocahontas*' Suite Wins Competition." New York Times (June 4, 1940), p.19:3.

Announcement of a suite from the ballet *Pocahontas* winning Juilliard School's annual competition for the best publication of orchestral works by American composers. The article also mentions Carter's work, *To Music*, winning the 1938 Choral contest by the WPA Federal Music Project.

C182.   Pollack, Howard. Harvard Composers: Essays on Walter Piston and His Students from Elliott Carter to Frederic Rzewski. Metuchen, NJ: Scarecrow Press, 1992.

C183.   Polling, Kees. "Elliott Carter in Gesprek met Kees Polling: Strijdvaardig Componist op Sleutelpositie Tussen Verenigde Staten en West-Europa." Mens en Melodie v.43 (January 1988), p.25-30.

A look at American composer, Elliott Carter, and his increasing popularity in Europe. (In Dutch)

C184.   Porter, Andrew. "Boris Redivivus." New Yorker v.50, no.5 (December 30, 1974), p.55.

A review of the premiere of Carter's *Brass Quintet* performed by the American Brass Quintet in which Porter states: "The score appears to spring from fruitful interaction between what brass instruments do best and the composer's own more 'abstract' concerns with multilayered music."

C185.   ----------. "Discourse Most Eloquent." New Yorker v.62, no.10 (April 28, 1986), p.96-99.

Review of recent performances including the New York premiere of Carter's *Penthode* by l'Ensemble InterContemporain. "Amid so much glitter and twitter, trillings and chirrupings, '*Penthode*' made an almost sober effect. . . . Its energy of thought was apparent at once. Repeated hearings reveal its elegance, lightness, and charm. The Ensemble performances were masterly."

C186.   ----------. "Duo." New Yorker v.51, no.7 (April 7, 1975), p.129-130.

Review of the premiere of Carter's *Duo for Violin and Piano* performed by Paul Zukofsky and Gilbert Kalish. [T]he Duo springs from contemplation of a fundamental contrast in the sound-producing methods of the violin and of the piano."

C187.   ----------. "Famous Orpheus." New Yorker (January 8, 1979), p.56-58, 61-
         63.

         Porter's critique of the *Syringa* premiere performed by Jan DeGaetani, Thomas
         Paul, Scott Kerney and the Speculum Musicae. He describes the piece as
         being "musically eloquent independent of its texts, the patterns of line, gesture,
         and timbre . . . made sense." Porter also analyses the Greek and English
         texts.

C188.   ----------. "Great Bridge, Our Myth." New Yorker v.53, no.3 (March 7,
         1977), p.101-104.

         Review of the premiere performance of Carter's *A Symphony of Three
         Orchestras* by the New York Philharmonic Orchestra. "We can praise [the
         Symphony] for its visionary aspiration. We can praise it for its refined, very
         delicate, and subtle workmanship. [W]e can praise the expressive quality of
         the melodies and of the instrumental colors."

C189.   ----------. "Mutual Ordering." New Yorker v.48, no.50 (February 3, 1973),
         p.82, 84-87.

         A review of Carter's *String Quartets Nos. 1, 2 and 3* upon the premiere
         performance of the third quartet by the Juilliard Quartet.

C190.   ----------. "Preludes to Felicity." New Yorker v.64, no.17 (June 13, 1988),
         p.92-95.

         Review of the premiere performance of Carter's *Enchanted Preludes*
         performed by the Da Capo Players. Carter, while introducing the piece said
         "he had tried to mirror some of Ann Santen's brightness, charm and
         irresistible enthusiasm."

C191.   ----------. "Quaternion." New Yorker v.62, no.40 (November 24, 1986),
         p.114, 116, 118, 120-121.

         Review of Carter's *String Quartet No. 4* performed by the Composers Quartet.
         "The movements are played without breaks, and they are articulated by
         chordal passages in which one can hear the building of the harmonies -- the
         pressure of note against note against note -- far more clearly than in the swift-
         moving textures that Carter has generally favored. This is one of the new
         things in the quartet: the dwelling on expressive intervals."

C192.   ----------. "Reflections." New Yorker v.52, no.3 (March 8, 1976), p.122,
         125-126.

         Review of the premiere of Carter's *A Mirror on Which to Dwell* performed by
         Susan Davenny Wyner and the Speculum Musicae.

C193.   ----------. "Riches in Little Room." New Yorker v.60, no.45 (December 24, 1984), p.62, 64-65.

Reviews of recent Carter performances and upcoming broadcasts including the American premiere of *Riconoscenza* by Eugene Drucker and *Canon for 4* by Paula Robison, Virgil Blackwell, Philip Setzer, and David Finckel. "*Riconoscenza*, a large adventure in small space, is concerned with seeing things in different and varied lights and looking back on what we've just experienced. "*Canon for 4* is at once musically denser and more readily charming. The charm derives in part from the play of instrumental timbres . . . and in part from the pleasures . . . of audible contrapuntal play."

C194.   ----------. "Songs with a Mind." New Yorker v.59, no.46 (January 2, 1984), p.84-86.

Review of the world premiere of *Changes* by David Starobin, the American Premiere of *In Sleep, In Thunder* by Jon Garrison and the Speculum Musicae, and a performance of *Triple Duo*.

C195.   ----------. "Tanglewood." New Yorker v.64, no.31 (September 19, 1988), p.92-95.

Review of a Tanglewood Music Center Orchestra concert including the premiere of Carter's *Remembrance* by John DiLutis. "The solemn, noble tones of the instrument (the trombone) are stirring. It is a born orator. Its utterance in *Remembrance* is neither pompous nor sentimental but thoughtful, ardent, and gravely impassioned."

C196.   ----------. "Thought-Executing Fires." New Yorker v.59, no.12 (May 9, 1983), p.114-118.

Carter's premiere of *Triple Duo* commissioned by BBC for the Fires of London, is compared and contrasted with Peter Maxwell Davies' Image, Reflection, Shadow. This "marks Carter's return to a pure instrumental ensemble."

C197.   Princeton Policy on Coeds Studied: Women Cannot be Ignored, Cohen Tells Graduates." New York Times (June 14, 1967), p.36:6.

Carter is awarded an honorary degree at the Princeton University commencement.

C198.   Probasco, Robert C.   A Study of Some Performance Problems in Contemporary Music: An Oboist's View of Berio, Carter and Stockhausen. M.A. thesis, University of Nebraska, 1968.

The technical difficulties of the performer are analyzed and discussed by examining six compositions by three composers including Carter's *Eight*

Etudes and a Fantasy and *Sonata for Flute, Oboe, Violoncello and Piano.*

C199.   Read, Gardner. "Some Problems of Rhythmic Notation." Journal of Music
Theory v.9, no.1 (Spring 1965), p.153-162.

Written in reply to Carter's "Letter to the Editor" (See: B73), Read agrees to
the need for standardization of musical notation suggested by Carter but
disagrees with his standard. Read suggests the use of Paul Hindemith's book
Elementary Training for Musicians (NY: Associated Music Publishers, 1949).

C200.   Reinhold, Robert. "Tradition Falls at Harvard [as] Women Join Men at
Graduation [Rites]." New York Times (June 12, 1970), p.24:3.

Carter is awarded an honorary degree at the Harvard graduation, the first such
graduation exercises with men and women combined. The write up is full of
incidences of public display.

C201.   Restagno, Enzo. Carter. Torino: EDT/Musica, 1989. Biography/interview
reprinted as: "Elliott Carter in Conversation with Enzo Restagno for
Settembre Musica, 1989." (See: B10)

A translation into Italian of 33 of Carter's writings. A 79 page
biography/interview is also included as well as a works list and a discography.

C202.   Rockwell, John. "American Intellectual Composers & the 'Ideal Public';
Elliott Carter." In: All American Music: Composition in the Late
Twentieth Century. New York: Alfred A. Knopf, 1983. p.37-46.

A review of Carter's musical career since 1951.

C203.   Rogers, Harold. "New Carter Concerto in Debut." Christian Science Monitor
v.69, no.3 (January 7, 1967), p.94.

Review of the premiere performance of Carter's *Piano Concerto* by Jacob
Lateiner and the Boston Symphony Orchestra. "Throughout its two
movements . . . one is impressed by the logic and order of Carter's mind,
even though the logic pursue a path trod and appreciated by only a few."

C204.   Rorem, Ned. "Messiaen and Carter on Their Birthdays." Tempo no.127
(December 1978), p.22-24. Reprinted as: "Messiaen and Carter at 70,"
In: The Listener v.100, no.2590 (December 14, 1978), p.806-807.

A tribute to Carter and Oliver Messiaen on their birthdays. Rorem compares
the two "modern masters" by contrasting their musical styles and training.

C205.   ----------. "Ned Rorem on Music: Elliott Carter." The New Republic v.166,
no.9 (February 26, 1972), p.22, 32. Reprinted In: Pure Contraption: A

Composer's Essays. By Ned Rorem. New York: Holt, Rinehart & Winston, 1974. p.23-26.

A review of Allen Edward's book-length interview with Carter entitled Flawed Words and Stubborn Sounds (See: B134). Rorem considers the book "pompous" and not an adequate reflection of Carter's importance.

C206.   Rosen, Charles. The Musical Languages of Elliott Carter. Washington, D.C.: Music Division, Research Services, Library of Congress, 1984.

Compiled by the Library of Congress in honor of Carter's 70th and 75th birthdays. Included is a lecture entitled "The Musical Languages of Elliott Carter," given by Charles Rosen at a performance of Carter's *Piano Sonata*. Rosen provides a detailed analysis of Carter's use of harmony and rhythm in his *Piano Sonata* to explain Carter's general compositional style. Also included is a reprint of Rosen's article "One Easy Piece." (See: C207) Rosen has also included "An Interview with Carter" in which Rosen and Carter discuss Carter's method of exploiting the character of each instrument in a composition, and "A Guide to Elliott Carter Research Materials at the Library of Congress Music Division" by Morgan Cundiff (See: C42, A6). Also included is a chronological list of works which includes only title and date, a comprehensive catalog of Elliott Carter materials at the Special Collections at the Library of Congress Music Division and a list of Library of Congress performances of Carter's works and a bibliography.

C207.   ----------. "One Easy Piece." New York Review of Books v.20, no.2 (February 22, 1973), p.25-29. Reprinted In: Composer (London) no.69 (Spring 1980), p.1-8. Reprinted as: "Un Morceau Facile: Le *Double Concerto* d'Elliott Carter," Translated by Will Pierre-Étienne, In: Critique no.408 (May 1981), p.496-505. Reprinted In: The Musical Languages of Elliott Carter. Washington, D.C.: Music Division, Library of Congress, 1984. p.21-31. (See: C206)

Charles Rosen, who has participated in most of the performances of Carter's *Double Concerto*, gives a personal review of Carter's "most brilliantly attractive and apparently most complex work."

C208.   Rothstein, Edward. "MacDowell Medal to Elliott Carter." New York Times (August 22, 1983), III, p.15:1.

Carter wins the Edward MacDowell medal for lifetime of achievement in music.

C209.   ----------. "Music: A Tribute to Elliott Carter, 75." New York Times (December 14, 1983), III, p.32:1.

A review of the American premiere of Carter's *In Sleep, In Thunder* performed by Jon Garrison and the Speculum Musicae. "Carter's music managed to celebrate the creation of art out of loss and pain, without becoming indulgent or nostalgic or obvious." The premiere of Carter's *Changes* by David Starobin also took place. "A virtuosic celebration of musical energy and transformation."

C210.   ----------. "Poetry and Music." New York Times (June 12, 1983), VII, p.51:1.

An essay showing Carter's use of literary texts as a poetic style to create his music.

C211.   ----------. "The Twilight Fantasies of Elliott Carter." The New Republic v.199, no.26 (December 26, 1988), p.23-28.

A glimpse of Carter's aspiring musical career and an analysis of his musical techniques and practices.

C212.   Ruby, Bjarne. "Ny Musik fra USA of Danmark Elliott Carter Hovedperson ved Musiknytår 1982." Cras Tidsskrift fur Kunst of Kulture v.29 (1981), p.91-94.

(In Danish)

C213.   Saez, Richard. "To Regain Wholeness: The Many and the One in Elliott Carter's Songs." Parnassus v.10, no.2 (Fall/Winter 1982), p.289-329.

Saez examines Carter's approach to songs by analyzing the structural integrity and psychological impetus of *A Mirror on Which to Dwell* and *Syringa*.

C214.   Salzman, Eric. "Music: Three Distinguished Works." New York Times (September 7, 1961), p.41:5.

Review of a concert on September 6, 1961, at the Metropolitan Museum of Art in New York. The concert was presented by the Fromm Foundation in conjunction with the Eighth Congress of the International Society of Musicology. Of the pieces performed was the premiere of Carter's *Double Concerto* by Ralph Kirkpatrick and Charles Rosen.

C215.   ----------. "Records Choice: Carter's *String Quartet No. 2* Earns Citation from New York Critics." New York Times (May 7, 1961), II, p.19:2.

Review of Carter's *String Quartet No. 2* upon the release of an RCA Victor recording. (See: D114)

C216.   ----------. "Unity in Variety: Elliott Carter Talks about His Aims in Writing Another String Quartet." New York Times (March 20, 1960), II, p.9:9.

Carter, having just completed his *String Quartet No. 2*, discusses the problems in writing music which is not only 'difficult' to listen to and to play, but also to write.

C216a.   Schiff, David. "Carter in the Seventies." Tempo no.130 (September 1979), p.2-10.

An examination of Carter's musical works of the 1970's. Schiff portrays this period as being "so adventurous in conception that there is little in the way of traditional musical terminology that can be used to describe their forms, harmonies, or even, as in the case of the most recent work, *Syringa*, their genre." Works discussed include: *A Symphony of Three Orchestras, Syringa*, and *A Mirror on Which to Dwell*.

C217.   Schiff, David. "Carter's New Classicism." College Music Symposium v.29 (1989), p.115-122.

Schiff examines Carter's *Oboe Concerto, Triple Duo, Penthode*, and *String Quartet No. 4* in light of Roland Barthes' book S/Z and Barthes' definition of the modern text and the classic text.

C218.   ----------. "Carter's *Violin Concerto*." Tempo no.174 (September 1990), p.22-24.

Review of the premiere performance of Carter's *Violin Concerto* performed by Ole Böhn and the San Francisco Symphony. "Mr. Böhn's pure tone and faultless intonation served the piece well - and expressively complex, dramatic in its outlines and yet reticent and spare in its details, as if a more continuous and articulated background had been erased, leaving only the most essential events."

C219.   ----------. "Elliott Carter: *A Mirror on Which to Dwell*." New York Arts Journal v.2 no.1 (September 1977), p.41-43.

A glimpse at the literary characteristics of Carter's *A Mirror on Which to Dwell*.

C220.   ----------. "Elliott Carter: America's Much-Honored Composer is Still Challenging Music at Age 75." Ovation (December 1983), p.12-14, 50-52.

In light of a year long celebration of Carter's 75th birthday, numerous performances of Carter's works are planned. This article offers an introduction to Elliott Carter and his music.

C221.   ----------. "Elliott Carter's *Harvest Home*." Tempo no.167 (December 1988), p.2-13.

A discussion and analysis of Carter's newer music with regard to harmony and structural rhythm. The author says this "serves as an essential up-date" to his book The Music of Elliott Carter. (See: C224)

C222.   ----------. "*In Sleep, In Thunder*': Elliott Carter's Portrait of Robert Lowell." Tempo no.142 (September 1982), p.2-9.

A discussion of Carter's work focusing on the selection and treatment of the text from six poems of Robert Lowell. Schiff also provides harmonic analysis of the composition which he says "constitute neither system nor general method . . . and [his harmonic procedures] are inseparable from the expressive and musical needs of the works in which they appear."

C223.   ----------. "Letters to the Editor." Tempo no.147 (December 1983), p.45.

Schiff replies to an article by David Harvey in which he corrects Harvey on the usefulness of using the concept of "tonic register positions of intervals" in Carter's *A Symphony of Three Orchestras*. (See: C98)

C224.   ----------. The Music of Elliott Carter. London: Eulenburg Books, 1983; New York: Da Capo Press, 1983. Reprinted in Italian with revisions by Edizioni Scientifichè Italiane, 1989. (I could not verify this translated publication.)

Schiff, a student of Carter at the Juilliard School, has written here the only book length analysis of Carter's music. Though there is only one short chapter labeled as a biography, biographical information is interspersed throughout the entire book. Basically chronological in nature, the book analyzes Carter's musical tendencies including metric modulation. The work also includes a chronological catalog of works and a lengthy bibliography and short discography.

C225.   ----------. "A Tribute to E.C." Newsletter (Institute for Studies in American Music v.17, no.2 (May 1988), p.1-2.

A celebration of Carter's 80th birthday; retrospective of Carter's musical accomplishments and a defense of Carter against music critics.

C226.   Schonberg, Harold C. "Carter, Cage, Reich . . . Speak to Me." New York Times (February 4, 1973), II, p.15:1.

Review of recent premiere performances including Carter's *String Quartet No. 3* performed January 23, 1973, by the Juilliard Quartet. Other premieres reviewed include P.M. Davies' Vesalii Icones, J. Cage's Cheap Imitation, and S. Reich's Four Organs.

C227.   ----------. "Carter Composition in World Premiere." New York Times (February 27, 1953).

Review of the premiere of Carter's *String Quartet No. 1* performed by the Walden Quartet. It "is a serious, complex, difficult, advanced and uncompromising. . . . [T]hese attributes are wrapped in a heavy overcoat of dissonance. The quartet owns a tight, intense feeling and also has some unconventional departures.

C228.   ----------. "Music: Bernstein Leads Carter Work." New York Times (February 6, 1970), p.27:1. Reprinted In: American Musical Digest v.1, no.5 (1970), p.26.

Review of the premiere on February 5, 1970, of Carter's *Concerto for Orchestra* commissioned by the New York Philharmonic for its 125th anniversary but the work was not completed until 1970.

C229.   ----------. "Music: Carter's Tomorrow Concerto." New York Times (January 7, 1967), p.21:1.

Review of the premiere of Carter's *Piano Concerto*. The concerto was performed on January 6, 1967, by Jacob Lateiner and the Boston Symphony. (See: D77)

C230.   ----------. "Music: Elliott Carter." New York Times (February 18, 1977), III, p.11:1.

Review of a concert including the premiere of Carter's *A Symphony of Three Orchestras* performed by the New York Philharmonic. "Mr. Carter never has made concessions, to his listeners. The dissonances are Ivesian, with everything coming together toward the end in smashing volleys of shrieking sound. It will take many hearings for the relationships of the score to assert themselves.

C231.   Schweitzer, Eugene William. Generation in String Quartets of Carter, Sessions, Kirchner, and Schuller: A Concept of Forward Thrust and Its Relationship to Structure in Aurally Complex Styles. Ph.D. diss., University of Rochester, Eastman School of Music, 1966.

"The purpose was to formulate through the study of contemporary works representing unusual difficulty of aural comprehension an approach to analysis of the elements contributing to a sense of purposeful forward thrust. This line of moving force was called the 'continuum of purpose,' and the process of contributing to its existence was designated 'generation.'"

C232.   Sevice, Alfred Roy Jr. A Study of the Cadence as a Factor in Musical Intelligibility in Selected Piano Sonatas by American Composers. Ph.D. diss., State University of Iowa, 1958.

A study of the cadence as used by American composers within their piano sonatas. Nineteen pages are devoted to Carter's use of the cadence in his

Piano Sonata.

C233.   Shawe-Taylor, Desmond.   "Desmond Shawe-Taylor at Covent Garden and
        Bath."   The Sunday Times (London) (June 8, 1980), p.37:4.

        Review of various performances at Covent Garden and at the Bath Festival.
        Included was the world premiere of Carter's *Night Fantasies* by Ursula
        Oppens.   "In this impressive piece, Carter seems to me to have regained the
        sense of flow and direction that I failed to recognize in his over complex
        Syringa."

C234.   ----------.   "A New Voice."   New Statesman and Nation v.50, no.1290
        (November 26, 1955), p.702-703.

        Review of Carter's *String Quartet No. 1* upon its performance by the Juilliard
        String Quartet.   "That only an intellectual type of composer could have
        conceived and carried through the vast structured plan of this quartet is
        undeniably true, and it is also true . . . that a powerful intellectual ferment
        seethes throughout the long work."

C235.   Shelness, Felicity A.   Composition: Piano Quartet. Analysis: *String Quartet
        No. 3* by Elliott Carter.   M.M. thesis, University of California at Davis,
        1978.

C236.   Shinn, Randall Alan.   An Analysis of Elliott Carter's *Sonata for Flute, Oboe,
        Cello, and Harpsichord* (1952).   D.M.A. diss., University of Illinois at
        Urbana-Champaign, 1975.

        Carter's sonata is analyzed as one of his "'middle period' works [in which] an
        interesting blend of tradition and innovation can be discovered."

C237.   "Sketches of the Pulitzer Prize Winners for 1960 in Letters, Music and
        Journalism: Elliott Carter."   New York Times (May 3, 1960), p.34:3.

        A short biographical sketch in honor of Carter winning a Pulitzer Prize in
        Music for his *String Quartet No. 2.*

C238.   "Sketches of the Winners of the 57th Pulitzer Prizes in Journalism and the
        Arts: Elliott C. Carter."   New York Times (May 8, 1973), p.32:1.

        Biographical sketch of Carter honoring him for receiving a pulitzer Prize for
        his *String Quartet No. 3.*

C239.   Skulsky, Abraham.   "Elliott Carter."   ACA Bulletin v.3, no.2 (Summer 1953),
        p.2-16.

        A review of Carter's early works showing his musical development.   The
        article also includes a list of works and gives quotes from reviews.

C240.   Small, Rosemary.   Elliott Carter's _'Eight Pieces for Four Timpani'_: Descriptive and Interpretative Analysis.   D.M.A. diss., University of Hartford, 1987.

C241.   Smith, Cecil. "Sights and Sounds of Spring." Theatre Arts v.31, no.6 (June 1947), p.34-36.

Review of recent ballets including Carter's _The Minotaur_ performed by the Ballet Society. "At first sight its visual aspects failed to measure up to Elliott Carter's well-composed music which has some of the rhythmic élan of Stravinsky and some of the constructional solidatity of Hindemith without really sounding like either."

C242.   Smith, Patrick J.   "N.Y.   Philharmonic: Carter Premiere."   High Fidelity/Musical America v.20, no.5 (May 1970), p.MA21, 24.

Review of the premiere of Carter's _Concerto for Orchestra_ performed by the New York Philharmonic. The "emphasis on clarity and rhythm, added to the already tough problems of metrical modulation through subdivision of beats, makes Carter's music a very high orchestral hurdle. The Philharmonic took the jump with the class of a top performance."

C243.   Sneerson, Grigorij.   "Elliott Carter."   In: Poetry Amerikanskikh Kompozitorov. Moskva: Muzyka, 1977. p.135-150.

One of nine biographical portraits including a discussion of Carter's music and its place in contemporary music history. (In Polish)

C244.   Soskin, Eileen.   Cadences and Formal Structure in Four American String Quartets: Elliott Carter: _String Quartet No. 3_; Andrew Imbrie: Fourth String Quartet; Fred Lerdahl: First String Quartet; Seymour Shifrin: Fifth String Quartet. Ph.D. diss., University of California, Berkeley, 1986.

"A cadence is that moment when a piece of music comes to rest, temporary or permanently, in contrast to the overall level of activity of the piece. Cadences are traditionally created by harmonic, rhythmic, melodic, dynamic and textural contrasts." (DAI v.48, no.5, p.1052 A)

C245.   "Speculum Musicae: Carter Prem." High Fidelity/Musical America v.26, no.6 (June 1976), p.MA27.

Review of the Speculum Musicae premiere performance of Carter's _A Mirror on Which to Dwell_. "Always a perfectionist in her wide repertory, Susan Davenny Wyner was in opulent voice and her interpretations displayed full measures of both foresight and spontaneity."

C246.   Stein, Don Allan. The Function of Pitch in Elliott Carter's *String Quartet No.*
         1 (Essay). [with] Lachrimae [original composition].   Ph.D. diss.,
         Washington University, 1981.

         "[E]xamines the role of pitch as a principal unifying factor in Carter's *String*
         Quartet No. 1." (DAI v.42, no.4, p.1371 A)

C247.   Steinberg, Michael. "Celebrating the Music of Elliott Carter." Symphony
         Magazine (January/February 1989), p.24-27, 98-100.

         A review of Carter's musical accomplishments in honor of his 80th birthday.

C248.   ----------. "Elliott Carter: An American Original at 70." Keynote v.2, no.10
         (December 1978), p.8-14.

         In light of Carter's 70th birthday and a series of broadcasts of Carter's works
         on WNCN Radio in honor of the occasion, this article highlights Carter's early
         musical development and career.

C249.   ----------. "Elliott Carter's *Second String Quartet.*" The Score and I.M.A.
         Magazine no.27 (July 1960), p.22-26. Reprinted as: "Elliott Carters 2.
         Streichquartett," In: Melos v.28, no.2 (1961), p.35-37.

         A review and general analysis of Carter's quartet upon its premiere
         performance on March 25, 1960, by the Juilliard String Quartet.

C250.   Stewart, Robert.   "Serial Aspects of Elliott Carter's *Variations for*
         Orchestra." Music Review v.34, no.1 (February 1973), p.62-65.

         Stewart shows that Carter's "limited use of serial technique [in his *Variations*
         for Orchestra] is evident and demonstrable." Even though Carter has said that
         "serialism plays no part whatsoever in his work."

C251.   Stone, Kurt. "Current Chronicle: New York." Musical Quarterly v.55, no.4
         (October 1969), p.559-572.

         A discussion of Carter's *Piano Concerto* including a review of the music and
         the recording made from tapes of the premiere performance by Jacob Lateiner
         and the Boston Symphony Orchestra.   (See: D77)   This discussion
         accompanies a general "recognition of the sixtieth
         birthday of its composer" by looking at Carter's *String Quartets Nos. 1 and*
         2 and his *Double Concerto.*

C252.   ----------. "Problems and Methods of Notation." Perspectives of New music
         v.1, no.2 (Spring 1963), p.9-31.

         Stone examines current (1963) trends in notating modern music. Though the
         article is not specific to Carter, Stone uses many examples of Carter's musical

notation while discussing tempo (*Variations for Orchestra*), rhythm (*String Quartet No. 2*), and meter (*Double Concerto*).

C253.   Straus, Noel. "New Carter Work Played by Sykes." <u>New</u> <u>York</u> <u>Times</u> (March 6, 1947), p.36:6.

Review of the premiere concert performance of Carter's *Piano Sonata* by James Sykes. "[T]hough earnestly presented, [Carter's Sonata] had little color or emotional life and was not free of blemished passages, nor without slips of memory."

C254.   "The Symphony: Is It Alive? Or Just Embalmed?" <u>New</u> <u>York</u> <u>Times</u> (September 22, 1968), II, p.25:1.

Excerpts from a symposium broadcast by the Eastern Educational Network and heard in New York on WRVR-FM. Lukas Foss, Elliott Carter and Leon Kirchner were panelists. Paul Hume was moderator. Carter states, "unless the situation changes very drastically, not only will there be no future for new music on the symphony orchestra world, but the symphony orchestra would itself die." (See: B42) for Carter's editorial concerning this article.

C255.   Swed, Mark. "The Difficulties and Rewards of Being Difficult." <u>New</u> <u>York</u> <u>Times</u> (November 27, 1988), II, p.27:1.

Written to detail some of the highlight performances celebrating Carter's 80th birthday; includes Carter's experiences and beliefs in writing for opera.

C256.   Taubman, Howard. "Music: Work by Carter." <u>New</u> <u>York</u> <u>Times</u> (March 26, 1960), p.14:1.

Review of the premiere performance on March 25, 1960, of Carter's *String Quartet No. 2* by the Juilliard String Quartet at the Juilliard School.

C257.   ----------. "Quartet with Art and Style." <u>New</u> <u>York</u> <u>Times</u> (April 3, 1960), II, p.9:1.

Taubman's article written after the premiere of Carter's *String Quartet No. 2*, performed by the Juilliard String Quartet, reviews both of Carter's String Quartets to date and reveals that with the appearance of the second quartet "[t]here is no doubt that this American is one of the outstanding composers of our time. He has forged this impressive position for himself through the shyest and most penetrating of forms -- chamber music."

C258.   Terry, Walter. "Ballet Society Produces Works by 3 Young Choreorgraphers [sic]." <u>New</u> <u>York</u> <u>Herald</u> <u>Tribune</u> (April 6, 1947), IV, p.2:1.

Review of three productions by the Ballet Society including the Highland Fling, the Zodiac and *The Minotaur*. "'The Minotaur' is one of the most beautiful productions I have ever seen. . . . The music . . . had the brightness and glow necessary to the dance plan but not . . . [the] necessary suggestion of the archaic, of the mysterious. . . . [The] choreography . . . was, unfortunately, far less interesting than the set and costumes. . . . [T]he ballet as a whole . . . seemed static and naive."

C259. Thomson, Virgil. "Music: Centenary Novelties." New York Herald Tribune (February 27, 1945), p.14:6.

Review of the centenary concert held February 25, 1945, and performed by Temple Emanu-El. Among the pieces performed includes Carter's *The Harmony of Morning* which was written for the concert.

C260. ----------. "Music: Contemporary Music: A Powerful Work." New York Herald Tribune (May 5, 1953), p.21:1.

Review of a concert held on May 4, 1953, performed by the Walden Quartet. Thomson mistakenly identifies the Walden Quartet as premiering *String Quartet No. 1.*

C261. ----------. "Music: Harpsichord Quartet: Serious and Lovely." New York Herald Tribune (November 11, 1953), p.19:5.

Review of a concert performed by the Harpsichord Quartet on November 10, 1953, including the premiere of Carter's *Sonata for Flute, Oboe, Violoncello and Harpsichord.*

C262. ----------. "Music: Masterpiece Revived." New York Herald Tribune (February 28, 1949), p.11:1.

Review of a concert on February 27, 1949, sponsored by the National Association for American Composers and Conductors. A brief review of the premiere of Carter's *Woodwind Quintet* performed by Martin Orenstein, David Abosch, Louis Paul, Pinson Bobo, and Mark Popkin is included.

C263. Time is Music. Directed by Frank Scheffer.

A film about Carter by the Dutch director. Carter first viewed the film in 1990.

C264. Tingley, George Peter. "Metric Modulation and Elliott Carter's *First String Quartet.*" Indiana Theory Review v.4, no.3 (Spring 1981), p.3-11.

Through the use of musical examples from Carter's *String Quartet No. 1,* Tingley discusses Carter's metric modulation.

C265. Trimble, Lester. "Elliott Carter." Stereo Review v.29, no.6 (December 1972), p.64-72.

An examination of how Carter has become "something of an admired mystery," and has come to be "at the very peak of the pyramid of creative excellence." Trimble discusses how Carter has created "a musical style, a technology, a language so entirely his own without either losing touch with the mainstream of contemporary expression or being drawn into some 'school' to which he would be just one more contributor."

C266.   "Two Arts Groups Make 24 Awards." New York Times (May 24, 1956), p.25:1.

Carter named as a member of the National Institute of Arts and Letters.

C267.   "2 Composers and Pianist Added to Naumburg Board." New York Times (March 3, 1965), p.34:3.

Announcement of Elliott Carter, among two others, of election to the Walter W. Naumburg Foundation Board.

C268.   UnRau, Mary Anne. Contemporary and Traditional Influences in the Elliott Carter Piano Concerto. M.M. thesis, University of Western Ontario, 1973.

C269.   Vamos, Roland V. An Analysis and Comparison of Elliott Carter's Three String Quartets. Ph.D. diss., Juilliard School, 1975.

C270.   Vars, Diane. Rhythmic Structure in Elliott Carter's String Quartet No. 1. M.M. thesis, Indiana University, 1973.

C271.   Walsh, Stephen. "Disagreeable Stimulus." The Listener v.94 (September 4, 1975), p.312-313.

A comparison and contrast between Carter's Concerto for Orchestra and Debussy's Jeux upon their performances in a week of Albert Hall proms. Carter's work is being performed by the New York Philharmonic under direction of Boulez.

C272.   Weber, J.F. Carter and Schumann. (Discography series; v.19). Utica, NY: The Author, 1978. p.1-10. Revised and expanded version reprinted as: "An Elliott Carter Discography," In: Association for Recorded Sound Collections Journal v.8, no.1 (1976), p.33-39.

Contains a 10 page discography of Carter's works listed by composition.

C273.   Weirich, Robert. "Who's Afraid of Elliott Carter?" American Music Teacher v.38, no.2 (November/December 1988), p.14-17, 59.

A glimpse of Carter's rise to musical success.

C274.   Whipple, Harold.   "An Elliott Carter Discography."   Perspectives of New
        Music v.20 (Fall/Winter 1981 - Spring/Summer 1982), p.169-181.

        A discography of recordings of Carter's music based on the discography
        appearing in the book Elliott Carter: Sketches and Scores in Manuscript.
        (See: B113) This discography includes performers, record label and number
        and date issued.

C275.   Whittal, Arnold.   "Elliott Carter."   In: First American Music Conference,
        Keele University, England, April 18-21, 1975.   Keele: University of
        Keele, 1977. p.82-98.

        One of many papers presented at the Conference.   The paper contrasts
        American music, especially that of Elliott Carter, and European music with
        respect to the neo-expressionistic style.

C276.   ----------.   "Post-Twelve-Note Analysis."   Proceedings of the Royal Music
        Association v.94 (1967-68), p.1-17.

        A thematic analysis of several "post-twelve-note" compositions including
        Carter's Double Concerto.   "[T]he work reveals a technique of distorted but
        related echoes which characterize each stage in the evolutionary sequence."

C277.   Wilhite, Carmen Irene.   Piano Sonata by Elliott Carter: A Foreshadowing of
        His Later Style; A Lecture Recital, Together with Three Recitals of
        Selected Works.   D.M.A. diss., North Texas State University, 1977.

        "The lecture recital was given January 22, 1977.   A discussion of Elliott
        Carter's Piano Sonata emphasized those compositional techniques which
        foreshadowed important compositional procedures in many of his later works."
        (DAI v.38, no.3 p.1115 A)

C278.   Wilson, Patrick.   "Elliott Carter: Eight Pieces for Four Timpani."   Percussive
        Notes v.23, no.1 (October 1984), p.63-65.

        An interview by Patrick Wilson with Carter in light of a performance of all
        eight movements the preceding evening.   Discussion includes performance
        problems, the rewriting of the six pieces for kettledrums, the addition of the
        'Adagio' and the 'Canto' pieces, definitive performances, and Carter's
        intentions of composing for percussion.

C279.   Young, Allen.   "Mozart and Elliott Carter in Colorado."   High
        Fidelity/Musical America v.16, no.10 (October 1966), p.MA20-21.

        Details Carter's involvement in the Aspen Conference on Contemporary Music
        held during the summer of 1966.

Appendix I

Archival Sources

This listing serves as a starting point for archival sources existing at the time of publication of this book. Numerous places hold a single program, letter, or interview. I have excluded these sources from this listing. Instead, I have sought to include locations for substantial unpublished resources. During correspondence to these archival respositories I requested information regarding how best to cite their collections for future scholars. I have included such information when provided. The nature of identifying archival sources is ongoing. This list is not meant to be definitive, but rather a starting place for the scholar.

A1.   Paul Sacher Stiftung
        Bibliothek
        Münsterpl 4
        4051 Basel, Switzerland
        Tel: (061) 256644

        The Elliott Carter Collection remains unprocessed. Letters to the Paul Sacher Stiftung regarding the contents of the collection were to no avail, although the Stiftung assured me that it has the largest collection on Carter in the world.

        The collection contains correspondence, manuscript scores, and programs. I was able to verify that materials which had been on permanent loan to the New York Public Library and the Library of Congress have now been pulled and transferred by Carter to the Stiftung.

        The following items previously at the Library of Congress are now presumed to be held by the Stiftung. Holograph scores, some with annotations, of: <u>Tarantella</u>, <u>To Music</u>, <u>Trio</u> (unfinished), <u>Voyage</u>, <u>Harvest Home</u>, <u>Let's Be Gay</u>, <u>Sophocles' Philoctetes</u>, <u>Prelude, Fanfare and Polka</u>, <u>The Rose Family</u>, sketch book containing: <u>Labyrinth</u>, from <u>The Minotaur?</u>, and <u>Invention</u>, sketch book containing easy pieces, counterpoint exercises, <u>Minotaur</u> sketches, and rounds, sketchbook containing: fanfares, counterpoint exercises, symphony, and chorus, sketchbook containing: <u>Mostellaria</u>, <u>Canonic Suite for 4 Clarinets</u>,

<u>Concerto</u> <u>for</u> <u>Orchestra</u>, <u>Piano</u> <u>Concerto</u>, <u>The</u> <u>Difference</u>, <u>Dust</u> <u>of</u> <u>Snow</u>, <u>Canon</u>, from <u>Easy</u> <u>Piano</u> <u>Pieces</u>, exercises and studies, <u>Folk</u> <u>Dance</u> <u>no.2</u>. (J.W. Bernard's "Interview with Elliott Carter" (See: B67) contains information regarding the transfer of these materials to the Paul Sacher Stiftung).

A2.   The Juilliard School
Lila Acheson Wallace Library
60 Lincoln Center Plaza
New York, NY 10023-6588
Tel: (212) 799-5000
Carter was a member of the composition faculty from 1966 to 1984. As such, correspondence from Carter to members of the School administration exist in the Schools' archival files.

A3.   Harvard University Archives
Pusey Library
Cambridge, Massachusetts 02138
Tel: (617) 495-2461
Carter received his MA in music in 1932 from Harvard. The University Archives does not retain Master's theses. My letter was forwarded to the Music Library but no response resulted. The University Archives does have two biographical sketches written by Carter entitled: <u>The 25th</u> <u>and</u> <u>50th</u> <u>Anniversary</u> <u>Report</u> <u>of</u> <u>the</u> <u>Harvard</u> <u>Class</u> <u>of</u> <u>1930</u>. (See: B42a, B42b)

A4.   Yale University
Music Library
P.O. Box 5469 Yale Station
New Haven, Connecticut 06520-5469
Tel: (203) 432-0492
1) Virgil Thomson Papers: 66 letters from Carter to Thomson, copies of five letters from Thomson to Carter, ten additional items possibly 3rd party letters regarding Carter.
2) Charles Ives Papers: Three letters from Carter to Ives, drafts or copies of ten letters from Charles or Harmony Ives to Carter. (See: B32)
3) Ralph Kirkpatrick Papers: Three letters from Carter to Kirkpatrick, photocopy of the holograph score to <u>Sonata</u> <u>for</u> <u>Harpsichord,</u> <u>Flute,</u> <u>Oboe,</u> <u>and</u> <u>Violoncello</u>, and <u>Concerto</u> <u>for</u> <u>Harpsichord</u> <u>and</u> <u>Piano</u> with an analysis of the composition by the composer.
4) Fred and Rose Plaut Archives: One letter from Carter to Fred Plaut, negatives and contact prints of 78 photos of Carter taken by Fred Plaut.

A5.   Broadcast Music, Inc.
Archives
320 West 57th Street
New York, NY 10019

Some photographs and correspondence exist in the Carl Haverlin Collection. The exact nature of the material is undefined.

A6.   Library of Congress
Music Division
Washington, D.C. 20540
Archival material of unknown quantity and type exist in the following collections: Koussevitzky, Coolidge, Hans Nathan (Correspondence), Finney Collection (ML94.F55), and Music Division Old Correspondence. Numerous holograph and manuscript scores had been held by the Library of Congress but were returned to the depositor (presumed to be Carter himself) in May 1988. These materials are now presumed to be at the Paul Sacher Stiftung. (See: C42, C206)

A7.   New York Public Library
Music Division
Fifth Avenue and 42nd Street
New York, NY 10018-2788
All manuscript scores which were on permanent loan to the Library have been returned to the depositor (Carter) and are now housed at the Paul Sacher Stiftung. The New York Public Library still has photographs and correspondence among its archival holdings. The following collections contain some material of unknown quantity: William Schuman Papers, Wallingford Riegger Correspondence, Composers Forum, League of Composers, and the Ross Lee Finney Collection. (See: C17)

A8.   The New York Public Library for the Performing Arts
Rodgers and Hammerstein Archives of Recorded Sound
40 Lincoln Center Plaza
New York, NY 10023-7498
Tel: (212) 870-1663
Many recorded lectures and interviews.
1)Lecture on his Third String Quartet, Rutgers, 1975. LT-10 3500-01
2)Fred Goldbeck interviews E. Carter concerning the Concerto for Orchestra, Paris, 1972. LT-7 1031
3)Interview with E. Carter concerning his Double Concerto, BBC, 1968. LT-7 1032-33
4)Virgil Thomson interviews E. Carter and Nicholas Nabokov, New York (WNCN) LT-7 1029-30
5)Interview with E. Carter at Oberlin, 1973 LT-7 1035
6)Elliott Carter's Variations for Orchestra performed by the Louisville Symphony Orchestra, 1960 LT-10-3318
7)Memorial Concert for Paul Jacobs February 24, 1984. "Elliott Carter Speaking about Paul Jacobs" LTC 659 no.1; Sonata for Flute, Oboe, Violoncello, Harpsichord performed by Harvey Sollberger, Stephen Taylor, Fred Sherry, Martin Goldray. LTC 659 no.2
8)Paul Jacobs Noncommercial Recordings Collection: Night Fantasies performed at the 92nd St. Y (November 11, 1981), Night Fantasies,

("Session for Nonesuch 79047 ... early 1982. This version not used"),
Night Fantasies (takes 1-156), Night Fantasies ("BBC") November 20,
1980, Sonata for Flute, Oboe, Cello, Harpsichord, recital (Brooklyn
College) December 7, 1973, Piano Sonata (takes 1-89) August 17, 1982
(See: C121)

A9.   "Music Criticism" a lecture read over the BBC as part of a series on
"Composers and Criticism," edited by Elaine Padmore (August 1972).
Reprinted in Stone p.310-318. (See: B133)

A10.   "Introduction to a Poetry Reading by W.H. Auden." Hunter College
Playhouse, January 1969. Reprinted in Stone, p.256-257. (See: B133)

A11.   "Brass Quintet: Introductory Talk for the BBC Premiere," October 20,
1974. Reprinted in Stone, p.322-325. (See: B133)

A12.   Other archival sources which may exist include:
1)Laboratory manuals on music written while a teacher at St. John's
College, Annapolis, MD, 1941. ("Manual of Musical Notation,"
"Musical Intervals and Scales," "The Greek Diatonic Scale," "The Just
Scale and its Uses."
2)Lecturer at the Illinois Festival, Urbana, IL, 1953.
3)Lecturer as the Ward Lucas Visiting Professor at Carleton College in
1966. (See: B47a)
4)While a professor in Analysis at Rutgers University, Carter had prepared
charts and graphs analyzing his String Quartet No.3
5)A small sketch book entitled "Attempts" (1970) shows Carter's thoughts
on pitch organization in his String Quartet No.3. This may be at Lincoln
Center for The Performing Arts.

Appendix II

Alphabetical List of Compositions

Adagio for Viola (or Violoncello) and Piano W58a
Anniversary W25
The Ball Room Guide W4
Bariolage W86
Birthday Fanfare for Sir William Glock's 70th W73
Birthday Flourish W81
Brass Quintet W71
The Bridge W20
Canon for 3: In Memoriam Igor Stravinsky W68
Canon for 4: Homage to William [Glock] W77
Canonic Suite for Four Clarinets W56b
Canonic Suite for Quartet of Alto Saxophones W56a
A Celebration of Some 100 x 150 Notes W21
Changes W76
Con Leggerezza Pensosa-Omaggio a Italo Calvino W83
Concerto for English Horn and Orchestra W7
Concerto for Orchestra W18
Concerto for Piano and Orchestra (Piano Concerto) W67
The Defense of Corinth W36
Difference W45
Double Concerto W16
Duo for Violin and Piano W70
Dust of Snow W42
Eight Etudes and a Fantasy W62
Eight Pieces for Four Timpani W63c
Elegy (for String Orchestra) W14
Elegy (for String Quartet) W58b
Elegy (for Viola (or Violincello) and Piano) W58a, W58d
Emblems W39
Enchanted Preludes W82
Esprit Rude/Esprit Doux W78

A Fantasy about Purcell's "Fantasia upon One Note" W72
The Harmony of Morning W37
Harvest Home W31
Heart not so Heavy as Mine W35
Holiday Overture W12
Immer Neu W88
In Sleep, In Thunder W48
Inner Song W87
Let's be Gay W32
The Line Gang W42
The Madrigal Book W33
The Minotaur W6
"The Minotaur" Suite W13
A Mirror on Which to Dwell W46
Mostellaria W2
Much Ado about Nothing W5
Musical Studies W55
Musicians Wrestle Everywhere W38
My Love is in a Light Attire W40
Night Fantasies W74
Oboe Concerto W22
Pastoral (for English Horn (or Viola or Clarinet) and Piano) W57
Pastoral (for English Horn, Marimba and String Orchestra) W23
Penthode W20
Philoctetes W1
Piano Concerto W67
Piano Sonata (1920's) W49
Piano Sonata (rev. 1982) W59
Pocahontas (for Orchestra) W3b
Pocahontas (for Piano Solo) W3a
Pocahontas Suite W10
Prelude, Fanfare and Polka W9
Quintet (for Piano and Winds) W85
Recitative and Improvisation W63b
Remembrance W24
Riconoscenza W79
The Rose Family W42
Scrivo In Vento W84
Six Pieces for Kettle Drums and Orchestra W63
Sonata (for Flute and Piano, 1934) W51
Sonata for Flute, Oboe, Violoncello, and Harpsichord W65
Sonata for Piano (Piano Sonata) W59
Sonata for Violoncello and Piano W61
String Quartet (1928) W50
String Quartet (1935) W52
String Quartet (1937) W54
String Quartet No.1 W64
String Quartet No.2 W66

String Quartet No.3 W69
String Quartet No.4 W80
[Suite for Timpani] W63a
Suite from the Ballet "The Minotaur" ("The Minotaur" Suite) W13
Suite from the Ballet "Pocahontas" ("Pocahontas" Suite) W10, W53
Symphony (1937) W8
Symphony No.1 W11
A Symphony of Three Orchestras W19
Syringa W47
Tarantella (for Male Chorus and Piano Four Hands) W29a
Tarantella (for Male Chorus and Orchestra) W29b
Tell Me, Where is Fancy Bred? W41
Three Occasions for Orchestra W26
Three Poems of Robert Frost W42
To Music W34
Tom and Lily W28
Trilogy W89
Triple Duo W75
12 Madrigals W34
Variations for Orchestra W15
Violin Concerto W27
Voyage (for Medium Voice and Piano) W43a
Voyage (for Voice and Small Orchestra) W43b
Warble for Lilac Time W44
Woodwind Quintet W60

Appendix III

Chronology of Compositions

1920's
  Joyce Settings (W40b)

1928
  My Love is in a Light Attire (W40a)
  String Quartet (W50)

Late 1920's
  Piano Sonata (W49)

1931
  Philoctetes (W1)

1934
  Sonata for Flute and Piano (W51)
  Tom and Lily (W28)

1935
  String Quartet (W52)

1936
  Mostellaria (W2a)
  Pocahontas for piano solo (W53a)
  Pocahontas (W3b)
  Tarantella for chorus and orchestra (W29a)
  Tarantella for chorus and piano four-hands (W29b)

1937
  The Ball Room Guide (W4)
  The Bridge (W30)
  Harvest Home (W31)

Concerto for English Horn and Orchestra (W7)
Let's Be Gay (W32)
Madrigal Book (W33)
To Music (W34)
Much Ado About Nothing (W5)
String Quartet (W54)
Symphony (W8)

1938
Heart Not so Heavy as Mine (W35)
Musical Studies (W55)
Prelude, Fanfare and Polka (W9)
Tell Me, Where is Fancy Bred? (W41)

1939
Canonic Suite for quartet of alto saxophones (W56a)
Pocahontas (ballet) (W3b)
Suite from the Ballet "Pocahontas" (W10a)

1940
Pastoral (W57a)

1941
The Defense of Corinth (W36)

1942
Symphony No. 1 (W11)

1943
Dust of Snow (W42)
Elegy for violoncello and piano (W14b)
The Line Gang (W42)
The Rose Family (W42)
Three Poems of Robert Frost (W42)
Voyage (W43a)
Warble for Lilac Time (W44)

1944
The Difference (W45)
The Harmony of Morning (W37)
Holiday Overture (W12)

1945
Musicians Wrestle Everywhere (W38)

1945-46
Piano Sonata (W59)

1946
   Elegy for string quartet (W58b)

1947
   Emblems (W39)
   The Minotaur (Ballet) (W6a)
   Suite from the Ballet "The Minotaur" (W13)

1948
   Sonata for Violoncello and Piano (W61)
   Woodwind Quintet (W60)

1949-50
   Eight Etudes and a Fantasy (W62)

1950
   Recitative and Improvisation (W63b)
   Six Pieces for Kettle Drums and Orchestra (W63a)

1950-51
   String Quartet No.1 (W64)

1952
   Elegy for string orchestra (W14a)
   Sonata for Flute, Oboe, Violoncello, and Harpsichord (W65)

1954
   Symphony No.1 (rev.) (W11)
   Warble for Lilac Time (rev.) (W44)

1954-55
   Variations for Orchestra (W15)

1955-56
   Canonic Suite for four clarinets (W56b)

1959
   String Quartet No.2 (W66)

1960
   Suite from the Ballet "Pocahontas" (rev.) (W10a)

1961
   Double Concerto (W16a)
   Elegy for viola and piano (W58d)
   Holiday Overture (rev.) (W12)

1964-65
  Piano Concerto (W17a)

1966
  Eight Pieces for Four Timpani (W63c)
  Sonata for Violoncello and Piano (rev.) (W61)

1967
  Piano Concerto reduction for two pianos (W67)

1968-69
  Concerto for Orchestra (W18)

1971
  Canon for 3: In Memoriam Igor Stravinsky (W68)
  String Quartet No.3 (W69)

1973-74
  Duo for Violin and Piano (W70)

1974
  Brass Quintet (W71)
  A Fantasy about Purcell's "Fantasia upon One Note" (W72)

1975
  A Mirror on Which to Dwell (W46)
  Voyage for voice and small orchestra (W43b)

1976
  A Symphony of Three Orchestras (W19)

1978
  Birthday Fanfare for Sir William Glock's 70th (W73)
  Syringa (W47)

1979
  Voyage for voice and small orchestra (rev.) (W43b)

1980
  Dust of Snow for voice and guitar (W42)
  The Line Gang for voice and chamber orchestra (W42)
  The Line Gang for voice and guitar (W42)
  Night Fantasies (W74)
  The Rose Family for vioce and guitar (W42)

1981
  Canonic Suite for quartet of alto saxophones (rev.) (W56a)
  In Sleep, In Thunder (W48)

1982
   Piano Sonata (rev.) (W59)

1982-83
   Triple Duo (W75)

1983
   Changes (W76)

1984
   Canon for 4: Homage to William [Glock] (W77)
   Esprit Rude/Esprit Doux (W78)
   Riconosenza - Per Goffredo Petrassi (W79)

1985
   Penthode (W20)

1985-86
   String Quartet No.4 (W80)

1986
   A Celebration of Some 100 x 150 Notes (W21)

1986-87
   Oboe Concerto (W22)

1988
   Birthday Flourish (W81)
   Enchanted Preludes (W82)
   Pastoral for English horn, marimba and string orchestra (W23a)
   Remembrance (W24)

1989
   Anniversary (W25)

1990
   Con Leggerezza Pensosa-Omaggio a Italo Calvino (W83)
   Violin Concerto (W27)

1991
   Scrivo In Vento (W84)

1992
   Bariolage (W86)
   Immer Neu (W88)
   Inner Song (W87)
   Quintet for piano and winds (W85)
   Trilogy (W89)

Appendix IV

Publisher's List

This list of music publishers of Carter's works is current as of December 1992.

Arrow Music Press
c/o Boosey & Hawkes, Inc.
24 West 57th Street
New York, NY 10019

Associated Music Publishers, Inc.
c/o Music Sales Corporation
24 East 22nd Street
New York, NY 10010

Boosey & Hawkes
24 East 21st St.
New York, NY 10010-7200

Broadcast Music, Inc.
320 W. 57th St.
New York, NY 10019

Edwin F. Kalmus & Company, Inc.
P.O. Box 5011
Boca Raton, FL 33433-8011

Harvard Music Department
Harvard University
Cambridge, MA 02138

Hendon Music, Inc.
c/o Boosey & Hawkes, Inc.
24 East 21st Street
New York, NY 10010-7200

Mercury Music Corporation
c/o Theodore Presser Company
Presser Place
Bryn Mawr, PA 19010

Merion Music, Inc.
c/o Theodore Presser Company
Presser Place
Bryn Mawr, PA 19010

Merrymount Press
c/o Theodore Presser Company
Presser Place
Bryn Mawr, PA 19010

Music Press
c/o Theodore Presser Company
Presser Place
Bryn Mawr, PA 19010

Peer International Corporation
Editorial Offices
810 Seventh Avenue, 9th floor
Sole Distributor in U.S. and Canada:
Theodore Presser Company
Presser Place
Bryn Mawr, PA 19010

Society for the Publication of American Music
P.O. Box 269
Wall Street Station
New York, NY

Theodore Presser Company
Presser Place
Bryn Mawr, PA 19010

Valley Music Press
Smith College
Northhampton, MA 01063

Index

About the Author

WILLIAM T. DOERING is Assistant Professor and Technical Services Librarian at Luther College in Decorah, Iowa.

Recent Titles in
Bio-Bibliographies in Music

Randall Thompson: A Bio-Bibliography
Caroline Cepin Benser and David Francis Urrows

André Messager: A Bio-Bibliography
John Wagstaff

Roy Harris: A Bio-Bibliography
Dan Stehman

Violet Archer: A Bio-Bibliography
Linda Hartig

Enrique Granados: A Bio-Bibliography
Carol A. Hess

Hans Rosbaud: A Bio-Bibliography
Joan Evans

Alec Wilder: A Bio-Bibliography
David Demsey and Ronald Prather

Alun Hoddinott: A Bio-Bibliography
Stewart R. Craggs

Elinor Remick Warren: A Bio-Bibliography
Virginia Bortin

Howard Hanson: A Bio-Bibliography
James E. Perone

Peter Sculthorpe: A Bio-Bibliography
Deborah Hayes

Germaine Tailleferre: A Bio-Bibliography
Robert Shapiro

Charles Wuorinen: A Bio-Bibliography
Richard D. Burbank